Dictionary of Birds of the United States

Buteo jamaicensis, red-tailed hawk

Dictionary of Birds
of the United States

SCIENTIFIC AND COMMON NAMES

Joel Ellis Holloway, M.D.

WITH ILLUSTRATIONS BY
George Miksch Sutton

TIMBER PRESS
Portland • Cambridge

Published in 2003 by
Timber Press, Inc.   Timber Press
The Haseltine Building   2 Station Road
133 S.W. Second Avenue, Suite 450   Swavesey
Portland, Oregon 97204-3527, U.S.A.   Cambridge CB4 5QJ, U.K.

ISBN 0-88192-600-0

Catalog records for this book are available from the Library of Congress and
the British Library.

Printed in Hong Kong

This work is dedicated to my wife, Twyla J. Smith, M.D.

CONTENTS

Preface   9

Acknowledgment   10

The Dictionary   11

Bibliography   221

Index   225

PREFACE

I have been interested in the translation of scientific names for many years. In my general reading, I would translate the names of dinosaurs, birds, mammals, flowers, trees, or any organisms as I came across them. The last dictionary of American bird names was published as a revised edition in 1985 (Choate 1985). The book was helpful but, because of all the nomenclature changes made over the years by the American Ornithologists' Union, the information was not up to date. Also, the book did not contain the birds of Hawaii or the rare, introduced, or escaped species found in the United States. Thus, I undertook the task of compiling a complete, single source of U.S. bird names.

This dictionary is meant to be a helpful companion book to bird guides and bird lists. It explains the scientific binomial and common names of the birds of the United States. The list of U.S. birds is based on *The Sibley Guide to Birds* (2000) by David Allen Sibley and *Hawaii's Birds* (1997) by the Hawaiian Audubon Society. Included are permanent and migratory birds, regional forms, introduced species, escaped exotics, and rare visitors. The spelling of the scientific and common names is based on *The American Ornithologists' Union Check-list of North American Birds* (7th ed.).

The bird names are alphabetized by genus and then by species epithet. The genus names are explained only in the first entry of that genus. The conventions of the cross-references are as follows: if a name has been explained within the genus, a cross-reference is listed. For example, the name *woodpecker* is explained under *Picoides albolarvatus*, the white-headed woodpecker; other woodpecker entries in the genus *Picoides* refer the reader back to *Picoides albolarvatus*. Cross-references contained within parentheses, for example (see *Amazona aestiva*) in the *Aratinga acuticaudata* entry, will lead the reader to additional information about the name.

All scientific binomial names are Latinized, and most come from classical Latin or Greek. In this work, when the original name is from the Greek, the name is written in the modern Greek alphabet and then transliterated. My source for the Greek was Liddell and Scott's *A Greek-English*

Lexicon (1996). Due to typographic considerations, the Greek words do not contain breathing marks. Many bird names are coined New Latin words, and some are from the local language of the bird's range. Other birds are named after people or mythological characters.

The section of the *International Code of Zoological Nomenclature* (4th ed.) titled "Validity of Names and Nomenclatural Acts," delineates the principle of priority. Briefly, the principle states that the oldest name given to an organism is the valid name. The name must be in a publication that has such status as required by the International Commission on Zoological Nomenclature. Once a name is established, it remains the valid name in spite of any mistakes, including misspellings, incorrect color designation, wrong location name, misunderstood myths and classical names, and nonsensical words.

The scientific names of animals and plants do not translate with ease or precision. In the past, the selected names were not peer reviewed as they are today. People might make up a name, usually from the Greek, that they thought had a certain meaning; unfortunately, many are complete nonsense. If a name was misspelled or nonsensical, once on record (that is, the first in print) all mistakes were set in stone. In some cases, the individual that assigned the name did not explain what it was supposed to mean, leaving later translators to try to figure out what he was thinking.

All of that being said, the vast majority of scientific bird names are interesting and appropriate. A name may hold fascinating clues about the bird's origin, its behavior, the sound of its call, its coloration, or other physical attributes. This book was written to be used as a dictionary, but hopefully a front-to-back reading will also prove to be both informative and entertaining.

Acknowledgment

This dictionary contains illustrations by the renowned ornithologist and bird artist George Miksch Sutton. I thank W. R. Johnson, D.D.S., for kindly allowing me to use these images in my book.

THE DICTIONARY

Accipiter cooperii   Cooper's Hawk

SCIENTIFIC NAME *Accipiter*, general Latin name for a bird of prey, especially a hawk + *cooperii*, for William C. Cooper (1798–1864), an American zoologist, collector, conchologist, and one of the founders of the New York Lyceum of Natural History.

COMMON NAME Cooper's, see scientific name. Hawk, from Anglo-Saxon *hafoc*, hawk, their name for this type of bird.

Accipiter gentilis   Northern Goshawk

SCIENTIFIC NAME *Accipiter* + *gentilis*, Latin for belonging to the same clan, noble. Used to mean born with noble qualities.

COMMON NAME Northern, for its natural range in the northern United States and Canada. Goshawk, from Anglo-Saxon *gos*, goose, and *hafoc*, hawk. This bird was thought to prey on geese.

Accipiter soloensis   Gray Frog-Hawk

SCIENTIFIC NAME *Accipiter* + *soloensis*, Latin for belonging to Solo, for the city of Solo in Java. Reference is to the region of the type specimen.

COMMON NAME Gray, for the slate-colored body. Frog, for the diet, which is composed almost entirely of frogs. Hawk, see *Accipiter cooperii*.

Accipiter striatus   Sharp-shinned Hawk

SCIENTIFIC NAME *Accipiter* + *striatus*, Latin for grooved, furrowed, striped. Refers to the stripes on this hawk's underside.

COMMON NAME Sharp-shinned, this bird has a raised ridge on the part of the leg that would correspond to the shin of a human. Most other bird's legs are rounded in this area. Hawk, see *Accipiter cooperii*.

13

Acridotheres cristatellus   Crested Myna

SCIENTIFIC NAME *Acridotheres*, a locust hunter, from Greek ακρις, *akris*, or ακριδ, *akrid*, a locust, and θηραν, *thēran*, to hunt or chase, in turn from θηρα, *thēra*, a hunt, a chase + *cristatellus*, from Latin *cristatus*, a crest, and the diminutive *-ellus*. Reference is to the small crest on this bird's forehead.

COMMON NAME Crested, see scientific name. Myna, from the Hindustani name for this bird, *maina*, a starling.

Acridotheres tristis   Common Myna

SCIENTIFIC NAME *Acridotheres* + *tristis*, Latin for of a character or aspect conveying gloom, shade, dark-colored things. Reference is to the dull plumage when compared to other mynas.

COMMON NAME Common, most common myna in its range. Myna, see *Acridotheres cristatellus*.

Acrocephalus familiaris   Nihoa Millerbird

SCIENTIFIC NAME *Acrocephalus*, from Greek ακρον, *akron*, a point, a peak, and κεφαλη, *kephalē*, head. Reference is to this genus having a more pointed head than other members of the subfamily Sylviinae + *familiaris*, Latin for well known, familiar.

COMMON NAME Nihoa, reference to the bird's natural range on the island of Nihoa in the Hawaiian archipelago. Millerbird, reference to the powdered grayish white plumage, like the clothes of a miller.

Actitis hypoleucos   Common Sandpiper

SCIENTIFIC NAME *Actitis*, from Greek ακτιτις, *aktitis*, a shore dweller + *hypoleucos*, from Greek υπο, *upo*, below, and λευκος, *leukos*, of color, white. Reference is to the white underparts in breeding plumage.

COMMON NAME Common, abundant in its range. Sandpiper, one who pipes on the sand. Piping is descriptive of its call, from Latin *pipare*, to chirp.

Actitis macularia   Spotted Sandpiper

SCIENTIFIC NAME *Actitis* + *macularia*, from Latin *maculo*, a spot, and *-arius*, possessing. Reference is to the spotted underparts of the breeding plumage.

COMMON NAME Spotted, descriptive of underparts in breeding plumage. Sandpiper, see *Actitis hypoleucos.*

Aechmophorus clarkii   Clark's Grebe

SCIENTIFIC NAME *Aechmophorus,* from Greek αιχμοφορος, *aikhmophoros,* one who carries a spear. Reference is to this bird's long, sharp bill + *clarkii,* for J. H. Clark (1830–?), an American surveyor and naturalist. This species was long considered the same as *Aechmophorus occidentalis;* it was recognized as a separate species in 1985.

COMMON NAME Clark's, see scientific name. Grebe, French for a crest of feathers on a bird's head, a comb. Reference is to the crest of some European species.

Aechmophorus occidentalis   Western Grebe

SCIENTIFIC NAME *Aechmophorus + occidentalis,* Latin for west or western. Reference is to the natural range in the western United States.

COMMON NAME Western, for its natural range in the western United States. Grebe, see *Aechmophorus clarkii.*

Aegolius acadicus   Northern Saw-whet Owl

SCIENTIFIC NAME *Aegolius,* from Greek αιγολιος, *aigolios,* a type of owl + *acadicus,* of Acadia (Nova Scotia), where the type specimen was found.

COMMON NAME Northern, for the natural range in the United States. Saw-whet, call sounds like the noise made when manually sharpening a saw. Owl, from Anglo-Saxon *ule,* owl, and from Latin *ululo,* to cry out (*ululo* is also Latin for the screech owl). Both words are onomatopoeic of the owl's call.

Aegolius funereus   Boreal Owl

SCIENTIFIC NAME *Aegolius + funereus,* Latin for of or appropriate to funerals, mourning. Reference is to the soft, bell-like call, reminiscent of a funeral bell.

COMMON NAME Boreal, from Latin *boreus,* in turn from Greek βορειος, *boreios,* northern. Reference is to this owl's natural range in the northern United States and Canada. Owl, see *Aegolius acadicus.*

Aeronautes saxatalis   White-throated Swift

SCIENTIFIC NAME *Aeronautes*, an air sailor, from Greek αερ, *aer*, air, and ναυτες, *nautes*, sailor + *saxatalis*, Latin for living among rocks.

COMMON NAME White-throated, descriptive. Swift, for its speedy flight.

Aethia cristatella   Crested Auklet

SCIENTIFIC NAME *Aethia*, from Greek αιθυια, *aithuia*, a diving bird, thought originally to be a shearwater + *cristatella*, a little crest, from Latin *cristatus*, a crest, and the diminutive *-ellus*. Reference is to the small crest on the forehead.

COMMON NAME Crested, has a small crest on the forehead. Auklet, a little auk, from Old Norse *alka*, their name for several different northern birds.

Aethia psittacula   Parakeet Auklet

SCIENTIFIC NAME *Aethia* + *psittacula*, a little parrot, diminutive of the Latin *psittacus*, a parrot, in turn from Greek ψιττακος, *psittakos*, a parrot. Reference is to the shape of the beak.

COMMON NAME Parakeet, Anglicized form of the French *perroquet*, one of their words for a parrot, used in English to describe the smaller types of parrot. Auklet, see *Aethia cristatella*.

Aethia pusilla   Least Auklet

SCIENTIFIC NAME *Aethia* + *pusilla*, from Latin *pusillus*, very small, tiny, wee. This is the United States' smallest auklet.

COMMON NAME Least, for the relatively small size. Auklet, see *Aethia cristatella*.

Aethia pygmaea   Whiskered Auklet

SCIENTIFIC NAME *Aethia* + *pygmaea*, Latin for of or belonging to the Pygmies, in turn from Greek Πυγμαιοι, *Pugmaioi*, a legendary race of dwarfs, usually living in Ethiopia, and thought to be in a never-ending war with the cranes of the area.

COMMON NAME Whiskered, for the small tuft of feathers on each side of the face. Auklet, see *Aethia cristatella*.

Agapornis roseicollis   Peach-faced Lovebird

SCIENTIFIC NAME *Agapornis*, a lovebird, from Greek αγαπη, *agapē*, love, and ορνις, *ornis*, bird + *roseicollis*, rose necked, from Latin *rosa*, a rose, and *collum*, neck. Reference is to the pink neck.

COMMON NAME Peach-faced, cheeks are the same rose color as the neck (see scientific name), which resembles the red found on a ripe peach. Lovebird, for the affection the pairs show for each other.

Agelaius phoeniceus   Red-winged Blackbird

SCIENTIFIC NAME *Agelaius*, from Greek αγελαιος, *agelaios*, belonging to a flock + *phoeniceus*, Latin for a dull scarlet, in turn from the Greek φοινικεος, *phoinikeos*, of the same meaning. This dye color was introduced to the Greeks by the Phoenicians, thus the name of the color. Reference is to the red wing-patch.

COMMON NAME Red-winged, male has a bright red wing-patch in breeding plumage. Blackbird, for the predominant black color.

Agelaius tricolor   Tricolored Blackbird

SCIENTIFIC NAME *Agelaius* + *tricolor*, Latin for having three colors. Reference is to the male breeding plumage: the body is all black, and there is a red and a white stripe on the shoulders.

COMMON NAME Tricolored, see scientific name. Blackbird, see *Agelaius phoeniceus*.

Aimophila aestivalis   Bachman's Sparrow

SCIENTIFIC NAME *Aimophila*, in 1837 William Swainson (1789–1855) named this genus, which at that time had only one species. He gave no details for the name. In 1954 M. F. Coble published *Introduction to Ornithological Nomenclature*, in which he translated *Aimophila* to mean blood loving. His basis was the Greek αιμα, *aima*, blood, and φιλος, *philos*, loving. Since then almost every translation source has accepted this derivation, and all have complained much about it making no sense. *The Oxford Greek-English Lexicon* (1996) lists αιμος, *aimos*, as meaning the same as δρυμος, *drumos*, a thicket. Thus, thicket loving, a name that refers to the habitat, appears to be the correct derivation. This same source lists αιμος, *aimos* as meaning the same as οβελισκους, *obeliskous*, a small spit, skewer, a nail, or anything shaped like a spit, that is, a thorn. *A Dictionary of Scientific Bird Names* (1991) lists "thorn" as the derivation. Although this is an etymological possibility, the bird's habitat suggests thicket loving over thorn loving + *aestivalis*, Latin for like the summer.

COMMON NAME Bachman's, John James Audubon (1785–1851) named this bird for Rev. John Bachman (1790–1874) of Charleston, South Carolina. The two families were close friends; Audubon's two sons married Bachman's daughters. Sparrow, from Anglo-Saxon *spearwa*, to flutter. Originally used to denote any small bird.

Aimophila botterii   Botteri's Sparrow

SCIENTIFIC NAME *Aimophila* + *botterii*, for Matteo Botteri (1808–1877), who collected the type specimen in Mexico.

COMMON NAME Botteri's, see scientific name. Sparrow, see *Aimophila aestivalis*.

Aimophila carpalis   Rufous-winged Sparrow

SCIENTIFIC NAME *Aimophila* + *carpalis*, Latin for pertaining to the wrist. The wrist area of the wing is rufous.

COMMON NAME Rufous-winged, from *rufus*, Latin for red of various shades, tawny. Reference is to the reddish brown on the wings. Sparrow, see *Aimophila aestivalis*.

Aimophila cassinii   Cassin's Sparrow

SCIENTIFIC NAME *Aimophila* + *cassinii*, in 1852 Samuel W. Woodhouse (1821–1904) named this bird for John Cassin (1813–1869), a Philadelphia ornithologist with a broad knowledge of the birds of the world.

COMMON NAME Cassin's, see scientific name. Sparrow, see *Aimophila aestivalis*.

Aimophila quinquestriata   Five-striped Sparrow

SCIENTIFIC NAME *Aimophila* + *quinquestriata*, having five stripes, from Latin *quinque*, five, and *striata*, from *striatus*, furrowed, grooved, striped. Reference is to the five white stripes on the head: one above each eye and three on the throat reaching the base of the beak.

COMMON NAME Five-striped, see scientific name. Sparrow, see *Aimophila aestivalis*.

Aimophila ruficeps — Rufous-crowned Sparrow

SCIENTIFIC NAME *Aimophila* + *ruficeps*, red headed, from Latin *rufus*, red of various shades, tawny, and *-ceps*, head, from Greek κεφαλη, *kephalē*, head. Reference is to the rufous crown.

COMMON NAME Rufous-crowned, descriptive. Sparrow, see *Aimophila aestivalis*.

Aix galericulata — Mandarin Duck

SCIENTIFIC NAME *Aix*, from Greek αιξ, *aix*, a kind of waterbird + *galericulata*, having a small cap, from Latin *galericulum*, a small cap. Reference is to the black crown, which looks like a skull cap.

COMMON NAME Mandarin, native range is in China. Duck, from Anglo-Saxon *duce*, a form of *ducan*, to duck or dive.

Aix sponsa — Wood Duck

SCIENTIFIC NAME *Aix* + *sponsa*, Latin for a woman betrothed, to be dressed up for a wedding. So named because of this bird's beautiful appearance.

COMMON NAME Wood, for the bird's habit of nesting in trees. Duck, see *Aix galericulata*.

Alauda arvensis — Sky Lark

SCIENTIFIC NAME *Alauda*, Latin name for the crested lark + *arvensis* from Latin *arvum*, a ploughed field, especially in contrast to a meadow, and *-ensis*, belonging to. Reference is to the birds being commonly seen around farms.

COMMON NAME Sky, for the extreme height of the male's courtship flight. Lark, from Middle English, a contraction of *lavercock*, the name for lark.

Alca torda — Razorbill

SCIENTIFIC NAME *Alca*, Latinized form of *alka* the Scandinavian, and Icelandic name for an auk + *torda*, the Latinized Swedish name for this bird.

COMMON NAME Razorbill, for the sharp edge of the thin maxilla.

Alectoris chukar   Chukar

SCIENTIFIC NAME *Alectoris*, from Greek αλεκτωρ, *alektōr*, a domestic cock. Reference is to the appearance + *chukar*, from Sanskrit *cakora*, a partridge. Thought to be an imitation of the call.

COMMON NAME Chukar, see scientific name.

Alectoris rufa   Red-legged Partridge

SCIENTIFIC NAME *Alectoris* + *rufa*, red, from Latin *rufus*, red of various shades, tawny. Reference is to the red legs.

COMMON NAME Red-legged, descriptive. Partridge, from Latin *perdix*, a partridge, in turn from Greek περδιξ, *perdix*, a partridge.

Alle alle   Dovekie

SCIENTIFIC NAME *Alle*, Swedish name for this bird + *alle*.

COMMON NAME Dovekie, diminutive of dove in Scottish. Reference is to this bird's small size.

Alopochen aegyptiacus   Egyptian Goose

SCIENTIFIC NAME *Alopochen*, a fox goose, from Greek αλωπεκ, *alōpek* or αλωπηξ, *alōpēx*, a fox, and χεν, *khen*, a goose. Reference is to the color of the breast, which resembles that of the red fox + *aegyptiacus*, Latin for of Egypt, its natural range.

COMMON NAME Egyptian, for the natural range. Goose, from Anglo-Saxon *gos*, the name for this type of bird.

Amandava amandava   Red Avadavat

SCIENTIFIC NAME *Amandava*, a corruption of Ahmadabad, the city in India from which these birds were first exported to Europe + *amandava*.

COMMON NAME Red, for the male's red breeding plumage. Avadavat, same as *Amandava*, see scientific name.

Amazilia beryllina   Berylline Hummingbird

SCIENTIFIC NAME *Amazilia*, for Amazili, an Inca heroine in the French novel *Les Incas, ou la destruction de l'Empire du Perou* (1777) by Jean François Marmontel. Name was given to a group of hummingbirds by the

French naturalist Rene P. Lesson (1794–1849). The natural range of this genus includes Peru, land of the Incas. Almost all sources call this a word of unknown origin or an attempt to Latinize Amazon + *beryllina*, from Greek βηρυλλος, *bērullos*, a sea-green gem, beryl (emerald and aquamarine are both types of beryl). Reference is to the bright green head and throat.

COMMON NAME Berylline, see scientific name. Hummingbird, for the buzzing hum of the wingbeats.

Amazilia violiceps — Violet-crowned Hummingbird

SCIENTIFIC NAME *Amazilia* + *violiceps*, violet headed, from Latin *violoceus*, violet colored, and *-ceps*, head, in turn from Greek κεφαλη, *kephalē*, head.

COMMON NAME Violet-crowned, descriptive. Hummingbird, see *Amazilia beryllina*.

Amazilia yucatanensis — Buff-bellied Hummingbird

SCIENTIFIC NAME *Amazilia* + *yucatanensis*, Latin for belonging to Yucatan, from Yucatan, the region of Mexico where the type specimen was collected.

COMMON NAME Buff-bellied, descriptive. Hummingbird, see *Amazilia beryllina*.

Amazona aestiva — Blue-fronted Parrot

SCIENTIFIC NAME *Amazona*, of the Amazon. Reference is to the natural range in South America + *aestiva*, of the summer, from Latin *aestas*, summer.

COMMON NAME Blue fronted, has a blue forehead, from Latin *frons*, the forehead. Parrot, from French *perrot*, a diminutive of Pierre (Peter), a pet name for this type of bird.

Amazona albifrons — White-fronted Parrot

SCIENTIFIC NAME *Amazona* + *albifrons*, having a white forehead, from Latin *albus*, white, and *frons*, forehead, front.

COMMON NAME White-fronted, has a white forehead. Parrot, see *Amazona aestiva*.

Amazona amazonica   Orange-winged Parrot

SCIENTIFIC NAME *Amazona* + *amazonica*, of the Amazon. Reference is to the natural range in South America.

COMMON NAME Orange-winged, has a prominent orange wing-speculum made up of the outer three secondaries. Parrot, see *Amazona aestiva*.

Amazona auropalliata   Yellow-naped Parrot

SCIENTIFIC NAME *Amazona* + *auropalliata*, *auro*, from Latin *aurosus*, of the color of gold, and *palliata*, from Latin *pallium*, a mantel or cover. Reference is to the yellow patch on the nape of the neck.

COMMON NAME Yellow-naped, descriptive. Parrot, see *Amazona aestiva*.

Amazona autumnalis   Red-lored Parrot

SCIENTIFIC NAME *Amazona* + *autumnalis*, Latin for autumn. Reference is to the colors of the plumage.

COMMON NAME Red-lored, descriptive (lores are the areas on each side of a bird's face from the bill to the eye). Parrot, see *Amazona aestiva*.

Amazona farinosa   Mealy Parrot

SCIENTIFIC NAME *Amazona* + *farinosa*, from Latin *farinosus*, dusted with flour or meal. Reference is to the flour-dusted appearance of the shoulders, back, and nape of the neck.

COMMON NAME Mealy, see scientific name. Parrot, see *Amazona aestiva*.

Amazona finschi   Lilac-crowned Parrot

SCIENTIFIC NAME *Amazona* + *finschi*, for Friedrich Hermann Otto Finsch (1839–1917), a German diplomat and author of *Die vogel ost Afrikas* (1870).

COMMON NAME Lilac-crowned, descriptive. Parrot, see *Amazona aestiva*.

Amazona ochrocephala   Yellow-crowned Parrot

SCIENTIFIC NAME *Amazona* + *ochrocephala*, Latin for having a pale yellow head, from Greek. ωχρος, *ōkhros*, pale yellow, and κεφαλη, *kephalē*, head.

COMMON NAME Yellow-crowned, descriptive. Parrot, see *Amazona aestiva*.

Amazona oratrix   Yellow-headed Parrot

SCIENTIFIC NAME *Amazona* + *oratrix*, Latin for a female suppliant. Reference is to the behavior.

COMMON NAME Yellow-headed, descriptive. Parrot, see *Amazona aestiva.*

Amazona ventralis   Hispaniolan Parrot

SCIENTIFIC NAME *Amazona* + *ventralis*, Latin for of the belly. Reference is to the maroon patch on the lower abdomen.

COMMON NAME Hispaniolan, natural range is the island of Hispaniola. Parrot, see *Amazona aestiva.*

Amazona viridigenalis   Red-crowned Parrot

SCIENTIFIC NAME *Amazona* + *viridigenalis*, green cheeked, from Latin *viridis*, green, and *gena*, cheek.

COMMON NAME Red-crowned, descriptive. Parrot, see *Amazona aestiva.*

Amazona xantholora   Yellow-lored Parrot

SCIENTIFIC NAME *Amazona* + *xantholora*, to have yellow lores (the area on each side of a bird's face from the bill to the eye), from Greek ξανθος, *xanthos*, yellow, and Latin *lorum*, a thong, a strip, or anything suggesting a thong.

COMMON NAME Yellow-lored, descriptive (lores are the areas on each side of a bird's face from the bill to the eye). Parrot, see *Amazona aestiva.*

Ammodramus bairdii   Baird's Sparrow

SCIENTIFIC NAME *Ammodramus*, sand runner, from Greek αμμος, *ammos*, sand, and δραμειν, *dramein*, to run + *bairdii*, for Spencer Fullerton Baird (1823–1887), secretary of the Smithsonian Institution and author of *Catalogue of North American Mammals* (1857) and *Catalogue of North American Birds* (1868).

COMMON NAME Baird's, see scientific name. Sparrow, from Anglo-Saxon *spearwa*, to flutter. Originally used to denote any small bird.

Ammodramus caudacutus   Saltmarsh Sharp-tailed Sparrow

SCIENTIFIC NAME *Ammodramus* + *caudacutus*, to have a sharp tail, from Latin *cauda*, tail, and *acutus*, sharp.

COMMON NAME Saltmarsh, for the habitat. Sharp-tailed, tail comes to a point. Sparrow, see *Ammodramus bairdii*.

Ammodramus henslowii   Henslow's Sparrow

SCIENTIFIC NAME *Ammodramus* + *henslowii*, for John Stevens Henslow (1796–1861), professor of botany at Cambridge University, England. He compiled *Catalogue of British Plants* (1829) and *Dictionary of Botanical Terms* (1857).

COMMON NAME Henslow's, see scientific name. Sparrow, see *Ammodramus bairdii*.

Ammodramus leconteii   Le Conte's Sparrow

SCIENTIFIC NAME *Ammodramus* + *leconteii*, for Dr. John Le Conte (1818–1891), a Georgia physician and president of the University of California at Berkeley. (His cousin Dr. John Lawrence Le Conte [1825–1883] had a thrasher named for him; see *Toxostoma lecontei*).

COMMON NAME Le Conte's, see scientific name. Sparrow, see *Ammodramus bairdii*.

Ammodramus maritimus   Seaside Sparrow

SCIENTIFIC NAME *Ammodramus* + *maritimus*, Latin for of or belonging to the sea, situated near the sea, coastal.

COMMON NAME Seaside, refers to the habitat. Sparrow, see *Ammodramus bairdii*.

Ammodramus nelsoni   Nelson's Sharp-tailed Sparrow

SCIENTIFIC NAME *Ammodramus* + *nelsoni*, for Edward W. Nelson (1855–1934), chief of the U.S. Biological Survey from 1916 to 1927.

COMMON NAME Nelson's, see scientific name. Sharp-tailed, tail tapers to a point. Sparrow, see *Ammodramus bairdii*.

Ammodramus savannarum   Grasshopper Sparrow

SCIENTIFIC NAME *Ammodramus* + *savannarum*, of the meadows, from Spanish *zavana*, in turn from a Carib Indian (Lesser Antilles, West Indies) word, *zavana*, a treeless plain. Reference is to the habitat.

COMMON NAME Grasshopper, the song sounds like the stridulation of a grasshopper. Sparrow, see *Ammodramus bairdii*.

Amphispiza belli   Sage Sparrow

SCIENTIFIC NAME *Amphispiza*, on both sides a finch, from Greek αμφι, *amphi*, on both sides, around, and σπιζα, *spiza*, a finch. A cryptic reference to the close relationship of this bird to others around it; it closely resembles some other sparrows in its range + *belli*, for John Graham Bell (1812–1889), a taxidermist who accompanied John James Audubon (1785–1851) on his Missouri River trip of 1843.

COMMON NAME Sage, for the habitat. Sparrow, from Anglo-Saxon *spearwa*, to flutter. Originally used to denote any small bird.

Amphispiza bilineata   Black-throated Sparrow

SCIENTIFIC NAME *Amphispiza* + *bilineata*, two lines, from Latin *bi*, two, and *linearis*, consisting of lines. Reference is to the two white lines on the head.

COMMON NAME Black-throated, descriptive; both sexes have black throats. Sparrow, see *Amphispiza belli*.

Anas acuta   Northern Pintail

SCIENTIFIC NAME *Anas*, Latin for duck + *acuta*, from Latin *acutus*, pointed or sharp. Reference is to the pointed tail.

COMMON NAME Northern, for its summer range in the northern United States and Canada. Pintail, for the long sharp tail of the adult male.

Anas americana   American Wigeon

SCIENTIFIC NAME *Anas* + *americana*, of America, to contrast it with the European species.

COMMON NAME American, see scientific name. Wigeon, from French *vigeon*, a small crane.

Anas bahamensis   White-cheeked Pintail

SCIENTIFIC NAME *Anas* + *bahamensis*, Latin for belonging to the Bahamas. Reference is to the natural range.

COMMON NAME White-cheeked, descriptive. Pintail, see *Anas acuta*.

Anas clypeata   Northern Shoveler

SCIENTIFIC NAME *Anas* + *clypeata*, to have a shield, from Latin *clypeus*, a shield. Reference is to the shield-shaped bill.

COMMON NAME Northern, for the natural range in the northern United States. Shoveler, reference is to the shape of the bill and how the bill is used when feeding.

Anas crecca   Green-winged Teal

SCIENTIFIC NAME *Anas* + *crecca*, to sound like a crow, from Greek κρεξ, *krex*, a type of land rail named for its call, which sounded like that of a crow. There is disagreement on this derivation: *kricka*, the Swedish name for this bird, thought to be onomatopoeic of the call, is also a possibility.

COMMON NAME Green-winged, has a bright green speculum. Teal, from Dutch *telen*, *teling* and the English *tele*, *teal*, to produce, to have a brood.

Anas cyanoptera   Cinnamon Teal

SCIENTIFIC NAME *Anas* + *cyanoptera*, dark blue wing, from Greek κυανος, *kuanos*, dark blue, a shade lighter than indigo, and πτερον, *pteron*, a feather, a bird's wing. Reference is to the blue upperwing, best seen in flight.

COMMON NAME Cinnamon, descriptive of the overall color. Teal, see *Anas crecca*.

Anas discors   Blue-winged Teal

SCIENTIFIC NAME *Anas* + *discors*, Latin for in conflict. Thought to be a reference to the call, but disagreement exists on this derivation because the call of this teal is not loud or unpleasant. The name may also refer to the noise the bird makes when taking off.

COMMON NAME Blue-winged, has a blue speculum. Teal, see *Anas crecca*.

Anas fulvigula   Mottled Duck

SCIENTIFIC NAME *Anas* + *fulvigula*, tawny throated, from Latin *fulvor*, tawny, and *gula*, throat.

COMMON NAME Mottled, refers to the mottled plumage. Duck, from Anglo-Saxon *duce*, a form of *ducan*, to duck or dive.

Anas clypeata, northern shoveler

Anas laysanensis Laysan Duck

SCIENTIFIC NAME *Anas* + *laysanensis*, Latin for belonging to Laysan, from Laysan Island in the Hawaiian archipelago.

COMMON NAME Laysan, see scientific name. Duck, see *Anas fulvigula*.

Anas penelope Eurasian Wigeon

SCIENTIFIC NAME *Anas* + *penelope*, according to Elliot Coues (1842–1899) and a few others, most probably a misspelling of the Greek πενελοψ, *penelops*, a type of duck or goose in the writings of Pliny. Just as probable and without needing to account for any misspelling, the name came from Penelope, daughter of Icarius and Polycaste. She was best known as the modest and faithful wife of Odysseus (Ulysses). As usual for myths, there are many versions of how she was saved from drowning by ducks or other waterbirds. Once this rescue occurred, Penelope became associated with these birds.

COMMON NAME Eurasian, for its natural range. Wigeon, see *Anas americana*.

Anas platyrhynchos   Mallard

SCIENTIFIC NAME *Anas* + *platyrhynchos*, to have a broad beak or snout, from Greek πλατυς, *platus*, broad, and ρυγχος, *rugkhos*, the snout or muzzle of an animal, the beak or bill of a bird.

COMMON NAME Mallard, from Old French *maslard*, a wild drake, Anglicized to *mallard*.

Anas querquedula   Garganey

SCIENTIFIC NAME *Anas* + *querquedula*, Latin for a kind of waterfowl, in turn from Greek κερκιθαλις, *kerkithalis*, of the same meaning. Thought to be onomatopoeic of the bird's call.

COMMON NAME Garganey, Italian name for this duck.

Anas rubripes   American Black Duck

SCIENTIFIC NAME *Anas* + *rubripes*, red footed, from Latin *ruber*, red, and *pes*, foot. Reference is to the orange-red feet and legs.

COMMON NAME American, for the natural range. Black, for the overall dark plumage (actually dark brown). Duck, see *Anas fulvigula*.

Anas strepera   Gadwall

SCIENTIFIC NAME *Anas* + *strepera*, from Latin *strepo*, to make a loud noise. Reference is to the loud call.

COMMON NAME Gadwall, origin is unknown. This has been the English name for this bird since at least the late seventeenth century.

Anas wyvilliana   Koloa or Hawaiian Duck

SCIENTIFIC NAME *Anas* + *wyvilliana*, for Sir Charles Wyville Thompson (1830–1882), chief of the Civilian Scientific Staff on HMS *Challenger* voyage of 1873–1876; named in his honor by Philip L. Sclater (1829–1913) from the type specimen collected on the Hawaiian Islands during that voyage.

COMMON NAME Koloa, the Hawaiian name for this duck. Hawaiian, for the natural range in the Hawaiian Islands. Duck, see *Anas fulvigula*.

Anhinga anhinga   Anhinga

SCIENTIFIC NAME *Anhinga*, Tupi Indian (upper Amazon Basin) name for this bird + *anhinga*.

COMMON NAME Anhinga, see scientific name.

Anous minutus — Black Noddy

SCIENTIFIC NAME *Anous*, from Greek ανους, *anous*, silly, without understanding, mindless. Reference is to the behavior of the bird, which is not fearful around humans and is thus easily caught and eaten + *minutus*, Latin for small in size. The black noddy is smaller than the brown noddy, which shares its range.

COMMON NAME Black, descriptive of the plumage. Noddy, a fool or simpleton, see genus name.

Anous stolidus — Brown Noddy

SCIENTIFIC NAME *Anous* + *stolidus*, Latin for insensible, dull, stupid. As with the genus name, reference is to its behavior around humans. The bird essentially ignores people and is easily caught.

COMMON NAME Brown, descriptive of the plumage. Noddy, see *Anous minutus*.

Anser albifrons — Greater White-fronted Goose

SCIENTIFIC NAME *Anser*, Latin for goose + *albifrons*, to have a white forehead, from Latin *albus*, white, and *frons*, forehead, front.

COMMON NAME Greater, larger than the European species, the lesser white-fronted goose. White-fronted, has a white forehead, a good field mark. Goose, from Anglo-Saxon *gos*, their name for this type of bird.

Anser anser — Graylag Goose

SCIENTIFIC NAME *Anser* + *anser*.

COMMON NAME Graylag, this gray goose lags behind the other geese in migration in Europe. Goose, see *Anser albifrons*.

Anser cygnoides — Swan Goose

SCIENTIFIC NAME *Anser* + *cygnoides*, to look like a swan, from Latin *cygnus*, a swan, in turn from Greek κυκνος, *kuknos*, a swan, and *-oides*, from Greek ειδος, *eidos*, to resemble.

COMMON NAME Swan Goose, see scientific name.

Anser indicus   Bar-headed Goose

SCIENTIFIC NAME *Anser* + *indicus*, Latin for of India, its natural range.

COMMON NAME Bar-headed, for the black bars on the white head. Goose, see *Anser albifrons*.

Anthus cervinus   Red-throated Pipit

SCIENTIFIC NAME *Anthus*, from Greek ανθος, *anthos*, a kind of bird. The mythological Anthus was killed by his father's horses, after which he was changed into a bird + *cervinus*, Latin for a deer or stag. Reference is to the rusty-colored (the color of a stag) throat of the male in breeding plumage.

COMMON NAME Red-throated, see scientific name. Pipit, French name for this type of bird, from Latin *pipio*, to peep.

Anthus rubescens   American Pipit

SCIENTIFIC NAME *Anthus* + *rubescens*, Latin for to become red. Reference is to the summer plumage.

COMMON NAME American, to differentiate it from the European species. Pipit, see *Anthus cervinus*.

Anthus spragueii   Sprague's Pipit

SCIENTIFIC NAME *Anthus* + *spragueii*, for Isaac Sprague (1811–1895), a highly skilled botanical draftsman who accompanied John James Audubon (1785–1851) on his Missouri River trip of 1843.

COMMON NAME Sprague's, see scientific name. Pipit, see *Anthus cervinus*.

Aphelocoma californica   Western Scrub-Jay

SCIENTIFIC NAME *Aphelocoma*, smooth hair, from Greek αφελης, *apheles*, smooth, and κομη, *kome*, hair of the head. This jay has no crest + *californica*, of California, for the region where the type specimen was collected, at the time a part of Mexico.

COMMON NAME Western, for the natural range in the United States and to contrast it with the Florida scrub-jay. Scrub, for the habitat. Jay, from French *geai*, a jay. Origin is unknown, but it may be onomatopoeic of the call.

Aphelocoma coerulescens   Florida Scrub-Jay

SCIENTIFIC NAME *Aphelocoma* + *coerulescens*, to become somewhat blue, a form of Latin *caeruleus*, blue or greenish blue, and *-escens*, somewhat like.

COMMON NAME Florida, for the natural range. Scrub-Jay, see *Aphelocoma californica*.

Aphelocoma insularis   Island Scrub-Jay

SCIENTIFIC NAME *Aphelocoma* + *insularis*, of an island, from Latin *insula*, an island. Reference is to its natural range, which is limited to Santa Cruz Island, California.

COMMON NAME Island, for the range on Santa Cruz Island, California. Scrub-Jay, see *Aphelocoma californica*.

Aphelocoma ultramarina   Mexican Jay

SCIENTIFIC NAME *Aphelocoma* + *ultramarina*, a shade of blue, from Latin *ultra*, beyond, and *mare, marinus*, the sea. According to *The Oxford English Dictionary* (1989) ultramarine blue is a pigment or coloring matter of various shades of blue, originally obtained from the mineral lapis lazuli and named with reference to the foreign origin of this mineral. That is, it came from beyond the sea.

COMMON NAME Mexican, for its common range. Jay, see *Aphelocoma californica*.

Aphriza virgata   Surfbird

SCIENTIFIC NAME *Aphriza*, called a false formation in *The Century Dictionary and Cyclopedia* (1913), John James Audubon (1785–1851) attempted to Latinize a word from Greek elements. The base words are αφρος, *aphros*, foam of the sea, and ζαω, ζην, *zaō, zēn*, live, therefore, to live in the sea foam. Reference is to the bird's behavior of feeding in the sea foam at the water's edge + *virgata*, a longitudinal band of color, a stripe. Reference is to the streaked back and breast of the summer plumage.

COMMON NAME Surfbird, for its habit of feeding along the surf line.

Aquila chrysaetos   Golden Eagle

SCIENTIFIC NAME *Aquila*, Latin for eagle + *chrysaetos*, golden eagle, from Greek χρυσοος, *khrusos*, golden, and αετος, *aetos*, an eagle. Reference is to the color of the head and neck.

COMMON NAME Golden, for the color of the feathers on the head and neck. Eagle, from French *aigle*, in turn from Latin *aquila*, an eagle.

Ara severa   Chestnut-fronted Macaw

SCIENTIFIC NAME *Ara*, part of the Tupi Indian (upper Amazon Basin) word for a macaw, *ararauna*. The *ara-* prefix is used in their language for several birds + *severa*, from Latin *severus*, stern, strict, severe. Reference is to the scolding call.

COMMON NAME Chestnut-fronted, has a chestnut-colored forehead. Macaw, origin obscure but probably from another Tupi word for a macaw, *macavuana*.

Aramus guarauna   Limpkin

SCIENTIFIC NAME *Aramus*, the origin of this word is listed as unknown in most references. *The Oxford Greek-English Lexicon* (1996) lists αραμος, *aramos*, as a form of ερωδιος, *erōdios*, a heron, the probable derivation because the body form is somewhat like that of a heron + *guarauna*, from the Spanish name of the region inhabited by the Guarauna (Warrau) Indians in Venezuela, where this bird is abundant.

COMMON NAME Limpkin, little limper, from Middle Dutch and Middle Low German *limp* plus the diminutive *-kin*. Reference is to the bird's gait, which resembles a limp.

Aratinga acuticaudata   Blue-crowned Parakeet

SCIENTIFIC NAME *Aratinga*, from one of the Tupi Indian (upper Amazon Basin) names for a parrot + *acuticaudata*, sharp tailed, from Latin *acutus*, sharp, and *cauda*, tail.

COMMON NAME Blue-crowned, has a blue forehead and partial blue crown. Parakeet, Anglicized form of the French *perroquet*, another name for a parrot (see *Amazona aestiva*). Used in English to describe smaller types of parrots.

Aratinga erythrogenys   Red-masked Parakeet

SCIENTIFIC NAME *Aratinga* + *erythrogenys*, red cheeked, from Greek ερυθρος, *eruthros*, red, and Greek γενυς, *genus*, jaw, cheek.

COMMON NAME Red-masked, appears to be wearing a red face mask. Parakeet, see *Aratinga acuticaudata*.

Aratinga holochlora Green Parakeet

SCIENTIFIC NAME *Aratinga* + *holochlora*, all green, from Greek ολοχλο-ρος, *olokhloros*, from ολο, *olo*, all, and χλορος, *khloros*, green.

COMMON NAME Green, descriptive of the overall color. Parakeet, see *Aratinga acuticaudata*.

Aratinga mitrata Mitred Parakeet

SCIENTIFIC NAME *Aratinga* + *mitrata*, from Latin *mitra*, in turn from Greek μιτρα, *mitra*, a head-band or turban, the type of hat worn by various religious leaders to denote a certain rank, originally a headdress with a ribbon tied under the chin. Reference is to the red on the head and sides of the face, thought to resemble a mitre and ribbon.

COMMON NAME Mitred, see scientific name. Parakeet, see *Aratinga acuticaudata*.

Aratinga weddellii Dusky-headed Parakeet

SCIENTIFIC NAME *Aratinga* + *weddellii*, for Hugh Algernon Weddell (1819–1877), a British botanist who studied the flora of South America.

COMMON NAME Dusky-headed, for the gray head. Parakeet, see *Aratinga acuticaudata*.

Archilochus alexandri Black-chinned Hummingbird

SCIENTIFIC NAME *Archilochus*, for Archilochus, a Greek lyric poet who specialized in lampoons and sarcastic poems of his contemporaries. He is credited with the invention of many new poetic meters and brought Iambic poetry to artistic heights. This name was given by Heinrich Gottlieb Ludwig Reichenbach (1793–1879), who gave several other hummingbird genus names honoring classical artists. Most sources break *Archilochus* down into two component Greek words and attempt a derivation from them: αρχι, *arkhi*, a chief, and λοχος, *lokhos*, an ambush or a group of men, usually military. Therefore the name was translated both as "chief ambusher" and "chief among men (birds)." This error was initiated by Edmund C. Jaeger in *A Source-Book of Biological Names and Terms* (1978) + *alexandri*, for M. M. Alexandre (fl. 1846), a French medical doctor who collected birds in Mexico in the 1840s.

COMMON NAME Black-chinned, for the large black chin-patch on the adult male. Hummingbird, for the buzzing hum of the wingbeats.

Archilochus colubris   Ruby-throated Hummingbird

SCIENTIFIC NAME *Archilochus* + *colubris*, probably a misspelling of *colibri*, both the French and Spanish word for hummingbird. The Latin *colubra*, serpent, is a highly unlikely choice.

COMMON NAME Ruby-throated, for the red throat of the adult male. Hummingbird, see *Archilochus alexandri*.

Ardea alba   Great Egret

SCIENTIFIC NAME *Ardea*, Latin for heron, in turn from Greek ερωδιος, *erōdios*, a heron + *alba*, white, from Latin *albus*, white. Reference is to the overall white color.

COMMON NAME Great, for the size; this is the United States' largest egret. Egret, from French *aigrette*, a diminutive of *aigron*, the name for the crest of feathers of these birds during the breeding season.

Ardea herodias   Great Blue Heron

SCIENTIFIC NAME *Ardea* + *herodias*, from Greek ερωδιος, *erōdios*, a heron.

COMMON NAME Great Blue, this is the United States' largest blue heron. Heron, from Old High German *haiger*, *heiger*, their name for this type of bird.

Arenaria interpres   Ruddy Turnstone

SCIENTIFIC NAME *Arenaria*, from Latin *harenarius*, of the sand. Reference is to the habitat along sandy shorelines + *interpres*, among other meanings, an interpreter of omens and oracles. This bird calls out to warn other birds of danger.

COMMON NAME Ruddy, has bright chestnut wings and back in the summer. Turnstone, descriptive of its feeding behavior: it turns over small stones searching for food.

Arenaria melanocephala   Black Turnstone

SCIENTIFIC NAME *Arenaria* + *melanocephala*, black headed, from Greek μελας, *melas*, black, and κεφαλη, *kephalē*, head.

COMMON NAME Black, the upperparts of this bird are black. Turnstone, see *Arenaria interpres*.

Asio flammeus Short-eared Owl

SCIENTIFIC NAME *Asio*, a form of the Latin *axio*, the little horned owl + *flammeus*, Latin for flaming, flame colored. Reference is to the tawny plumage. There is also a Hawaiian subspecies, *sandwichensis*. The Sandwich Islands was an old name for the Hawaiian Islands; they were named for John Montagu, fourth earl of Sandwich (1718–1792), the first lord of the British Admiralty.

COMMON NAME Short-eared, for the small feather tufts on top of the head, almost indiscernible, certainly much shorter than those of the long-eared owl. Owl, from Anglo-Saxon *ule*, owl, and from Latin *ululo*, to cry out. Both words are onomatopoeic of the owl's call.

Asio otus Long-eared Owl

SCIENTIFIC NAME *Asio* + *otus*, from Greek οτος, *otos*, the eared or horned owl.

COMMON NAME Long-eared, for the long feather tufts on top of the head that resemble ears. Owl, see *Asio flammeus*.

Asturina nitida Gray Hawk

SCIENTIFIC NAME *Asturina*, to look like a goshawk, from *Astur*, an old genus name for the goshawk, and -*ina*, like or belonging to + *nitida*, from Latin *nitidus*, bright, shining. Reference is to the light plumage.

COMMON NAME Gray, for the overall color. Hawk, from Anglo-Saxon *hafoc*, hawk, their name for this type of bird.

Athene cunicularia Burrowing Owl

SCIENTIFIC NAME *Athene*, of Athene (Athena), the Greek goddess, to whom the owl was sacred + *cunicularia*, from Latin *cunicularius*, a miner. The root word is *cuniculus*, a rabbit, a subterranean passage, mine, tunnel, burrow. Reference is to the nesting sites.

COMMON NAME Burrowing, for its nesting site in burrows. Owl, from Anglo-Saxon *ule*, owl, and from Latin *ululo*, to cry out. Both words are onomatopoeic of the owl's call.

Auriparus flaviceps Verdin

SCIENTIFIC NAME *Auriparus*, a gold titmouse, from Latin *aurum*, gold, and *parus*, a titmouse + *flaviceps*, yellow headed, from Latin *flavus*, pale yellow, and -*ceps*, head, from Greek κεφαλη, *kephalē*, head. Reference is to the yellow face and head.

COMMON NAME Verdin, French for yellowhammer, their common name for this bird.

Aythya affinis   Lesser Scaup

SCIENTIFIC NAME *Aythya*, a diving bird, Latinized from Greek αιθυια, *aithuia*, a kind of diving bird. According to Elliot Coues (1842–1899), this is a blatant mistake in the transliteration from Greek to Latin and the name should be *Æthyia* not *Aythya* + *affinis*, Latin for adjacent or related to. Reference is to the greater scaup, which this bird resembles.

COMMON NAME Lesser, smaller than the greater scaup but only slightly. Scaup, Scottish for a ledge in the ocean that at times may be partially exposed above water. This bird feeds on the shellfish that live on such a ledge.

Aythya americana   Redhead

SCIENTIFIC NAME *Aythya* + *americana*, of America.

COMMON NAME Redhead, for the male's red head.

Aythya collaris   Ring-necked Duck

SCIENTIFIC NAME *Aythya* + *collaris*, from Latin *collare*, a neck band or collar. Reference is to the faint ring at the base of the neck on the male in breeding plumage.

COMMON NAME Ring-necked, for the faint line of lighter color at the base of the neck on the male in breeding plumage. Duck, from Anglo-Saxon *duce*, a form of *ducan*, to duck or dive.

Aythya fuligula   Tufted Duck

SCIENTIFIC NAME *Aythya* + *fuligula*, from Latin *fuligo*, soot, and the diminutive -*ulus*, thus, a little sooty; or from *fuligo*, soot, and *gula*, throat, thus, sooty neck. Both refer to the color of the bird.

COMMON NAME Tufted, for the prominent crest on the back of the male's head in breeding plumage. Duck, see *Aythya collaris*.

Aythya marila — Greater Scaup

SCIENTIFIC NAME *Aythya* + *marila*, charcoal black, from Latin *marile*, embers of charcoal, the color of charcoal. Reference is to the male's black head and neck in summer plumage.

COMMON NAME Greater, this bird is slightly larger than the lesser scaup. Scaup, see *Aythya affinis*.

Aythya valisineria — Canvasback

SCIENTIFIC NAME *Aythya* + *valisineria*, eel grass; Alexander Wilson (1766–1813) gave this name to the canvasback because it prefers to eat eel grass, *Vallisneria americana*. This plant genus was named for Antonio Vallisnieri (1661–1730), an Italian physician, botanist, and prolific scientific author. Wilson misspelled the name when he assigned it to this duck but, because of the principle of priority, the mistake stands.

COMMON NAME Canvasback, for the off-white color on the back that resembles undyed canvas.

Baeolophus atricristatus — Black-crested Titmouse

SCIENTIFIC NAME *Baeolophus*, having a small crest, from Greek βαιος, *baios*, short, small, and λοφος, *lophos*, used by Homer to mean a crest on top of a bird's head, whether made up of feathers, as the lark's crest, or of flesh, as seen on a cock + *atricristatus*, Latin for black crested, from *ater*, black, dark colored, and *cristatus*, with a crest.

COMMON NAME Black-crested, descriptive. Titmouse, a small small bird, from Icelandic *tittr*, anything small, and Anglo-Saxon *mase*, a name used for small birds.

Baeolophus bicolor — Tufted Titmouse

SCIENTIFIC NAME *Baeolophus* + *bicolor*, Latin for having two colors. This bird is gray on top and has a conspicuous buff stripe on each side.

COMMON NAME Tufted, English for a lock of hair. Reference is to the crest on the head. Titmouse, see *Baeolophus atricristatus*.

Baeolophus inornatus — Oak Titmouse

SCIENTIFIC NAME *Baeolophus* + *inornatus*, Latin for plain, unadorned. When this scientific name was given, this titmouse was dull in color when compared to the other two described at that time, the bridled titmouse and the tufted titmouse.

COMMON NAME Oak, for the general habitat. Titmouse, see *Baeolophus atricristatus*.

Baeolophus ridgwayi Juniper Titmouse

SCIENTIFIC NAME *Baeolophus* + *ridgwayi*, for Robert Ridgway (1850–1929), an American ornithologist who wrote *The Birds of North and Middle America* (1901–1919).

COMMON NAME Juniper, for the general habitat. Titmouse, see *Baeolophus atricristatus*.

Baeolophus wollweberi Bridled Titmouse

SCIENTIFIC NAME *Baeolophus* + *wollweberi*, for Wollweber (fl. 1840), a German naturalist who collected the type specimen.

COMMON NAME Bridled, for the color pattern on the head, which makes it look like it is wearing a bridle. Titmouse, see *Baeolophus atricristatus*.

Bartramia longicauda Upland Sandpiper

SCIENTIFIC NAME *Bartramia*, for William Bartram (1739–1823), an American naturalist. Under the patronage of John Fothergill, a wealthy English botanist, Bartram traveled throughout the southeastern United States collecting specimens of the fauna and flora, which he drew, wrote about, and shipped to his benefactor in England + *longicauda*, long tailed, from Latin *longus*, long, and *caudum*, tail.

COMMON NAME Upland, the parts of the country away from the sea. Sandpiper, one who pipes on the sand. Piping is descriptive of its call, from Latin *pipare*, to chirp.

Basileuterus culicivorus Golden-crowned Warbler

SCIENTIFIC NAME *Basileuterus*, from the Greek βασιλευτερυς, *basileuterus*, more kingly, from βασιλευς, *basileus*, a king or chief. This word was used by Aristotle to describe a small bird + *culicivorus*, gnat eater, from Latin *culicis*, a tiny gnat, and *vorus*, to eat, from *voro*, to swallow ravenously, devour.

COMMON NAME Golden-crowned, for the yellow stripe on the crown. Warbler, for the trills and quavers of its song.

Basileuterus rufifrons Rufous-capped Warbler

SCIENTIFIC NAME *Basileuterus* + *rufifrons*, to have a red forehead, from Latin *rufus*, various shades of red, tawny, and *frons*, forehead, front.

COMMON NAME Rufous-capped, for the red patches on the top of the head. Warbler, see *Basileuterus culicivorus*.

Bombycilla cedrorum Cedar Waxwing

SCIENTIFIC NAME *Bombycilla*, meant to be Latin for silk-tail (from the German common name for this bird, *seidenschwanz*, silk-tail), from Latin *bombyx*, silk, and *cilla*, thought by Louis Pierre Vieillot (1748–1831), who named the bird, to mean tail. He took the word from the Latin *motacilla*, the wagtail, but *-illa* of this word is a diminutive attached to *motacis*, mover. Thus, the "c" in Vieillot's *-cilla* belongs to the root word *motacis*, not to the suffix as he supposed + *cedrorum*, from Latin *cedrus*, the cedar or juniper tree.

COMMON NAME Cedar, reference is to this bird's preference for juniper (commonly called cedar) cones as food. Waxwing, for the red drop-shaped tips on the secondary flight feathers that look like drops of red wax. These are actually where the feather shafts extend beyond the vanes.

Bombycilla garrulus Bohemian Waxwing

SCIENTIFIC NAME *Bombycilla* + *garrulus*, Latin for talkative, chattering. This name was chosen because it is the genus name for the European jay, which this waxwing resembles.

COMMON NAME Bohemian, a gypsy, a vagabond, a wanderer; this bird migrates in large flocks that descend to feed together. Waxwing, see *Bombycilla cedrorum*.

Bonasa umbellus Ruffed Grouse

SCIENTIFIC NAME *Bonasa*, from Latin *bonasus*, a species of wild ox, the European bison, in turn from Greek βοναοος, *bonasos*, of the same meaning. Reference is to this bird's drumming, which was thought to sound similar to the bellowing of a bull. In *A Source-Book of Biological Names and Terms* (1978). Edmund C. Jaeger suggests the unlikely possibility of the Latin *bonus*, good, and *assum*, a roast + *umbellus*, from Latin *umbella*, a sunshade, parasol, an umbrella. Reference is to the umbrella shape of the feathers that make up the ruff around the neck.

COMMON NAME Ruffed, for the ruff of feathers around the neck. Grouse, origin unknown but thought to be from French *griais*, speckled gray.

Botaurus lentiginosus   American Bittern

SCIENTIFIC NAME *Botaurus*, Medieval Latin for *bittern*, to roar like a bull, from Latin *boo*, in turn from Greek βοαω, *boaō*, to shout or roar, and from Latin *taurus*, in turn from Greek ταυρος, *tauros*, a bull. Reference is to the bird's call, which was thought to resemble the bellowing of a bull. The Latin *boatum tauri*, the bellowing of a bull (of the same derivation as above) has also been suggested. Most references give the derivation as Latin *bos*, an ox, and *taurus*, a bull, therefore, ox-bull. This is etymologically possible but is certainly a tangential reference to this bird's call + *lentiginosus*, freckled, from Latin *lentigo*, a lentil-shaped spot.

COMMON NAME American, to contrast it with the European bittern. Bittern, from Old English transcending through *buttour*, *butorius*, and *botaurus* to *bittern* (see genus derivation).

Brachyramphus brevirostris   Kittlitz's Murrelet

SCIENTIFIC NAME *Brachyramphus*, having a short beak, from Greek βραχυς, *brakhus*, short, and ραμφος, *ramphos*, the snout or muzzle of an animal, the beak or bill of a bird, in turn derived from ραμφις, *ramphis*, a hook + *brevirostris*, short beak, from Latin *brevis*, short, and rostrum, the snout or muzzle of an animal, the beak or bill of a bird.

COMMON NAME Kittlitz's, for Friedrich Heinrich Kittlitz (1779–1874), a German Naval officer who collected the type specimen of this bird. Murrelet, diminutive of murre, a type of auk, guillemot, or puffin, depending on the geographic region in which the word is used.

Brachyramphus marmoratus   Marbled Murrelet

SCIENTIFIC NAME *Brachyramphus* + *marmoratus*, Latin for marbled. Reference is to the mottled breeding plumage.

COMMON NAME Marbled, see scientific name. Murrelet, see *Brachyramphus brevirostris*.

Brachyramphus perdix   Long-billed Murrelet

SCIENTIFIC NAME *Brachyramphus* + *perdix*, from Greek περδιξ, *perdix*, a partridge. In Greek mythology Perdix (Talos) was the nephew of Daedalus, whose name means "artful craftsman" and who is probably best known for making wings for himself and his son Icarus. Pedrix was apprenticed to Daedalus in his workshop. He outdid his uncle by inventing the saw (after studying the protrusions on the spine of a fish) and then the compass and potter's wheel. Daedalus was so jealous of these accomplishments that, when he had the chance, he pushed Perdix from a great height. Athena saw this and changed Perdix into a partridge while he was still in the air. Reference is to the size.

COMMON NAME Long-billed, has a longer bill than any of the other murrelets. Murrelet, see *Brachyramphus brevirostris*.

Branta bernicla   Brant

SCIENTIFIC NAME *Branta*, sources differ in their opinions as to the derivation of this word. *The Oxford English Dictionary* (1989) states that the origin is not known with certainty. *The Dictionary of American Bird Names* (1985) says it comes from Anglo-Saxon *bernan* or *brennan*, to burn, in reference to the dark, burnt color of the plumage, and mentions a possible corruption of Greek βρενθα, *brentha*, an unknown waterbird. *A Source-Book of Biological Names and Terms* (1978) agrees with the *bernan* derivation. *The Century Dictionary and Cyclopedia* (1913) and *A Dictionary of Scientific Bird Names* (1991) list the Icelandic or Old Norse *brandgas*, a dark or burnt-appearing goose, as the root. Regardless of which root word is actually correct, the consensus is that *Branta* refers to a burnt or dark appearance of the plumage + *bernicla*, Middle Latin for barnacle. In European folklore it was believed that these geese hatched from barnacles. The birds migrated to the north and returned in the spring with their offspring. Because nothing but ocean was thought to exist to the north of Europe, the belief arose that these geese must have hatched from something in the sea.

COMMON NAME Brant, same as *Branta*, see scientific name.

Branta canadensis   Canada Goose

SCIENTIFIC NAME *Branta* + *canadensis*, Latin for belonging to Canada. Reference is to the breeding range.

COMMON NAME Canada, for the breeding range. Goose, from Anglo-Saxon *gos*, their name for this type of bird.

Branta leucopsis   Barnacle Goose

SCIENTIFIC NAME *Branta* + *leucopsis*, having a white face, from Greek λευκος, *leukos*, of color, white, and οψις, *opsis*, face, eye, appearance. Reference is to the white face of this goose.

COMMON NAME Barnacle, these geese were thought to have hatched from barnacles (see *Branta bernicla*). Goose, see *Branta canadensis*.

Branta canadensis, Canada goose

Branta sandvicensis — Nene or Hawaiian Goose

SCIENTIFIC NAME *Branta* + *sandvicensis*, of the Sandwich Islands, an old name for the Hawaiian Islands. They were named for John Montagu, the fourth earl of Sandwich (1718–1792), First Lord of the British Admiralty.

COMMON NAME Nene, the Hawaiian name for this bird. Hawaiian, endemic to Hawaii. Goose, see *Branta canadensis*.

Brotogeris chiriri — Yellow-chevroned Parakeet

SCIENTIFIC NAME *Brotogeris*, having the voice of a human, from Greek βροτος, *brotos*, mortal man, and γηρυς, *gērus*, voice, speech. Reference is to this bird's ability to mimic human speech + *chiriri*, the Guarani Indian (eastern lowlands of South America) name for this bird. The name is imitative of the song.

COMMON NAME Yellow-chevroned, has yellow greater coverlets on the wings that are chevron shaped. Parakeet, Anglicized form of the French *perroquet*, another name for a parrot (see *Amazona aestiva*). Used in English to describe smaller types of parrots.

Brotogeris versicolurus   White-winged Parakeet

SCIENTIFIC NAME *Brotogeris* + *versicolurus*, having a tail that changes colors, from Latin *versicolor*, having colors that change over time or from the viewing angle, and from Greek ουρος, *ouros*, tailed. Reference is to the two colors of the tail, which is green when viewed from above and greenish blue when viewed from below. According to the *Oxford Greek-English Lexicon* (1996), ουρος, *ouros*, should not be used for the tail of a bird but is restricted to other animals.

COMMON NAME White-winged, has white secondaries and inner primaries that show best during flight. Parakeet, see *Brotogeris chiriri*.

Bubo virginianus   Great Horned Owl

SCIENTIFIC NAME *Bubo*, Latin for a horned owl, from Greek βυας, *buas*, the horned or eagle owl (Pliny), in turn from Greek βυζο, *buzo*, to hoot + *virginianus*, Latin for pertaining to Virginia, from Virginia. Reference is to the region of the type specimen.

COMMON NAME Great, for its size. Horned, has tufts of feathers on top of the head that resemble horns. Owl, from Anglo-Saxon *ule*, owl, and from Latin *ululo*, to cry out. Both words are onomatopoeic of the owl's call.

Bubulcus ibis   Cattle Egret

SCIENTIFIC NAME *Bubulcus*, Latin for a cowherd, of or pertaining to cattle. Reference is to the feeding habits of this bird: it walks along with cattle and feeds on the insects the herd stirs up + *ibis*, Latin for the ibis, in turn from Greek ιβις, *ibis*, from the Egyptian name for this bird. Reference is to the bird's appearance, which is somewhat like an ibis.

COMMON NAME Cattle, for its feeding habits around cattle. Egret, from French *aigrette*, a diminutive of *aigron*, the name for the crest of feathers of these birds during the breeding season.

Bucephala albeola   Bufflehead

SCIENTIFIC NAME *Bucephala*, bull headed, Latinized from Greek βους, *bous*, ox or bull, and κεφαλη, *kephalē*, head. Reference is to the shape of the head of this genus, which was thought to resemble the head of the American buffalo + *albeola*, little white, a diminutive of the Latin *albus*, white. Reference is to the white patch on the back of the head.

COMMON NAME Bufflehead, a corrupted contraction of *buffalo head*. The shape of this bird's head is reminiscent of the head of a buffalo.

Bucephala clangula   Common Goldeneye

SCIENTIFIC NAME *Bucephala* + *clangula*, a small noise, a diminutive of the Latin *clangor*, noise. Reference is to the sound of the wingbeats in flight.

COMMON NAME Common, for its wide distribution. Goldeneye, has yellow irises.

Bucephala islandica   Barrow's Goldeneye

SCIENTIFIC NAME *Bucephala* + *islandica*, Latinized form of Iceland, one of the breeding grounds for this bird.

COMMON NAME Barrow's, for Sir John Barrow (1764–1848), Secretary of the British Admiralty and founder of the Royal Geographic Society. Point Barrow, Alaska, was also named for him. Goldeneye, see *Bucephala clangula*.

Bulweria bulwerii   Bulwer's Petrel

SCIENTIFIC NAME *Bulweria*, for James Bulwer (1794–1879) a British naturalist, artist, a fellow of the Linnaean Society, and an ordained priest. He collected the type specimen of this bird in Madeira, Portugal + *bulwerii*.

COMMON NAME Bulwer's, see scientific name. Petrel, a diminutive of Peter, little Peter. Named for St. Peter, who was said to walk on water. This bird appears to walk on the surface of the sea as it lands on the water; this walking also stirs up small fish, the petrel's food.

Buteo albicaudatus   White-tailed Hawk

SCIENTIFIC NAME *Buteo*, Latin for a species of hawk, a buzzard + *albicaudatus*, white tailed, from Latin *albus*, white, and *caudatus*, tailed.

COMMON NAME White-tailed, descriptive. Hawk, from Anglo-Saxon *hafoc*, hawk, their name for this type of bird.

Buteo albonotatus   Zone-tailed Hawk

SCIENTIFIC NAME *Buteo* + *albonotatus*, clearly marked white, from Latin *albus*, white, and *notatus*, clearly marked, defined. Reference is to the white bands on the tail.

COMMON NAME Zone-tailed, for the white bands on the tail. Hawk, see *Buteo albicaudatus*.

Buteo brachyurus   Short-tailed Hawk

SCIENTIFIC NAME *Buteo* + *brachyurus*, short tailed, from Greek βραχυς, *brakhus*, short, and ουρος, *ouros*, tail. According to the *Oxford Greek-English Lexicon* (1996), ουρος, *ouros* should not be used for the tail of a bird but is restricted to other animals.

COMMON NAME Short-tailed, descriptive. Hawk, see *Buteo albicaudatus*.

Buteo jamaicensis   Red-tailed Hawk

SCIENTIFIC NAME *Buteo* + *jamaicensis*, Latin for belonging to Jamaica. Reference is to the site of the collection of the type specimen.

COMMON NAME Red-tailed, dorsal aspect of the tail is orange-red. Hawk, see *Buteo albicaudatus*.

Buteo lagopus   Rough-legged Hawk

SCIENTIFIC NAME *Buteo* + *lagopus*, hare's foot, from Greek λαγως, *lagōs*, a hare, and πους, *pous*, foot. Reference is to the feather-covered legs. *Lagopus* is also Latin for a ptarmigan, a grouse with feathers on its legs.

COMMON NAME Rough-legged, descriptive of the feather-covered legs. Hawk, see *Buteo albicaudatus*.

Buteo lineatus   Red-shouldered Hawk

SCIENTIFIC NAME *Buteo* + *lineatus*, Latin for striped. Reference is to the black and white bands on the tail and dorsum of the wings.

COMMON NAME Red-shouldered, the cinnamon-colored breast spills over onto the shoulders. Hawk, see *Buteo albicaudatus*.

Buteo platypterus   Broad-winged Hawk

SCIENTIFIC NAME *Buteo* + *platypterus*, broad winged, from Greek πλατυς, *platus*, broad, flat, wide, and πτερον, *pteron*, a feather, a bird's wing.

COMMON NAME Broad-winged, descriptive. Hawk, see *Buteo albicaudatus*.

Buteo regalis   Ferruginous Hawk

SCIENTIFIC NAME *Buteo* + *regalis*, Latin for royal, regal, kingly. In this case the scientific name was taken from the locale where the type specimen was collected, the village of Real del Monte in Mexico. *Real* is Spanish for royal.

COMMON NAME Ferruginous, from Latin *ferrugo*, iron rust. Reference is to the reddish plumage. Hawk, see *Buteo albicaudatus*.

Buteo solitarius   'Io or Hawaiian Hawk

SCIENTIFIC NAME *Buteo* + *solitarius*, Latin for solitary. Reference is to this hawk being the only native *Buteo* in Hawaii.

COMMON NAME 'Io, the Hawaiian name for this hawk. Hawaiian, for the natural range. Hawk, see *Buteo albicaudatus*.

Buteo swainsoni   Swainson's Hawk

SCIENTIFIC NAME *Buteo* + *swainsoni*, for William Swainson (1789–1855), a British naturalist and artist. He published *Zoological Illustrations* (1820–1823) and was a strong advocate of the quinary system of taxonomy, a failed method of classifying plants and animals.

COMMON NAME Swainson's, see scientific name. Hawk, see *Buteo albicaudatus*.

Buteogallus anthracinus   Common Black-Hawk

SCIENTIFIC NAME *Buteogallus*, a chicken hawk, from Latin *buteo*, a kind of hawk, and *gallus*, the domestic cock. This genus was so named because its first species *Buteogallus aequinoctialis*, of South and Central America, was thought to look like a chicken, not because this hawk preyed on chickens + *anthracinus*, Latin for coal black, in turn from Greek ανθραξ, *anthrax*, coal. Reference is to the overall black color.

COMMON NAME Common, abundant in its range. Black, for the color of the plumage. Hawk, from Anglo-Saxon *hafoc*, hawk, their name for this type of bird.

Butorides virescens   Green Heron

SCIENTIFIC NAME *Butorides*, to look like a bittern. *Butor* was an Old English word for a bittern, which came through Old French and is thought to

Buteo swainsoni, Swainson's hawk

be related to the rare Latin *butionemin* of the same meaning. Some sources list *butor* and *butio* as Middle Latin for a bittern. *-ides*, from Greek ειδος, *eidos*, means to resemble + *virescens*, from Latin *viresco*, to become green. Reference is to the green back.

COMMON NAME Green, for the green back. Heron, from Old High German *haiger*, *heiger*, a heron.

Cacatua galerita   Sulphur-crested Cockatoo

SCIENTIFIC NAME *Cacatua*, Latinized form of *kakatua*, the Malay name for a cockatoo + *galerita*, Latin for wearing a *galerus*, a cap or hat made of skin, a ceremonial cap. Reference is to the yellow crest, which is only visible when flared.

COMMON NAME Sulphur-crested, has a yellow head crest. Cockatoo, from the Malay *kakatua*, their name for this bird. Imitative of the call.

Cairina moschata — Muscovy Duck

SCIENTIFIC NAME *Cairina*, from Italian *cairino*, a native of Cairo, Egypt, for the mistaken belief that this duck was native to that region + *moschata*, from Latin *moschatus*, musky. Reference is to the scent of this duck.

COMMON NAME Muscovy, intended to mean connected with musk. Duck, from Anglo-Saxon *duce*, a form of *ducan*, to duck or dive.

Calamospiza melanocorys — Lark Bunting

SCIENTIFIC NAME *Calamospiza*, reed finch, from Greek καλαμος, *kalamos*, reed, and σπιζα, *spiza*, finch. Reference is to the habitat + *melanocorys*, black lark, from Greek μελας, *melas*, black, and κορυς, *korus*, a shortened form of κορυδος, *korudos*, a lark.

COMMON NAME Lark, like a lark, it sings while flying. Bunting, the origin of this word is unknown, but *The Oxford English Dictionary* (1989) suggests the Scandinavian *buntin*, short and thick, plump.

Calcarius lapponicus — Lapland Longspur

SCIENTIFIC NAME *Calcarius*, spurred, from Latin *calcar*, a cock's spur. Reference is to the long claw on the hind toe + *lapponicus*, of Lapland, the site where the type specimen was collected.

COMMON NAME Lapland, see scientific name. Longspur, for the long claw on the hind toe.

Calcarius mccownii — McCown's Longspur

SCIENTIFIC NAME *Calcarius* + *mccownii*, for John Porter McCown (1815–1879), a Captain in the U.S. Army who discovered this bird in Texas in 1851.

COMMON NAME McCown's, see scientific name. Longspur, see *Calcarius lapponicus*.

Calcarius ornatus — Chestnut-collared Longspur

SCIENTIFIC NAME *Calcarius* + *ornatus*, Latin for richly adorned. Reference is to the male's attractive breeding plumage.

COMMON NAME Chestnut-collared, for the male's chestnut-colored nape in breeding plumage. Longspur, see *Calcarius lapponicus*.

Calcarius pictus   Smith's Longspur

SCIENTIFIC NAME *Calcarius* + *pictus*, Latin for painted. Reference is to the bright colors of the male's breeding plumage.

COMMON NAME Smith's, for Gideon B. Smith (1793–1867), an American editor and author. As a friend of John James Audubon (1785–1851), who named this bird for him, Smith was the agent who sold and distributed the octavo edition of Audubon's *Birds of America*. Longspur, see *Calcarius lapponicus*.

Calidris acuminata   Sharp-tailed Sandpiper

SCIENTIFIC NAME *Calidris*, from Greek καλιδρις, *kalidris*, a form of οκαλι-δρις, *skalidris*, used by Aristotle for a speckled waterbird + *acuminata*, from Latin *acuminatus*, sharp, pointed, tapering. Reference is to the shape of the tail.

COMMON NAME Sharp-tailed, descriptive. Sandpiper, one who pipes on the sand. Piping is descriptive of its call, from Latin *pipare*, to chirp.

Calidris alba   Sanderling

SCIENTIFIC NAME *Calidris* + *alba*, Latin for white. Reference is to the white underparts.

COMMON NAME Sanderling, little bird of the sand, from *sand*, the habitat, -*er*, a German suffix for one who has to do with, and the Anglo-Saxon diminutive -*ling*.

Calidris alpina   Dunlin

SCIENTIFIC NAME *Calidris* + *alpina*, of the mountains, from Latin *alpinus*, the mountains of northern Italy, by extension any mountainous area. Reference to this bird breeding in alpine or cool areas.

COMMON NAME Dunlin, little dark brown one, a diminutive of Anglo-Saxon *dunn*, dark brown.

Calidris bairdii   Baird's Sandpiper

SCIENTIFIC NAME *Calidris* + *bairdii*, for Spencer Fullerton Baird (1823–1887), secretary of the Smithsonian Institution and author of *Catalogue of North American Mammals* (1857) and *Catalogue of North American Birds* (1868).

COMMON NAME Baird's, see scientific name. Sandpiper, see *Calidris acuminata*.

Calidris canutus   Red Knot

SCIENTIFIC NAME *Calidris* + *canutus*, for King Canute of Denmark (995–1035). To prove the flattering claims of his great power were wrong, Canute went to the seaside and commanded the tide not to come in. When the tide came in, he advised his subjects to take note of what little power he actually possessed. Reference is to this bird's habit of feeding along the tide line.

COMMON NAME Red, for the reddish brown face and underparts. Knot, a form of Canute, see scientific name.

Calidris ferruginea   Curlew Sandpiper

SCIENTIFIC NAME *Calidris* + *ferruginea*, rusty, from Latin *ferrugo*, iron rust. Reference is to the rusty-colored breeding plumage.

COMMON NAME Curlew, for the bill, which is shaped like that of a curlew. Sandpiper, see *Calidris acuminata*.

Calidris fuscicollis   White-rumped Sandpiper

SCIENTIFIC NAME *Calidris* + *fuscicollis*, dark necked, from Latin *fuscus*, dark colored, dusky, and *collum*, neck. This is a misleading scientific name because this bird does not have a distinctive dark neck.

COMMON NAME White-rumped, descriptive. Sandpiper, see *Calidris acuminata*.

Calidris himantopus   Stilt Sandpiper

SCIENTIFIC NAME *Calidris* + *himantopus*, from Greek ιμαντοπους, *imantopous*. This word has two meanings: spindle shanked, which means very thin legs, and a kind of waterbird, by extension one with very thin legs (*Oxford Greek-English Lexicon* 1996). Most other references give thong foot, from ιμαντ, *imant*, thong, and πους, *pous*, foot.

COMMON NAME Stilt, for its long, thin legs. Sandpiper, see *Calidris acuminata*.

Calidris maritima   Purple Sandpiper

SCIENTIFIC NAME *Calidris* + *maritima*, from Latin *maritimus*, of or belonging to the sea. Reference is to its habitat along rocky seashores.

COMMON NAME Purple, the feathers on the shoulders sometimes reflect a purple iridescence in the sunlight. Sandpiper, see *Calidris acuminata*.

Calidris mauri   Western Sandpiper

SCIENTIFIC NAME *Calidris + mauri*, for Ernesto Mauri (1791–1836), an Italian botanist and friend of Charles Bonaparte (1803–1857), who named this bird for him. Mauri was the director of the botanical gardens in Rome and coauthor, with Bonaparte, of *Iconografia della Fauna Italica* (1832–1841).

COMMON NAME Western, more common in the western United States. Sandpiper, see *Calidris acuminata*.

Calidris melanotos   Pectoral Sandpiper

SCIENTIFIC NAME *Calidris + melanotos*, having a black back, from Greek μελας, *melas*, black, and νωτον, *nōton*, back. Reference is to the dark back of the breeding plumage.

COMMON NAME Pectoral, for the inflatable sac on the male's chest that is used to increase the resonance of his mating call. Sandpiper, see *Calidris acuminata*.

Calidris minuta   Little Stint

SCIENTIFIC NAME *Calidris + minuta*, from Latin *minutus*, small in size or amount. Reference is to this bird's small size when compared to most other sandpipers.

COMMON NAME Little, for the size. Stint, origin obscure, but the English word *stint* is derived from *stunt* and when applied to this group of birds could be a reference to the size.

Calidris minutilla   Least Sandpiper

SCIENTIFIC NAME *Calidris + minutilla*, very small, from Latin *minutulus*, very small, tiny.

COMMON NAME Least, for the size; this is the smallest sandpiper in the United States. Sandpiper, see *Calidris acuminata*.

Calidris ptilocnemis   Rock Sandpiper

SCIENTIFIC NAME *Calidris + ptilocnemis*, feather leg armor, from Greek πτιλον, *ptilon*, a feather, especially the soft downy feathers under the covering feathers, and κνημιδες, *knēmides,* a piece of armor worn over the shins by a Greek soldier. Reference is to the soft feathers covering this bird's leg from the knee to the heel, an area usually devoid of feathers in other birds.

COMMON NAME Rock, for the habitat along rocky shorelines. Sandpiper, see *Calidris acuminata.*

Calidris pusilla   Semipalmated Sandpiper

SCIENTIFIC NAME *Calidris + pusilla,* from Latin *pusillus,* very small in size, tiny, wee.

COMMON NAME Semipalmated, half-palmed, from Latin *semi,* half, and *palma,* the palm. Reference is to the partially webbed foot. Sandpiper, see *Calidris acuminata.*

Calidris ruficollis   Red-necked Stint

SCIENTIFIC NAME *Calidris + ruficollis,* red necked, from Latin *rufus,* red of various shades, tawny, and *collis,* neck. Reference is to the color of the neck in breeding plumage.

COMMON NAME Red-necked, see scientific name. Stint, see *Calidris minuta.*

Calidris subminuta   Long-toed Stint

SCIENTIFIC NAME *Calidris + subminuta,* below small, very small, from Latin *sub,* below, and *minuta,* small in size or amount. If the *sub-* prefix is used to mean near, this can also be translated as closely related to *Calidris minuta.*

COMMON NAME Long-toed, the toes are slightly longer than other stints. Stint, see *Calidris minuta.*

Calidris temminckii   Temminck's Stint

SCIENTIFIC NAME *Calidris + temminckii,* for Coenraad Jacob Temminck (1778–1858), a Dutch ornithologist, author, and director of the natural history museum in Leyden.

COMMON NAME Temminck's, see scientific name. Stint, see *Calidris minuta.*

Calidris tenuirostris   Great Knot

SCIENTIFIC NAME *Calidris* + *tenuirostris*, having a slender bill, from Latin *tenuis*, slender, and *rostrum*, the snout or muzzle of an animal, the beak or bill of a bird.

COMMON NAME Great, for the size; it is larger than the red knot. Knot, see *Calidris cantus*.

Callipepla californica   California Quail

SCIENTIFIC NAME *Callipepla*, beautifully robed, from Greek καλλι, καλος, *kalli, kalos*, beautiful, and πεπλος, *peplos*, any woven cloth used for a covering, including a woman's or man's robe. Reference is to the male's plumage + *californica*, of California, the type specimen was collected in California, at the time part of Mexico.

COMMON NAME California, see scientific name. Quail, from Old French *quaille*, quail, imitative of the call of the European species.

Callipepla gambelii   Gambel's Quail

SCIENTIFIC NAME *Callipepla* + *gambelii*, for William Gambel (1819–1849), an American ornithologist and adventurer who spent several years in California and who collected the type specimen.

COMMON NAME Gambel's, see scientific name. Quail, see *Callipepla californica*.

Callipepla squamata   Scaled Quail

SCIENTIFIC NAME *Callipepla* + *squamata*, scaly, from Latin *squamatus*, covered with scales. Reference is to the pattern of the plumage.

COMMON NAME Scaled, for the pattern of the plumage. Quail, see *Callipepla californica*.

Calonectris diomedea   Cory's Shearwater

SCIENTIFIC NAME *Calonectris*, beautiful swimmer, from Greek καλλι, καλος, *kalli, kalos*, beautiful, and νεκτρις, *nektris*, a swimmer + *diomedea*, for Diomedes, a Greek warrior-hero who traveled and fought accompanied by two companions, Sthenelus and Euryalus. One version of the myth has him disappearing in the islands of the Adriatic now named for him (Insulae Diomedeae) following a war with Troy. His companions were changed into herons, known as the Birds of Diomedes.

COMMON NAME Cory's, for Charles Barney Cory (1857–1921), an American ornithologist and author. He started the *Birds of the Americas* series and wrote *The Birds of the Bahama Islands* (1880), *The Birds of Haiti and San Domingo* (1885), and *The Birds of the West Indies* (1889). Shearwater, for the flight pattern, which passes swiftly and close to (that is, shears) the surface of the water.

Calothorax lucifer   Lucifer Hummingbird

SCIENTIFIC NAME *Calothorax*, beautiful chest, from Greek καλλι, καλος, *kalli, kalos*, beautiful, and θοραξ, *thorax*, chest. In fact, this bird has a beautiful purple anterior neck, the chest is gray + *lucifer*, Latin for light bringing or light bearing. Reference is to the bright purple gorget, which resembles a small torch when viewed from the front. In Latin, Lucifer means light-bearing or refers to the planet Venus, the bright morning star. The confusion of Lucifer with Satan was caused by a misreading of Isaiah 14:12, "How art thou fallen from heaven, O Lucifer, Son of the morning: how art thou cut down to the ground, which didst weaken the nations." This verse was actually a prophecy directed to Nebuchadnezzar, then king of Babylon, predicting what would be said to him at his defeat and death.

COMMON NAME Lucifer, see scientific name. Hummingbird, for the buzzing hum of the wingbeats.

Calypte anna   Anna's Hummingbird

SCIENTIFIC NAME *Calypte*, a veil or headdress, from Greek καλυπτρη, *kaluptrē*, a veil or headdress, a bridal veil. Reference is to the male's iridescent elongated gorgets and crown, which give the appearance of an elegant veil + *anna*, named by Rene P. Lesson (1794–1849) for Anna de Belle Massena (1806–1896), duchess of Rivoli, France.

COMMON NAME Anna's, see scientific name. Hummingbird, for the buzzing hum of the wingbeats.

Calypte costae   Costa's Hummingbird

SCIENTIFIC NAME *Calypte* + *costae*, for Louis Marie Pantaleon Costa (1806–1864), Marquis de Beau-Regard, who had a great interest in hummingbirds. This bird was named for him by Jules Bourcier (1797–1873).

COMMON NAME Costa's, see scientific name. Hummingbird see *Calypte anna*.

Camptostoma imberbe — Northern Beardless-Tyrannulet

SCIENTIFIC NAME *Camptostoma*, bent mouth, from Greek καμψος, καμπτως, *kampsos*, *kamptōs*, crooked or bent, and στομα, *stoma*, mouth. Reference is to the shape of the beak, which is not really bent but has a shape more like that of a titmouse (compressed) rather than like most other flycatchers (depressed) + *imberbe*, from Latin *imberbis*, beardless. This bird has short rictal bristles at the base of the bill, in contrast with the long bristles usual of flycatchers.

COMMON NAME Northern, for the range in northern Mexico. Beardless, see scientific name. Tyrannulet, a little *Tyrannus*, resembles a smaller version of some members of this genus of flycatchers.

Campylorhynchus brunneicapillus — Cactus Wren

SCIENTIFIC NAME *Campylorhynchus*, curved beak, from Greek καμπυλος, *kampulos*, curved or bent like a bow, and ρυγχος, *rugkhos*, a snout or muzzle of an animal, the beak or bill of a bird + *brunneicapillus*, brown haired, from Latin *brunneus*, brown, and *capillus*, hair of the head. Reference is to the brown crown.

COMMON NAME Cactus, for the site of the nests, which are commonly found in cacti or other thorny shrubs. Wren, from Anglo-Saxon *wraenna*, their name for this type of bird.

Caprimulgus carolinensis — Chuck-will's-widow

SCIENTIFIC NAME *Caprimulgus*, a goat milker, from Latin *capra*, a female goat, and *mulgeo*, to milk an animal. This name came from Greek folklore, adopted by the Romans, that these birds would come to small groups of goats in the evening and suck milk from them. They were of course fluttering around to feed on insects disturbed by the goats + *carolinensis*, Latin for of the Carolina colonies, an area encompassing the southeastern United States. Reference is to the region of the type specimen.

COMMON NAME Chuck-will's-widow, onomatopoeic of the call.

Caprimulgus ridgwayi — Buff-collared Nightjar

SCIENTIFIC NAME *Caprimulgus* + *ridgwayi*, for Robert Ridgway (1850–1929), the American ornithologist who wrote *The Birds of North and Middle America* (1901–1919).

COMMON NAME Buff-collared, has a buff-colored ring around the neck. Nightjar, a corruption of *night-churr*. This bird is crepuscular and nocturnal, and the call is a whirring ("churr") noise.

Caprimulgus vociferus   Whip-poor-will

SCIENTIFIC NAME *Caprimulgus* + *vociferus*, from Latin *vociferatus*, a loud cry. Reference is to the call.

COMMON NAME Whip-poor-will, onomatopoeic of the call.

Caracara cheriway   Crested Caracara

SCIENTIFIC NAME *Caracara*, Tupi Indian (upper Amazon Basin) name for this bird; onomatopoeic of the call + *cheriway*, the Carib Indian (Lesser Antilles, West Indies) name for this bird; also meant to be onomatopoeic.

COMMON NAME Crested, descriptive. Caracara, see scientific name.

Cardellina rubrifrons   Red-faced Warbler

SCIENTIFIC NAME *Cardellina*, a little finch, diminutive of the Latin *carduelis*, goldfinch, a kind of finch + *rubrifrons*, to have a red forehead, from Latin *ruber*, red, and *frons*, forehead, front.

COMMON NAME Red-faced, descriptive. This is a more apt description than the scientific name. Warbler, for the trills and quavers of the song.

Cardinalis cardinalis   Northern Cardinal

SCIENTIFIC NAME *Cardinalis*, so named because the red of the male was thought to resemble the red robes of a Roman Catholic cardinal + *cardinalis*.

COMMON NAME Northern, for the natural range in the United States. Cardinal, see scientific name.

Cardinalis sinuatus   Pyrrhuloxia

SCIENTIFIC NAME *Cardinalis* + *sinuatus*, from Latin *sinuo*, to form a curve, curved. Reference is to the downcurved maxilla.

COMMON NAME Pyrrhuloxia, taken from the old genus name for this bird. There are two possible derivations, both of which mean essentially the same thing. First, from Greek πυρρουλας, *pyrr(h)oulas*, a red bird, the bullfinch, and λοξος, *loxos*, slanting, crosswise, oblique, in reference to the shape of the beak. Second, from Greek πυρρος, *pyrr(h)os*, flame colored, and λοξος, *loxos*, slanting crosswise, oblique. Red and flame refer to the male's plumage, and oblique refers to the shape of the beak.

Carduelis carduelis European Goldfinch

SCIENTIFIC NAME *Carduelis*, Latin for goldfinch, from Latin *carduus*, thistle, the seeds of which are a favorite food of the goldfinch + *carduelis*.

COMMON NAME European, for the natural range; it is an escaped exotic in the United States. Gold, for the yellow color all goldfinches have to a greater or lesser degree. Finch, from Anglo-Saxon *finc*, their name for this bird, an imitation of the call. Other languages have similar names for the finch for the same reason.

Carduelis flammea Common Redpoll

SCIENTIFIC NAME *Carduelis* + *flammea*, from Latin *flamma*, a flame. Reference is to the red crown.

COMMON NAME Common, more common in the shared portion of their ranges that the hoary redpoll. Redpoll, for the red crown, from Middle English *pol*, head.

Carduelis hornemanni Hoary Redpoll

SCIENTIFIC NAME *Carduelis* + *hornemanni*, for Jens Wilken Hornemann (1770–1841), a Danish botanist and the lead author of the fourteen-volume *Flora Danica* (1805–1841).

COMMON NAME Hoary, to become gray-haired or to turn white, from Anglo-Saxon *har*, of the same meaning. Reference is to the gray and white streaks in the plumage. Redpoll, see *Carduelis flammea*.

Carduelis lawrencei Lawrence's Goldfinch

SCIENTIFIC NAME *Carduelis* + *lawrencei*, for George Newbold Lawrence (1806–1895), who worked with John Cassin (1813–1869) collecting birds on the Pacific Railroad surveys. He assisted in writing the section on birds for the *Pacific Railroad Reports* (1853–1854).

COMMON NAME Lawrence, see scientific name. Goldfinch, see *Carduelis carduelis*.

Carduelis pinus Pine Siskin

SCIENTIFIC NAME *Carduelis* + *pinus*, Latin for pine, the favorite nesting place of this bird.

COMMON NAME Pine, for the nesting site. Siskin, named after the European siskin. The origin of *siskin* is unclear, probably onomatopoeic; many

European languages have similar names for this bird, which usually translate as a chirper or a small bird.

Carduelis psaltria   Lesser Goldfinch

SCIENTIFIC NAME *Carduelis* + *psaltria*, from Greek ψαλτρια, *psaltria*, a female harp player. Reference is to the call.

COMMON NAME Lesser, for the size; this is the smallest of all American goldfinches. Goldfinch, see *Carduelis carduelis*.

Carduelis tristis   American Goldfinch

SCIENTIFIC NAME *Carduelis* + *tristis*, Latin for sad, depressed. Reference is to the call.

COMMON NAME American, to separate it from the European goldfinch, a colony of which was introduced into the United States but failed to survive. Goldfinch, see *Carduelis carduelis*.

Carpodacus cassinii   Cassin's Finch

SCIENTIFIC NAME *Carpodacus*, fruit biter, from Greek καρπος, *karpos*, fruit, and δακος, *dakos*, biter. Reference is to the preferred diet of berries, fruits, and seeds + *casinii*, for John Cassin (1813–1869), a Philadelphia ornithologist with a broad knowledge of the birds of the world.

COMMON NAME Cassin's, see scientific name. Finch, from Anglo-Saxon *finc*, their name for this bird, an imitation of the call. Other languages have similar names for the finch for the same reason.

Carpodacus mexicanus   House Finch

SCIENTIFIC NAME *Carpodacus* + *mexicanus*, Latin for pertaining to Mexico, from Mexico. Reference is to the region of the type specimen.

COMMON NAME House, commonly found around houses. Finch, see *Carpodacus cassinii*.

Carpodacus purpureus   Purple Finch

SCIENTIFIC NAME *Carpodacus* + *purpureus*, Latin for purple. Reference is to the male, which looks like he was splashed with purple dye.

COMMON NAME Purple, see scientific name. Finch, see *Carpodacus cassinii*.

Cathartes aura — Turkey Vulture

SCIENTIFIC NAME *Cathartes*, Latinized from Greek καθαρτης, *kathartēs*, a cleanser or purifier. Reference is to the scavenging done by the vulture + *aura*, Latinized form of *auroura*, the Mexican Indian name for this bird.

COMMON NAME Turkey, resembles a turkey because of its bare red head and dark feathers. Vulture, from Latin *vulturus*, a tearer. Reference is to the feeding habits.

Catharus bicknelli — Bicknell's Thrush

SCIENTIFIC NAME *Catharus*, from Greek καθαρος, *katharos*, physically clean, spotless, pure. Reference is to the sharp, clear, brown and white plumage on the type bird of this genus, *Catharus aurantiirostris* + *bicknelli*, for E. P. Bicknell (1859–1925), the ornithologist who first described this bird in the Catskill Mountains of New York. He was a founder of the American Ornithologists' Union.

COMMON NAME Bicknell's, see scientific name. Thrush, from Middle English *thrusch*, their name for this type of bird.

Catharus fuscescens — Veery

SCIENTIFIC NAME *Catharus* + *fuscescens*, to be dark or dusky, from Latin *fuscus*, dark colored, somber, dusky, and *-escens*, somewhat like. Reference is to the color of the plumage.

COMMON NAME Veery, imitative of the call.

Catharus guttatus — Hermit Thrush

SCIENTIFIC NAME *Catharus* + *guttatus*, Latin for containing drops or drop-like masses, spotted, speckled as with raindrops. Reference is to the spotted breast of this bird.

COMMON NAME Hermit, for its solitary habits. Thrush, see *Catharus bicknelli*.

Catharus minimus — Gray-cheeked Thrush

SCIENTIFIC NAME *Catharus* + *minimus*, Latin for least, smallest. This is not an appropriate scientific name because this bird is the largest in the genus *Catharus*.

COMMON NAME Gray-cheeked, descriptive. Thrush, see *Catharus bicknelli*.

Catharus ustulatus Swainson's Thrush

SCIENTIFIC NAME *Catharus* + *ustulatus*, scorched, from Latin *ustulo*, to partially burn, char, scorch. Reference is to the brownish, singed color of the plumage.

COMMON NAME Swainson's, for William Swainson (1789–1855), a British naturalist and artist. He published *Zoological Illustrations* (1820–1823) and was a strong advocate of the quinary system of taxonomy, a failed method of classifying plants and animals. Thrush, see *Catharus bicknelli*.

Catherpes mexicanus Canyon Wren

SCIENTIFIC NAME *Catherpes*, to creep down, from Greek καθερπο, καθερο, *katherpo*, *kathero* to creep down, steal down. Reference is to its habit of creeping down rock faces + *mexicanus*, Latin for pertaining to Mexico. Reference is to the region of the type specimen.

COMMON NAME Canyon, for the habitat. Wren, from Anglo-Saxon *wraenna*, their name for this type of bird.

Catoptrophorus semipalmatus Willet

SCIENTIFIC NAME *Catoptrophorus*, a mirror bearer, from Greek κατοπτρον, *katoptron*, a mirror, and φορος, *phoros*, to bear. Reference is to the white patches on the wings + *semipalmatus*, from Latin *semi*, half, and *palma*, palm. Reference is to the partially webbed feet.

COMMON NAME Willet, imitative of the call.

Centrocerus minimus Gunnison Sage-Grouse

SCIENTIFIC NAME *Centrocerus*, pointed tail, from Greek κεντρον, *kentron*, any sharp point, and κερκος, *kerkos*, a tail, here used in error: this word is used specifically for the tail of a beast not a bird + *minimus*, Latin for least, smallest. This grouse is smaller than *Centrocerus urophasianus*.

COMMON NAME Gunnison, for the Gunnison Valley in Colorado, which has the largest population of these birds. Named for John William Gunnison (1812–1853), who explored the region in 1853. Sage, for the habitat. Grouse, origin unknown but thought to come from French *griais*, speckled gray.

Centrocerus urophasianus Greater Sage-Grouse

SCIENTIFIC NAME *Centrocerus* + *urophasianus*, pheasant tail, from Greek ουρα, *oura*, tail, and φασιανος, *phasianos*, a pheasant. According to the

Oxford Greek-English Lexicon (1996), ουρα, *oura* should not be used for the tail of a bird but is restricted to other animals. Named for the River Phasis, the region from which these birds were first brought back to Greece. Descriptive, the tail resembles that of a pheasant.

COMMON NAME Greater, larger than *Centrocerus minimus*. Sage-Grouse, see *Centrocerus minimus*.

Cepphus columba   Pigeon Guillemot

SCIENTIFIC NAME *Cepphus*, from Greek κεπφος, *kepphos*, a light sea bird, thought to be a storm-petrel + *columba*, Latin for pigeon or dove, in turn from Greek κολυμβος, *kolumbos*, a diver, a kind of sea bird. It is not known how or why the meaning changed when this word passed from Greek to Latin. Strangely the original Greek meaning fits this bird perfectly. Reference is to the size of this guillemot.

COMMON NAME Pigeon, from Old French *pijon*, a young bird, in turn from Latin *pipio*, to peep. Reference is to the size, which is about the same as a pigeon. Guillemot, little William, a diminutive of the French Guillaume.

Cepphus grylle   Black Guillemot

SCIENTIFIC NAME *Cepphus* + *grylle*, the local name for this bird on the Baltic island of Gotland, Sweden, where the type specimen was collected.

COMMON NAME Black, for the color of the breeding plumage. Guillemot, see *Cepphus columba*.

Cerorhinca monocerata   Rhinoceros Auklet

SCIENTIFIC NAME *Cerorhinca*, horn-nose, from Greek κερας, *keras*, the horn of an animal, and ρυγχος, *rugkhos*, the snout or muzzle of an animal, the beak or bill of a bird + *monocerata*, one horn, from Greek μονος, *monos*, single, and κερας, *keras*, the horn of an animal. Reference for both the genus and species names is the single hornlike protrusion at the base of the bill.

COMMON NAME Rhinoceros, meaning is the same as for *Cerorhinca*; note that the two Greek elements that make up these two words are simply reversed. Auklet, a little auk.

Certhia americana   Brown Creeper

SCIENTIFIC NAME *Certhia*, from Latin *certhius*, a creeper, in turn from Greek κερθιος, *kerthios*, used by Aristotle to mean a little bird; later authors associated it with the common tree creeper. Reference is to its habit of creeping up tree trunks searching for food + *americana*, of America, for the natural range.

COMMON NAME Brown, for the color of the plumage. Creeper, see scientific name.

Ceryle alcyon   Belted Kingfisher

SCIENTIFIC NAME *Ceryle*, from Greek κηρυλος, *kērulos*, a fabulous sea bird of the halcyon type. The halcyon, or *kērulos*, was a kingfisher with mythical properties attributed to it. It was thought by the Greeks to breed and nest on the ocean during the winter calm period. This calm lasted fourteen days, seven days were used for breeding and nest building followed by seven days to lay eggs and rear their young. This period of calm surrounding the winter solstice was known as the halcyon days. Fantastic descriptions of what were believed to be the nests of these birds were described by Aristotle and Plutarch. Another version of this myth has the birds nesting on the ocean as the actual cause of the midwinter calm seas + *alcyon*, for the Greek mythological character Alcyone, the daughter of Aeolus, a mortal. Her husband, Ceyx, was half divine, being the son of Eosphorus, the morning star. There are two major forms of this myth. The first has Alcyone and Ceyx playing gods and calling each other Zeus and Hera. This behavior so vexed Zeus that he turned Alcyone into a kingfisher and Ceyx into a gannet. The second form has Ceyx drowned at sea; the grief stricken Alcyone then throws herself into the sea to join him. In sympathy for her great love, Zeus turns them both into kingfishers.

COMMON NAME Belted, for the blue band across the male's chest that looks like a belt. Kingfisher, the king, chief, or best of fishers.

Ceryle torquata   Ringed Kingfisher

SCIENTIFIC NAME *Ceryle* + *torquata*, from Latin *torquatus*, wearing a collar or necklace. Reference is to the white ring around the neck.

COMMON NAME Ringed, for the white ring around the neck. Kingfisher, see *Ceryle alcyon*.

Cettia diphone   Japanese Bush-Warbler

SCIENTIFIC NAME *Cettia*, named by Charles Bonaparte (1803–1857) for Francesco Cetti (1726–1778), an Italian Jesuit priest, naturalist, and author + *diphone*, two voices, from Greek δι, *di*, two, and φωνεω, φωνη, *phōneō*, *phōnē*, produce a sound or tone, speak. Reference is to the call.

COMMON NAME Japanese, for the natural range. Bush, for the habitat. Warbler, for the trills and quavers of its song.

Chaetura pelagica   Chimney Swift

SCIENTIFIC NAME *Chaetura*, hair-tail or bristle-tail, from Greek χαιτη, *khaitē*, loose or flowing hair, a horse's mane, and ουρα, *oura*, tail. According to the *Oxford Greek-English Lexicon* (1996), ουρα, *oura* should not be used for the tail of a bird but is restricted to other animals. Reference is to the hairlike spines on the ends of the tail feathers + *pelagica*, from Greek πελαγιος, *pelagios*, of the sea. This is a land bird, and there is much speculation about other meanings of the word. One possibility is an original misspelling by Carl Linnaeus (1707–1778) of the name Pelasgi, an ancient nomadic tribe of Greece. This derivation would refer to the migratory habits of this bird and not to the sea at all. Linnaeus spelled this specific name *pelagtea* in 1758 and *pelasgia* in 1766, and these two spellings are at the root of the controversy.

COMMON NAME Chimney, for the nesting sites. Swift, for its speedy flight.

Chaetura vauxi   Vaux's Swift

SCIENTIFIC NAME *Chaetura* + *vauxi*, for William Sansom Vaux (1811–1882), who amassed a great collection of both archaeological material and minerals, which he later donated to the Philadelphia Academy of Natural Sciences.

COMMON NAME Vaux's, see scientific name. Swift, see *Chaetura pelagica*.

Chamaea fasciata   Wrentit

SCIENTIFIC NAME *Chamaea*, from Greek χαμαι, *khamai*, on the ground. Reference is to its feeding habits + *fasciata*, from Latin *fascia*, a ribbon or band. This bird has indistinct streaks on the breast and tail.

COMMON NAME Wren, from Anglo-Saxon *wraenna*, their name for this type of bird. Tit, Middle English for something small, especially a bird.

Charadrius alexandrinus   Snowy Plover

SCIENTIFIC NAME *Charadrius*, from Greek χαραδριος, *kharadrios*, a yellow bird dwelling in clefts, thought to be the stone curlew, from, χαραδρα, *kharadra*, a ravine or cleft. This bird nests in ravines or gullies. In ancient Greece the sight of this bird was thought to cure jaundice, the association being the yellow color of both + *alexandrinus*, of Alexandria, Egypt, where the type specimen was collected.

COMMON NAME Snowy, for its pale plumage. Plover, from Latin *pulvia*, rain. Although many have tried, there is no good explanation for this derivation.

Charadrius hiaticula — Common Ringed Plover

SCIENTIFIC NAME *Charadrius* + *hiaticula*, a cleft dweller, from Latin *hiatus*, a cleft, and *-cola*, to live, dwell. Reference is to the nesting sites.

COMMON NAME Common, abundant in its range. Ringed, for the black ring around the base of the neck. Plover, see *Charadrius alexandrinus*.

Charadrius melodus — Piping Plover

SCIENTIFIC NAME *Charadrius* + *melodus*, from Greek μελωδος, *melōdos*, musical, melodious. Reference is to the song.

COMMON NAME Piping, for the call. Plover, see *Charadrius alexandrinus*.

Charadrius mongolus — Mongolian Plover

SCIENTIFIC NAME *Charadrius* + *mongolus*, of Mongolia, for the natural range.

COMMON NAME Mongolian, for the natural range. Plover, see *Charadrius alexandrinus*.

Charadrius montanus — Mountain Plover

SCIENTIFIC NAME *Charadrius* + *montanus*, Latin for of or belonging to the mountains, a mountain dweller. Reference is to the breeding range.

COMMON NAME Mountain, for the breeding range. Plover, see *Charadrius alexandrinus*.

Charadrius morinellus — Eurasian Dotterel

SCIENTIFIC NAME *Charadrius* + *morinellus*, a little fool, from Greek μωρος, *mōros*, dull, stupid, foolish, and the diminutive Latin *-ellus*. Reference is to its being easily caught for food.

COMMON NAME Eurasian, for the natural range. Dotterel, a little foolish fellow, Old French diminutive of Middle Dutch *dote*, *dotard*, a foolish fellow. Reference is the same as for the species name.

Charadrius semipalmatus — Semipalmated Plover

SCIENTIFIC NAME *Charadrius* + *semipalmatus*, half-palmed, from Latin *semi*, half, and *palma*, the palm. Reference is to the partially webbed feet.

COMMON NAME Semipalmated, see scientific name. Plover, see *Charadrius alexandrinus*.

Charadrius vociferus — Killdeer

SCIENTIFIC NAME *Charadrius* + *vociferus*, from Latin *vociferatus*, a loud cry. Reference is to the call.

COMMON NAME Killdeer, imitative of the call.

Charadrius wilsonia — Wilson's Plover

SCIENTIFIC NAME *Charadrius* + *wilsonia*, for Alexander Wilson (1766–1813), known as the father of American ornithology. He initiated the first series on birds of the eastern United States, *American Ornithology* (1808–1814).

COMMON NAME Wilson's, see scientific name. Plover, see *Charadrius alexandrinus*.

Chasiempis sandwichensis gayi — Oahu 'Elepaio

SCIENTIFIC NAME *Chasiempis*, mouth open for a mosquito or a gnat, from Greek χασμα, *khasma*, an open, gaping mouth, and εμπις, *empis*, a mosquito or gnat + *sandwichensis*, of the Sandwich Islands, an old name for the Hawaiian Islands, named for John Montagu, fourth earl of Sandwich (1718–1792), First Lord of the British Admiralty + *gayi*, for Claude Gay (1800–1873), a French botanist who did fieldwork in Chile.

COMMON NAME Oahu, for the island of Oahu in the Hawaiian archipelago, the natural range of this bird. 'Elepaio, the Hawaiian name for this bird, onomatopoeic of the call.

Chasiempis sandwichensis sandwichensis — Hawaii 'Elepaio

SCIENTIFIC NAME *Chasiempis* + *sandwichensis*, see *Chasiempis sandwichensis gayi* + *sandwichensis*

COMMON NAME Hawaii, for the island of Hawaii, the natural range of this bird. 'Elepaio, see *Chasiempis sandwichensis gayi*.

Chasiempis sandwichensis sclateri   Kauai 'Elepaio

SCIENTIFIC NAME *Chasiempis* + *sandwichensis*, see *Chasiempis sandwichensis gayi* + *sclateri*, for Philip Lutley Sclater (1829–1913), an English ornithologist, a prolific author, and secretary of the Zoological Society in London.

COMMON NAME Kauai, for the island of Kauai in the Hawaiian archipelago, the natural range of this bird. 'Elepaio, see *Chasiempis sandwichensis gayi*.

Chen caerulescens   Snow Goose

SCIENTIFIC NAME *Chen*, from Greek χην, *khēn*, the wild goose + *caerulescens*, Latin for becoming or verging on blue or greenish blue. This goose has two color phases, one white and one blue, termed snow goose and blue goose, respectively.

COMMON NAME Snow, for the white-phase plumage. Goose, from Anglo-Saxon *gos*, their name for this type of bird.

Chen canagica   Emperor Goose

SCIENTIFIC NAME *Chen* + *canagica*, for Kanaga Island of the Aleutian chain, where the original specimen was collected.

COMMON NAME Emperor, origin unknown but probably refers to the handsome, imperial appearance of the plumage when contrasted with most other geese. Goose, see *Chen caerulescens*.

Chen rossii   Ross's Goose

SCIENTIFIC NAME *Chen* + *rossii*, for Bernard Rogan Ross (1827–1874), an officer of the Hudson Bay Company. John Cassin (1813–1869) named this goose for him.

COMMON NAME Ross's, see scientific name. Goose, see *Chen caerulescens*.

Chlidonias leucopterus   White-winged Tern

SCIENTIFIC NAME *Chlidonias*, a misspelling of the Greek χελιδων, χελιδον, *khelidōn, khelidon*, a swallow. The correct spelling would be *Chelidonias*. The principle of priority allows the mistake to remain + *leucopterus*, white winged, from Greek λευκοπτερυς, *leukopterus*, white winged, in turn from λευκο, *leuko*, white, and πτερος, *pteros*, a feather, a bird's wing. Reference is to the white wings of the breeding plumage.

COMMON NAME White-winged, descriptive. Tern, from Old Norse *taerne*, their name for this type of bird.

Chlidonias niger — Black Tern

SCIENTIFIC NAME *Chlidonias* + *niger*, Latin for black. Reference is to the color of the breeding plumage.

COMMON NAME Black, for the black breeding plumage. Tern, see *Chlidonias leucopterus*.

Chloroceryle americana — Green Kingfisher

SCIENTIFIC NAME *Chloroceryle*, green kingfisher, from Greek χλωρος, *khlōros*, green, and κηρυλος, *kērulos*, a kingfisher (see *Ceryle alcyon*). Reference is to the greenish back + *americana*, of America.

COMMON NAME Green, for the greenish back. Kingfisher, the king, chief, or best of fishers.

Chondestes grammacus — Lark Sparrow

SCIENTIFIC NAME *Chondestes*, grain eater, from Greek χονδρος, *khondros*, grain, specifically hulled wheat or spelt, and εδεστες, *edestes*, eater + *grammacus*, a line or stroke in drawing. Reference is to a line on the head.

COMMON NAME Lark, for the song, which is like that of the lark. Sparrow, from Anglo-Saxon *spearwa*, to flutter. Originally used to denote any small bird.

Chondrohierax uncinatus — Hook-billed Kite

SCIENTIFIC NAME *Chondrohierax*, cartilage hawk, from Greek χονδρο, *khondro*, gristle, cartilage, and ιεραξ, *ierax*, a hawk or falcon. The Greek χονδρο, *khondro*, is a root word of several meanings (see *Chondestes grammacus*); however, when followed by a consonant in English scientific nomenclature, its meaning is cartilage (*Century Dictionary and Cyclopedia*, 1913). This single member of the genus lacks a bony shield above the eye that is found in other kites + *uncinatus*, Latin for furnished with hooks or barbs. Reference here is to the hooked bill.

COMMON NAME Hook-billed, descriptive. Kite, from Anglo-Saxon *cyta*, their name for this type of bird. The kite that is flown on a string was so named because it appeared to hang in the air like this bird.

Chondestes grammacus, lark sparrow

Chordeiles acutipennis — Lesser Nighthawk

SCIENTIFIC NAME *Chordeiles*, lyre note in the evening, from Greek χορδη, *khordē*, the cord of a lyre, a musical note, and δειλη, *deilē*, the evening. Some sources list χορος, *khoros*, a dance, and δειλη, *deilē*, the evening, with reference to the flight pattern of the nighthawk. *Chordeiles* is a Latinized term coined by William Swainson (1789–1855); he intended the name to refer to the call of the bird at twilight. A more proper spelling would have been *Chordodiles*, which would have avoided the confusion of χορδη, *khordē*, lyre note with χορος, *khoros*, dance + *acutipennis*, pointed wing, from Latin *acutus*, pointed, sharp, and *penna*, wing, feather. Reference is to the sharp tip of the wing.

COMMON NAME Lesser, smaller than the common nighthawk. Night, hunts insects at dusk. Hawk, from Anglo-Saxon *hafoc*, a hawk, their name for this type of bird.

Chordeiles gundlachii — Antillean Nighthawk

SCIENTIFIC NAME *Chordeiles* + *gundlachii*, for Juan Gundlach (1810–1896), the Cuban ornithologist who wrote *Catalogo de los Aves Cubanas* (1873).

COMMON NAME Antillean, for its natural range. Nighthawk, see *Chordeiles acutipennis*.

Chordeiles minor   Common Nighthawk

SCIENTIFIC NAME *Chordeiles* + *minor*, smaller, this name was assigned when this was the only nighthawk known in the United States; it was smaller than the only other known member of this family, the European nightjar.

COMMON NAME Common, this is the most common nighthawk in the United States. Nighthawk, see *Chordeiles acutipennis*.

Cinclus mexicanus   American Dipper

SCIENTIFIC NAME *Cinclus*, from Greek κιγκλος, *kigklos*, a type of water-bird mentioned by Aristotle and others that bobbed its tail up and down. Of interest, the Greek word κιγκλιζω, *kigklizō*, means to wag the tail as the bird *kigklos* does. Reference is to the bobbing behavior when standing on rocks at a streamside + *mexicanus*, Latin for pertaining to Mexico, from Mexico. The name refers to the range of the type specimen.

COMMON NAME American, to differentiate it from the Eurasian dipper. Dipper, for the bobbing (dipping) behavior of this bird while standing at the edge of a stream.

Circus cyaneus   Northern Harrier

SCIENTIFIC NAME *Circus*, from Greek κιρκος, *kirkos*, a circle or ring, a kind of hawk or falcon that flies in circles. Reference is to its circling flight pattern + *cyaneus*, dark blue, from Greek κυανος, *kuanos*, dark blue. Reference is to the bluish gray on the male's back.

COMMON NAME Northern, for the summer range in Canada and the northern United States. Harrier, for the hunting behavior of flying close to the ground and harrying its prey.

Cistothorus palustris   Marsh Wren

SCIENTIFIC NAME *Cistothorus*, rock rose leaper, from Greek κισθος, κιστος, *kisthos, kistos*, the rock rose (*Helianthemum*) and θωυρος, *thōuros*, rushing, leaping. Reference is to its movement around a common perch + *palustris*, from Latin *paluster*, marshy, marshland.

COMMON NAME Marsh, for the habitat. Wren, from Anglo-Saxon *wraenna*, a wren.

Cistothorus platensis   Sedge Wren

SCIENTIFIC NAME *Cistothorus* + *platensis*, for the Spanish territory of Río de la Plata, where the type specimen was collected. This territory was the approximate region of present-day Argentina, Uruguay, and Paraguay.

COMMON NAME Sedge, for the habitat. Wren, from Anglo-Saxon *wraenna*, a wren.

Clangula hyemalis   Long-tailed Duck

SCIENTIFIC NAME *Clangula*, a small noise, a diminutive of Latin *clangor*, the crying, clamor, and screaming of various birds, noise. Reference is to its constant calling + *hyemalis*, wintry, from Latin *hiems*, winter. Reference is to the winter range along the northern portions of both U.S. coasts.

COMMON NAME Long-tailed, for the male's distinctive long and tapering tail. Duck, from Anglo-Saxon *duce*, a form of *ducan*, to duck or dive.

Coccothraustes vespertinus   Evening Grosbeak

SCIENTIFIC NAME *Coccothraustes*, grain crusher, from Greek κοκκος, *kokkos*, grain or seed, and θραυω, *thrauō*, to break in pieces, shatter. Reference is to the feeding habit of crushing seeds in its large beak. This genus was formerly named *Hesperiphona*, which is Greek for voice in the evening, certainly a more elegant name + *vespertina*, from Latin *vespertinus*, of or belonging to the evening.

COMMON NAME Evening, sings in the evening. Grosbeak, for the large beak, from French *gros*, large, and *bec*, beak.

Coccyzus americanus   Yellow-billed Cuckoo

SCIENTIFIC NAME *Coccyzus*, to call "cuckoo," from Greek κοκκυζω, *kokkuzō*, to cry "cuckoo," in turn from κοκκυξ, *kokkux*, a cuckoo. The name is onomatopoeic of the male's call + *americanus*, pertaining to America, from America. Reference is to the natural range.

COMMON NAME Yellow-billed, descriptive. Cuckoo, an imitation of the call.

Coccyzus erythropthalmus   Black-billed Cuckoo

SCIENTIFIC NAME *Coccyzus* + *erythropthalmus*, red eyed, from Greek ερυθρος, *eruthros*, red, and οφθαλμος, *ophthalmos*, the eye. Reference is to the red orbital ring.

COMMON NAME Black-billed, descriptive. Cuckoo, see *Coccyzus americanus*.

Coccyzus minor
Mangrove Cuckoo

SCIENTIFIC NAME *Coccyzus + minor*, Latin for smaller. Although there is no real difference in size between the birds of this genus, it does have the shortest wingspan in the genus by 1/2 inch. The name came from the type specimen being smaller than normal members of the species, which was not discovered until after the name had been accepted.

COMMON NAME Mangrove, for the habitat in the mangrove swamps of its range in southern Florida. Cuckoo, see *Coccyzus americanus*.

Coereba flaveola
Bananaquit

SCIENTIFIC NAME *Coereba*, Tupi Indian (upper Amazon Basin) name for this and other small birds + *flaveola*, little yellow, a diminutive of Latin *flavus*, yellow. Reference is to the yellow rump and belly of this small bird.

COMMON NAME Banana, refers to the yellow on the rump and belly. Quit, a Jamaican native word for any small bird.

Colaptes auratus
Northern Flicker

SCIENTIFIC NAME *Colaptes*, to peck as a bird, to chisel, Latinized by William Swainson (1789–1855) from Greek κολαπτειν, *kolaptein*, to peck as birds, carve, chisel, in turn from κολαπτηρ, *kolaptēr*, to chisel, carve, engrave + *auratus*, from Latin *aurathus*, overlaid with gold, gilded. This species name originally belonged only to the yellow-shafted flicker, and *auratus* referred to the yellow on the undersurface of the wings.

COMMON NAME Northern, for the summer range in Canada and the northern United States. Flicker, from Anglo-Saxon *flicerian*, fluttering of birds.

Colaptes chrysoides
Gilded Flicker

SCIENTIFIC NAME *Colaptes + chrysoides*, to resemble gold, from Greek χρυσος, *khrusos*, gold, and ειδος, *eidos*, that which is seen, form or shape. Reference is to the gold crown.

COMMON NAME Gilded, overlaid wholly or in parts with a thin coating of gold. Reference is to the gold crown. Flicker, see *Colaptes auratus*.

Colibri thalassinus   Green Violet-ear

SCIENTIFIC NAME *Colibri*, Latinized form of the French *colibre*, a hummingbird. This is also a Spanish and probably originally a Carib Indian (Lesser Antilles, West Indies) word for hummingbird + *thalassinus*, Latin for resembling the sea in color. Reference is to the body color.

COMMON NAME Green, for the predominant body color. Violet-ear, for the violet ear-patch.

Colinus virginianus   Northern Bobwhite

SCIENTIFIC NAME *Colinus*, a quail, Latinized form of the Spanish *colin*, a quail, this in turn from *zolin*, the Nahuatl Indian (Mexico) word for this bird + *virginianus*, Latin for pertaining to Virginia, from Virginia. Reference is to the region of the type specimen.

COMMON NAME Northern, for the natural range. Bobwhite, an imitation of the call.

Columba fasciata   Band-tailed Pigeon

SCIENTIFIC NAME *Columba*, Latin for pigeon or dove + *fasciata*, banded, from Latin *fascia*, a strip of material, a ribbon, a band. Reference is to the banded tail.

COMMON NAME Band-tailed, has gray tips on the tail feathers that form a striking band when the tail is spread in flight. Pigeon, from Old French *pijon*, a young bird, in turn from Latin *pipio*, to peep.

Columba flavirostris   Red-billed Pigeon

SCIENTIFIC NAME *Columba* + *flavirostris*, yellow billed, from Latin *flavus*, yellow, and *rostrum*, the snout or muzzle of an animal, the beak or bill of a bird. Reference is to the yellow tip on the bill.

COMMON NAME Red-billed, descriptive. Pigeon, see *Columba faciata*.

Columba leucocephala   White-crowned Pigeon

SCIENTIFIC NAME *Columba* + *leucocephala*, white headed, from Greek λευκο, *leuko*, of color, white, and κεφαλη, *kephalē*, head. Reference is to the white crown.

COMMON NAME White-crowned, descriptive. Pigeon, see *Columba fasciata*.

Columba livia Rock Dove

SCIENTIFIC NAME *Columba* + *livia*, grayish blue, from Latin *lividus*, of a dull or grayish blue, slate colored. Reference is to the overall color of the plumage.

COMMON NAME Rock, nests in rocky cliffs. Dove, from Anglo-Saxon *dufan*, to dive, for its irregular flight pattern.

Columbina inca Inca Dove

SCIENTIFIC NAME *Columbina*, a little dove, a diminutive of the Latin *columba*, a pigeon or dove + *inca*, named by Rene P. Lesson (1794–1849), who apparently confused the land of the Inca (Peru) with the land of the Aztec (Mexico), where this bird is found in large numbers.

COMMON NAME Inca, see scientific name. Dove, from Anglo-Saxon *dufan*, to dive, for its irregular flight pattern.

Columbina passerina Common Ground-Dove

SCIENTIFIC NAME *Columbina* + *passerina*, sparrowlike, from Latin *passerinus*, of or for sparrows. Reference is to the small size of this dove.

COMMON NAME Common, abundant in its range. Ground, spends most of its time on the ground. Dove, see *Columbina inca*.

Columbina talpacoti Ruddy Ground-Dove

SCIENTIFIC NAME *Columbina* + *talpacoti*, Tupi Indian (upper Amazon Basin) name for this bird.

COMMON NAME Ruddy, for the overall reddish color of the plumage. Ground-Dove, see *Columbina passerina*.

Contopus cooperi Olive-sided Flycatcher

SCIENTIFIC NAME *Contopus*, short footed, from Greek κοντος, *kontos*, short, and πους, *pous*, foot. Reference is to the relatively short tarsi of this genus (the tarsi in birds corresponds to the foot in humans; what we commonly call the foot of a bird is actually the toes) + *cooperi*, for William C. Cooper (1798–1864), a zoologist, collector, conchologist, and one of the founders of the New York Lyceum of Natural History.

COMMON NAME Olive-sided, descriptive. Flycatcher, for the habit of catching insects in the air.

Contopus pertinax   Greater Pewee

SCIENTIFIC NAME *Contopus* + *pertinax*, Latin for having a firm grip, tenacious, obstinate. This name was assigned without comment and has no good explanation. Perhaps it was some observed characteristic of the type specimen.

COMMON NAME Greater, for the size; this is the largest of the pewees. Pewee, an imitation of the call of the eastern wood-pewee, the first of this genus to be described.

Contopus sordidulus   Western Wood-Pewee

SCIENTIFIC NAME *Contopus* + *sordidulus*, little dirty one, from Latin *sordidus*, dirty, and *-ulus*, a diminutive suffix. Reference is to the dusky plumage.

COMMON NAME Western, for the range in the western United States. Wood, lives in forests. Pewee, see *Contopus pertinax*.

Contopus virens   Eastern Wood-Pewee

SCIENTIFIC NAME *Contopus* + *virens*, greenish, from Latin *virere*, to be green. Reference is to the light green underparts.

COMMON NAME Eastern, for the range in the eastern United States. Wood-Pewee, see *Contopus sordidulus*.

Copsychus malabaricus   White-rumped Shama

SCIENTIFIC NAME *Copsychus*, a blackbird, from Greek κοψιχος, *kopsikhos*, a blackbird; therefore, the spelling of the translation from Greek should be *Copsichus* not *Copsychus* + *malabaricus*, from Malabar, for the Malabar Coast on the Arabian Sea, where this bird was first identified.

COMMON NAME White-rumped, descriptive. Shama, from the Hindi (India) name for this type of bird.

Coragyps atratus   Black Vulture

SCIENTIFIC NAME *Coragyps*, raven vulture, from Greek κοραξ, *korax*, raven, and γυψ, *gups*, vulture. Reference is to the black color, like that of a raven + *atratus*, Latin for dark, dingy, clothed in black. Reference is to the dark plumage.

COMMON NAME Black, for the overall color of the plumage. Vulture, from Latin *vulturus*, a tearer. Reference is to this bird's feeding habits.

Coragyps atratus, black vulture

Corvus brachyrhynchos American Crow

SCIENTIFIC NAME *Corvus*, Latin for raven, in turn from Greek κοραξ, *korax*, a raven + *brachyrhynchos*, short beak, from Greek βραχυς, *brakhus*, short, and ρυγχος, *rugkhos*, the snout or muzzle of an animal, the beak or bill of a bird. Reference is to the beak of this bird being shorter than that of a raven, which it much resembles.

COMMON NAME American, native to America. Crow, from Anglo-Saxon *crawe*, a crow, onomatopoeic of its call.

Corvus caurinus Northwestern Crow

SCIENTIFIC NAME *Corvus* + *caurinus*, Latin for of or belonging to the northwest wind. Reference is to its range in the northwestern United States and Canada.

COMMON NAME Northwestern, see scientific name. Crow, see *Corvus brachyrhynchos*.

Corvus corax Common Raven

SCIENTIFIC NAME *Corvus* + *corax*, a raven, from Greek κοραξ, *korax*, a raven.

COMMON NAME Common, most common raven in its range. Raven, from Anglo-Saxon *hraefn*, a raven, onomatopoeic of the call.

Corvus cryptoleucus Chihuahuan Raven

SCIENTIFIC NAME *Corvus* + *cryptoleucus*, hidden white, from Greek κρυπτος, *kruptos*, hidden, and λευκος, *leukos*, of color, white. Reference is to the white bases of the neck feathers, these are usually hidden and only seen when the feathers are ruffled or windblown.

COMMON NAME Chihuahuan, for the state in Mexico where this bird is abundant. Raven, see *Corvus corax*.

Corvus hawaiiensis 'Alala or Hawaiian Crow

SCIENTIFIC NAME *Corvus* + *hawaiiensis*, Latin for belonging to the island of Hawaii.

COMMON NAME 'Alala, the Hawaiian name for this bird. Hawaiian, it is native to the island of Hawaii. Crow, see *Corvus brachyrhynchos*.

Corvus imparatus   Tamaulipas Crow

SCIENTIFIC NAME *Corvus* + *imparatus*, Latin for not prepared, unready. This seems to be a vague reference by James Lee Peters (1889–1952) to the mistaken nomenclature of *Corvus mexicanus* being applied to this bird at one time. The implication is that those making the mistake were not properly prepared.

COMMON NAME Tamaulipas, for Tamaulipas, Mexico, the northern part of its range. Crow, see *Corvus brachyrhynchos*.

Corvus monedula   Eurasian Jackdaw

SCIENTIFIC NAME *Corvus* + *monedula*, Latin for the jackdaw.

COMMON NAME Eurasian, for its natural range. Jack, British slang for a saucy fellow. Daw, from Old English *dawe*, their name for this bird.

Corvus ossifragus   Fish Crow

SCIENTIFIC NAME *Corvus* + *ossifragus*, one who breaks bones, from Latin *os*, genitive *ossis*, bone, and *frango*, to break, shatter, smash. Reference is to the feeding habit of breaking open shellfish.

COMMON NAME Fish, scavenges dead fish along the shoreline. Crow, see *Corvus brachyrhynchos*.

Coturnicops noveboracensis   Yellow Rail

SCIENTIFIC NAME *Coturnicops*, to look like a quail, from Latin *coturnix*, a quail, and Greek ωψ, *ōps*, eye, face, appearance + *noveboracensis*, belonging to New York, from Latin *nova*, new, *Eboracum*, the Roman name for York, England, and *-ensis*, belonging to. This bird is rarely sighted in New York, the locale of the type specimen.

COMMON NAME Yellow, plumage is yellowish brown. Rail, from French *rale*, their name for this type of bird.

Coturnix japonica   Japanese Quail

SCIENTIFIC NAME *Coturnix*, Latin for quail + *japonica*, of Japan, for the natural range.

COMMON NAME Japanese, for the natural range. Quail, from Old French *quaille*, quail, imitative of the call of the European species.

Crotophaga ani   Smooth-billed Ani

SCIENTIFIC NAME *Crotophaga*, tick eater, from Greek κροτων, *krotōn*, a tick, and φαγειν, *phagein*, to eat. In addition to ticks, this bird eats other arthropods as well + *ani*, Tupi Indian (upper Amazon Basin) name for this type of bird.

COMMON NAME Smooth-billed, to contrast it with the groove-billed ani. Ani, see scientific name.

Crotophaga sulcirostris   Groove-billed Ani

SCIENTIFIC NAME *Crotophaga* + *sulcirostris*, grooved beak, from Latin *sulcus*, a furrow, a groove, a wrinkle, and *rostrum*, the snout or muzzle of an animal, the beak or bill of a bird. Reference is to the heavily grooved beak of this species.

COMMON NAME Groove-billed, see scientific name. Ani, see *Crotophaga ani*.

Cyanocitta cristata   Blue Jay

SCIENTIFIC NAME *Cyanocitta*, a dark blue chattering bird, a jay from Greek κυανος, *kuanos*, dark blue, and κιττα, a form of κισσα, *kissa*, a chattering bird, the jay + *cristata*, from Latin *cristatus*, with a crest.

COMMON NAME Blue, for the overall color of the plumage. Jay, from French *geai*, a jay. Origin is unknown, onomatopoeia of the call is a possibility.

Cyanocitta stelleri   Steller's Jay

SCIENTIFIC NAME *Cyanocitta* + *stelleri*, for Georg Wilhelm Steller (1709–1746), a German botanist and medical doctor. He accompanied Vitus Bering (1680–1741) on his 1740 expedition to Alaska and collected the type specimen of this jay on that trip.

COMMON NAME Steller's, see scientific name. Jay, see *Cyanocitta cristata*.

Cyanocompsa parellina   Blue Bunting

SCIENTIFIC NAME *Cyanocompsa*, dark blue and attractive, from Greek κυανος, *kuanos*, dark blue, and κομψη, *kompsē*, elegance, prettiness + *parellina*, violet, from Modern Latin *parellinus*, violet colored.

COMMON NAME Blue, for the color of the male's plumage. Bunting, the origin of this word is unknown, but *The Oxford English Dictionary* (1989) suggests the Scandinavian *buntin*, short and thick, plump.

Cyanocorax morio   Brown Jay

SCIENTIFIC NAME *Cyanocorax*, a dark blue raven, from Greek κυανος, *kuanos*, dark blue, and κοραξ, *korax*, a raven. This genus name originated with *Cyanocorax yncas*, which has some bright blue areas on it head + *morio*, strictly translated, Latin for an idiot kept as a laughing stock, a fool. However, that was not the intent of this species name. This is a contraction of *mormorion*, a brown gemstone. Reference is to the overall brown color.

COMMON NAME Brown, for the overall color of the plumage. Jay, from French *geai*, a jay. Origin is unknown, onomatopoeia of the call is a possibility.

Cyanocorax yncas   Green Jay

SCIENTIFIC NAME *Cyanocorax* + *yncas*, of the Incas. The first specimens were from Peru.

COMMON NAME Green, for the overall color of the plumage. Jay, see *Cyanocorax morio*.

Cygnus atratus   Black Swan

SCIENTIFIC NAME *Cygnus*, a form of Latin *cycnus*, a swan, in turn from Greek κυκνος, *kuknos*, a swan + *atratus*, Latin for dark, dingy, clothed in black. Reference is to the black plumage.

COMMON NAME Black, for the overall color of the plumage. Swan, the Anglo-Saxon name for this type of bird.

Cygnus buccinator   Trumpeter Swan

SCIENTIFIC NAME *Cygnus* + *buccinator*, from Latin *bucinator*, a trumpeter. Reference is to the call.

COMMON NAME Trumpeter, for the call. Swan, see *Cygnus atratus*.

Cygnus columbianus   Tundra Swan

SCIENTIFIC NAME *Cygnus* + *columbianus*, pertaining to Columbia, from Columbia. Reference is to the Columbia River, where Lewis and Clark discovered the type specimen.

COMMON NAME Tundra, for its summer range. Swan, see *Cygnus atratus*.

Cygnus cygnus   Whooper Swan

SCIENTIFIC NAME *Cygnus* + *cygnus*.

COMMON NAME Whooper, for the call. Swan, see *Cygnus atratus*.

Cygnus olor   Mute Swan

SCIENTIFIC NAME *Cygnus* + *olor*, Latin for a swan.

COMMON NAME Mute, quieter than most swans but not actually mute.
Swan, see *Cygnus atratus*.

Cynanthus latirostris   Broad-billed Hummingbird

SCIENTIFIC NAME *Cynanthus*, flower dog, from Greek κυων, κυνος, *kuōn*,
kunos, a dog, and ανθος, *anthos*, a blossom, a flower. Reference is to the
feeding behavior; in his *Dictionary of American Bird Names* (1985)
Choate suggests that this bird "hounds" the flowers it feeds on + *latirostris*,
broad billed, from Latin *latus*, wide, broad, and *rostrum*, the snout or muzzle of an animal, the beak or bill of a bird.

COMMON NAME Broad-billed, has a wider bill than most hummingbirds.
Hummingbird, for the buzzing hum of the wingbeats.

Cypseloides niger   Black Swift

SCIENTIFIC NAME *Cypseloides*, to look like a *Cypselus*, the genus of the
European swift, from Greek κυψελος, *kupselos*, the swift, and ειοδος, *eiodos*, to resemble + *niger*, Latin for black.

COMMON NAME Black, for the overall color. Swift, for its speedy flight.

Cyrtonyx montezumae   Montezuma Quail

SCIENTIFIC NAME *Cyrtonyx*, curved claws, from Greek κυρτος, *kurtos*,
convex, curved, and ονυξ, *onux*, a nail or claw. Reference is to the long,
curved claws of this bird + *montezumae*, for Montezuma II (1466–1520),
the last Aztec ruler of Mexico. The type specimen was collected in Mexico.

COMMON NAME Montezuma, see scientific name. Quail, from Old French
quaille, imitative of the call of the European species.

Dendragapus obscurus   Blue Grouse

SCIENTIFIC NAME *Dendragapus*, tree lover, from Greek δενδρον, *dendron*,
a tree, and αγαπαω, *agapaō*, treat with affection, receive with outward

signs of love. Reference is to the habitat in forests + *obscurus*, in this sense, Latin for dim, dark or dingy in color. Reference is to the dark plumage.

COMMON NAME Blue, for the bluish gray underparts. Grouse, origin unknown but thought to come from French *griais*, speckled gray.

Dendrocygna autumnalis   Black-bellied Whistling-Duck

SCIENTIFIC NAME *Dendrocygna*, tree swan, from Greek δενδρον, *dendron*, a tree, and from Latin *cygnus*, a form of *cycnus*, a swan, in turn from Greek κυκνος, *kuknos*, a swan. Reference is to the tree-perching by some birds in this genus and to the longer swanlike necks when compared to other ducks + *autumnalis*, Latin for of autumn. Reference is to the autumn colors of brown and orange of the plumage and bill.

COMMON NAME Black-bellied, descriptive. Whistling, for the call. Duck, from Anglo-Saxon *duce*, a form of *ducan*, to duck or dive.

Dendrocygna bicolor   Fulvous Whistling-Duck

SCIENTIFIC NAME *Dendrocygna* + *bicolor*, Latin for having two colors. Reference is to the different colors of the back and the underparts.

COMMON NAME Fulvous, Latin for brown, between a dull yellow and a reddish brown, tawny, sandy. Reference is to the reddish brown plumage. Whistling-Duck, see *Dendrocygna autumnalis*.

Dendroica caerulescens   Black-throated Blue Warbler

SCIENTIFIC NAME *Dendroica*, tree dwelling, from Greek δενδρον, *dendron*, a tree, and οικος, *oikos*, a house, any dwelling place. Reference is to the favored habitat in forests + *caerulescens*, Latin for becoming or verging on blue or greenish blue. Reference is to the male's body color.

COMMON NAME Black-throated, descriptive. Blue, for the male's predominant body color. Warbler, for the trills and quavers of the song.

Dendroica castanea   Bay-breasted Warbler

SCIENTIFIC NAME *Dendroica* + *castanea*, Latin for chestnut, in turn from Greek καστανα, *kastana*, a chestnut tree, a chestnut. Reference is to the chestnut-colored breast.

COMMON NAME Bay-breasted, descriptive of the color of part of the breast (bay is used mainly in horses to describe a reddish brown body color with a black mane and tail). Warbler, see *Dendroica caerulescens*.

Dendroica cerulea   Cerulean Warbler

SCIENTIFIC NAME *Dendroica* + *cerulea*, sky blue, a form of *caeruleus*, blue or greenish blue. Reference is to the male's body color.

COMMON NAME Cerulean, see scientific name. Warbler, see *Dendroica caerulescens.*

Dendroica chrysoparia   Golden-cheeked Warbler

SCIENTIFIC NAME *Dendroica* + *chrysoparia*, gold cheeked, from Greek χρυσος, *khrusos*, gold, and παρειον, παρεια, *pareion, pareia*, cheek. Reference is to the bright yellow cheeks.

COMMON NAME Golden-cheeked, descriptive. Warbler, see *Dendroica caerulescens.*

Dendroica coronata   Yellow-rumped Warbler

SCIENTIFIC NAME *Dendroica* + *coronata*, Latin for adorned with a wreath or crown. Reference is to the male's yellow crown in breeding plumage.

COMMON NAME Yellow-rumped, both sexes have yellow rumps. Warbler, see *Dendroica caerulescens.*

Dendroica discolor   Prairie Warbler

SCIENTIFIC NAME *Dendroica* + *discolor*, Latin for differing in color, of different colors, variegated in color. Reference is to the black, yellow, and red of the plumage.

COMMON NAME Prairie, in the Florida pine forests, used to refer to a low grassy opening in the pine woods. This bird is a year-round resident in Florida, and the name refers to these birds frequenting these prairies. Warbler, see *Dendroica caerulescens.*

Dendroica dominica   Yellow-throated Warbler

SCIENTIFIC NAME *Dendroica* + *dominica*, for Santo Domingo, an old name for the island of Hispaniola, where the type specimen was collected.

COMMON NAME Yellow-throated, both sexes have yellow throats. Warbler, see *Dendroica caerulescens.*

Dendroica discolor, prairie warbler

Dendroica fusca — Blackburnian Warbler

SCIENTIFIC NAME *Dendroica* + *fusca*, from Latin *fuscus*, dark colored, dusky. Reference is to the body color.

COMMON NAME Blackburnian, named by Johann Georg Gmelin (1748–1804) for Anna Blackburn (1740–1793), an English patron of ornithology who had a private museum for her collections. The scientific name that he gave at that time was *Motacilla blackburniae*. A prior name of *Motacilla fusca* by P. L. S. Muller (1725–1776) was discovered, so Miss Blackburn lost the species name given in her honor but she did retain the common name. Warbler, see *Dendroica caerulescens*.

Dendroica graciae — Grace's Warbler

SCIENTIFIC NAME *Dendroica* + *graciae*, for Grace Darlington Coues (1847–1939). Her brother, Elliot Coues (1842–1899), collected the type specimen of this warbler and asked Spencer Fullerton Baird (1823–1887) to name it after his sister.

COMMON NAME Grace's, see scientific name. Warbler, see *Dendroica caerulescens*.

Dendroica kirtlandii   Kirtland's Warbler

SCIENTIFIC NAME *Dendroica* + *kirtlandii*, for Jared Potter Kirtland (1793–1877), a physician, zoologist, professor, and one of the founders of the Cleveland Medical College.

COMMON NAME Kirtland's, see scientific name. Warbler, see *Dendroica caerulescens*.

Dendroica magnolia   Magnolia Warbler

SCIENTIFIC NAME *Dendroica* + *magnolia*, for the magnolia tree from which Alexander Wilson (1766–1813) shot the type specimen.

COMMON NAME Magnolia, see scientific name. Warbler, see *Dendroica caerulescens*.

Dendroica nigrescens   Black-throated Gray Warbler

SCIENTIFIC NAME *Dendroica* + *nigrescens*, from Latin *nigrescere*, to become dark in color, blacken. Reference is to the overall gray and black of the plumage.

COMMON NAME Black-throated, for the male's black throat-patch. Gray, for the dominant overall color. Warbler, see *Dendroica caerulescens*.

Dendroica occidentalis   Hermit Warbler

SCIENTIFIC NAME *Dendroica* + *occidentalis*, of the west, for the range in the United States.

COMMON NAME Hermit, lives and feeds high in conifer trees, where it is difficult to find. This bird is not solitary in its habits. Warbler, see *Dendroica caerulescens*.

Dendroica palmarum   Palm Warbler

SCIENTIFIC NAME *Dendroica* + *palmarum*, Latin for of the palms. The first specimens were found in palm trees in Hispaniola.

COMMON NAME Palm, see scientific name. Warbler, see *Dendroica caerulescens*.

Dendroica pensylvanica   Chestnut-sided Warbler

SCIENTIFIC NAME *Dendroica* + *pensylvanica*, of Pennsylvania, where the type specimen was collected. The principle of priority allows the misspelling to stand.

COMMON NAME Chestnut-sided, both sexes have chestnut-colored sides, color is especially pronounced in breeding plumage. Warbler, see *Dendroica caerulescens*.

Dendroica petechia Yellow Warbler

SCIENTIFIC NAME *Dendroica* + *petechia*, from Italian *petecchia*, a spot on the face, a freckle. In English, *petechiae* is used to refer specifically to small red or purple spots in the skin containing blood. Reference is to the reddish streaks on the male's breast.

COMMON NAME Yellow, for the overall color of the plumage. Warbler, see *Dendroica caerulescens*.

Dendroica pinus Pine Warbler

SCIENTIFIC NAME *Dendroica* + *pinus*, Latin for a pine tree. Reference is to the habitat.

COMMON NAME Pine, for the habitat. Warbler, see *Dendroica caerulescens*.

Dendroica striata Blackpoll Warbler

SCIENTIFIC NAME *Dendroica* + *striata*, Modern Latin for striped, from Latin *stria*, a groove, furrow or channel. Reference is to the stripes on the body.

COMMON NAME Blackpoll, black headed, from Middle English *pol*, head. Reference is to the black cap. Warbler, see *Dendroica caerulescens*.

Dendroica tigrina Cape May Warbler

SCIENTIFIC NAME *Dendroica* + *tigrina*, Latin for to look like a tiger. Reference is to the brown stripes on the yellow breast.

COMMON NAME Cape May, the type specimen was collected in Cape May County, New Jersey. Warbler, see *Dendroica caerulescens*.

Dendroica townsendi Townsend's Warbler

SCIENTIFIC NAME *Dendroica* + *townsendi*, for John Kirk Townsend (1809–1851), an ornithologist from Philadelphia who traveled and collected birds in the western United States. He was the author of *Narrative of a Journey across the Rocky Mountains* (1839), in which he wrote descriptions of some of the new birds he found.

COMMON NAME Townsend's, see scientific name. Warbler, see *Dendroica caerulescens*.

Dendroica virens Black-throated Green Warbler

SCIENTIFIC NAME *Dendroica* + *virens*, green, from Latin *vireo*, to be green. Reference is to the olive-green back.

COMMON NAME Black-throated, for the male's black throat-patch. Green, for the olive-green back. Warbler, see *Dendroica caerulescens*.

Dolichonyx oryzivorus Bobolink

SCIENTIFIC NAME *Dolichonyx*, long claw, from Greek δολιχος, *dolikhos*, long, and ονυξ, *onux*, talon, claw, nail. Reference is to the relatively long claws of this bird + *oryzivorus*, rice eater, from Latin *oryza*, rice, in turn from Greek ορυζα, *oruza*, rice, and Latin *voro*, to swallow ravenously, devour.

COMMON NAME Bobolink, onomatopoeic of the call.

Dryocopus pileatus Pileated Woodpecker

SCIENTIFIC NAME *Dryocopus*, a woodpecker, from Greek δρυοκοπος, *druokopos*, a form of δρυοκολαπτης, *druokolaptēs*, a woodpecker, from δρυς, *drus*, oak tree, and κοπος, *kopos*, striking, beating. There is disagreement on this derivation, and κοπις, *kopis*, a chopper or cleaver is favored by some authors. Breaking apart the base word δρυοκολαπτης, *druokolaptēs*, gives the clearer translation to chisel or peck like a bird on an oak tree, δρυς, *drus*, oak tree, and κολαπτης, *kolaptes*, in turn from κολαπτηρ, *kolaptēr*, to chisel, to peck as a bird + *pileatus*, a form of the Latin *pilleatus*, wearing a pilleus. A pilleus was a felt cap worn as a sign of manumission; if the person was still a slave, it was worn as a sign that his vendor did not guarantee him. Reference is to the large red crest.

COMMON NAME Pileated, see scientific name. Woodpecker, descriptive of the feeding and nesting behavior.

Dumetella carolinensis Gray Catbird

SCIENTIFIC NAME *Dumetella*, a little thicket, a diminutive of the Latin *dumetum*, a clump of thorn or similar bushes, a thicket. Reference is to the habitat + *carolinensis*, Latin for belonging to the Carolinas. Reference is to the Carolina colonies, an area encompassing the southeastern United States, where the type specimen was collected.

COMMON NAME Gray, for the overall color of the plumage. Catbird, for part of the call that sounds like a cat mewing.

Egretta caerulea   Little Blue Heron

SCIENTIFIC NAME *Egretta*, from Old French *aigrette*, an egret or small heron, a diminutive of *aigron*, a heron + *caerulea*, from Latin *caeruleus*, blue or greenish blue. Reference is to the overall color of the plumage.

COMMON NAME Little, smaller than the great blue heron. Blue, for the overall color of the plumage. Heron, many languages have a name for this bird that is close to *heron*, for example, from Middle English *heiroun* and *heyron* and the Old French *aigron* and *hairon*. Many are thought to come from the Old High German name for this bird, *heiger* or *heigir*.

Egretta garzetta   Little Egret

SCIENTIFIC NAME *Egretta* + *garzetta*, the Italian name for this bird.

COMMON NAME Little, for the size when compared to the great egret. Egret, from Old French *aigrette*, an egret or small heron, a diminutive of *aigron*, a heron.

Egretta rufescens   Reddish Egret

SCIENTIFIC NAME *Egretta* + *rufescens*, from Latin *rufesco*, to become reddish or tawny. Reference is to the reddish plumage of the head and neck.

COMMON NAME Reddish, see scientific name. Egret, see *Egretta garzetta*.

Egretta thula   Snowy Egret

SCIENTIFIC NAME *Egretta* + *thula*, an Araucano Indian (south-central Chile) word assigned to this bird when it was first described in 1782. The word was actually used by the Araucano as the name for the black-necked swan, *Cygnus melanocoryphus*, so it was incorrectly applied here as a species name.

COMMON NAME Snowy, descriptive of the white plumage. Egret, see *Egretta garzetta*.

Egretta tricolor   Tricolored Heron

SCIENTIFIC NAME *Egretta* + *tricolor*, Latin for having three colors. Reference is to the slate-colored neck and body, the white rump and underparts, and the reddish brown anterior neck.

COMMON NAME Tricolored, see scientific name. Heron, see *Egretta caerulea*.

Elanoides forficatus Swallow-tailed Kite

SCIENTIFIC NAME *Elanoides*, to look like a kite, from Greek ελανος, *elanos*, a form of ικτινος, *iktinos*, a kite, and ειοδος, *eiodos*, that which is seen, shape or form + *forficatus*, deeply forked, from Latin *forceps*, *forfex*, or *forpex*, forceps, tongs, shears or scissors, and *-atus*, to have. Reference is to the deeply forked tail. The appropriate use of *forficate* when referring to a bird's tail is when the depth of the fork equals or exceeds the length of the shortest tail feather (*Century Dictionary and Cyclopedia*, 1913).

COMMON NAME Swallow-tailed, the tail resembles that of a swallow. Kite, from Anglo-Saxon *cyta*, their name for this type of bird. The kite that is flown on a string was so named because it appeared to hang in the air like the bird.

Elanus leucurus White-tailed Kite

SCIENTIFIC NAME *Elanus*, a kite, from Greek ελανος, *elanos*, a form of ικτινος, *iktinos*, a kite + *leucurus*, white tailed, from Greek λευκουρος, *leukouros*, white tailed, from λευκος, *leukos*, of color, white, and ουρα, *oura*, tail. According to the *Oxford Greek-English Lexicon* (1996), ουρα, *oura* should not be used for the tail of a bird but is restricted to other animals.

COMMON NAME White-tailed, descriptive. Kite, see *Elanoides forficatus*.

Emberiza rustica Rustic Bunting

SCIENTIFIC NAME *Emberiza*, from Old German *embritz*, a bunting + *rustica*, when applied to animals, wild as opposed to domesticated.

COMMON NAME Rustic, of or pertaining to the country. Bunting, the origin of this word is unknown, but *The Oxford English Dictionary* (1989) suggests the Scandinavian *buntin*, short and thick, plump.

Empidonax alnorum Alder Flycatcher

SCIENTIFIC NAME *Empidonax*, mosquito or gnat master, from Greek εμπις, εμπιδ, *empis*, *empid*, a mosquito or gnat, and αναξ, *anax*, lord, master, king, son or brother of a king, hero, leader of the gods. Reference is to the feeding habits of this genus of flycatchers + *alnorum*, of alders, from Latin *alnus*, an alder. Reference is to the nesting habitat.

COMMON NAME Alder, for the nesting habitat. Flycatcher, for the habit of catching insects in the air.

Empidonax difficilis   Pacific-slope Flycatcher

SCIENTIFIC NAME *Empidonax* + *difficilis*, Latin for hard to deal with, difficult. Reference is to members of this genus looking so much alike that the species are difficult to separate.

COMMON NAME Pacific-slope, for the natural range in the United States. Flycatcher, see *Empidonax alnorum*.

Empidonax flaviventris   Yellow-bellied Flycatcher

SCIENTIFIC NAME *Empidonax* + *flaviventris*, yellow bellied, from Latin *flavus*, yellow, especially pale yellow or golden, and *venter, ventris*, the lower part of the human torso, belly, abdomen, the underside of animals. Reference is to the yellowish olive breast and belly, a common mark in this genus.

COMMON NAME Yellow-bellied, see scientific name. Flycatcher, see *Empidonax alnorum*.

Empidonax fulvifrons   Buff-breasted Flycatcher

SCIENTIFIC NAME *Empidonax* + *fulvifrons*, tawny front, from Latin *fulvus*, brown, ranging between a dull yellow and a reddish brown, tawny, sandy, and *frons*, forehead, front. Refers to the tawny breast.

COMMON NAME Buff-breasted, descriptive. Flycatcher, see *Empidonax alnorum*.

Empidonax hammondii   Hammond's Flycatcher

SCIENTIFIC NAME *Empidonax* + *hammondii*, for William Alexander Hammond (1828–1900), surgeon general of the U.S. Army (1862–1864). John Xantus (1825–1894) named this bird for Hammond for his help in giving Xantus the opportunity to do fieldwork in the western United States.

COMMON NAME Hammond's, see scientific name. Flycatcher, see *Empidonax alnorum*.

Empidonax minimus   Least Flycatcher

SCIENTIFIC NAME *Empidonax* + *minimus*, Latin for smallest or very small in size or amount. Reference is to the size of this bird, although the buff-breasted flycatcher is just as small.

COMMON NAME Least, smallest, see scientific name. Flycatcher, see *Empidonax alnorum*.

Empidonax oberholseri — Dusky Flycatcher

SCIENTIFIC NAME *Empidonax* + *oberholseri*, for Harry Church Oberholser (1870–1963), an ornithologist who classified and named a large number of new species by working with skins and not in the field. His ability to detect subtle differences in specimens was said to be unmatched.

COMMON NAME Dusky, for the gray back. Flycatcher, see *Empidonax alnorum*.

Empidonax occidentalis — Cordilleran Flycatcher

SCIENTIFIC NAME *Empidonax* + *occidentalis*, Latin for west or western. Reference is to the natural range in the United States.

COMMON NAME Cordilleran, a diminutive of Spanish *cuerda*, a rope or string. Refers to the main mountain axis of a continent. In the United States this is used for the Rocky Mountains, the Sierra Nevada, and the Coast and Cascade Ranges. Reference is to the natural range along the Rocky Mountain chain. Flycatcher, see *Empidonax alnorum*.

Empidonax traillii — Willow Flycatcher

SCIENTIFIC NAME *Empidonax* + *traillii*, for Thomas Stewart Traill (1781–1862), a Scottish physician who taught medical jurisprudence, was a founder of the Royal Institution of Liverpool, and edited the eighth edition of the *Encyclopedia Britannica*. He protested the neglect of the natural history collections by the British Museum and managed to get them sent to the newly formed, free-standing Museum of Natural History. John James Audubon (1785–1851) named this bird for him.

COMMON NAME Willow, for the preferred nesting site. Flycatcher, see *Empidonax alnorum*.

Empidonax virescens — Acadian Flycatcher

SCIENTIFIC NAME *Empidonax* + *virescens*, Latin for to turn green. Reference is to the olive-green back.

COMMON NAME Acadian, originally the range was erroneously believed to include Nova Scotia; the name has been retained, however. Flycatcher, see *Empidonax alnorum*.

Empidonax wrightii   Gray Flycatcher

SCIENTIFIC NAME *Empidonax* + *wrightii*, for Charles Wright (1811–1885), a successful self-taught botanist and prolific collector. Asa Gray (1810–1888), of Harvard, published some of his work in *Plantae Wrightianae*. Spencer Fullerton Baird (1823–1887) named this bird for him.

COMMON NAME Gray, for the overall color of the plumage. Flycatcher, see *Empidonax alnorum*.

Eremophila alpestris   Horned Lark

SCIENTIFIC NAME *Eremophila*, desert loving, from Greek ερημος, *erēmos*, when referring to places, desert, and φιλος, *philos*, loving. Reference is to the habitat + *alpestris*, belonging to the mountains, from Latin *Alpes*, a form of *Alpis*, the high mountains of northern Italy, by extension any mountain range. Reference is to the breeding grounds in the mountains.

COMMON NAME Horned, for the tufts of feathers on the head that look like horns. Lark, from Middle English, a contraction of *lavercock*, the name for lark.

Estrilda astrild   Common Waxbill

SCIENTIFIC NAME *Estrilda*, from Afrikaans *astrild*, *estrelda*, *astrelda*, and *astrilda*, their names for the African waxbill. William Swainson (1789–1855) took this name from the name Carl Linnaeus (1707–1778) had assigned to the African waxbill, *Loxia astrild* + *astrild*, same as genus name.

COMMON NAME Common, most common waxbill in its range. Waxbill, for the bright red bill that looks like a stick of sealing wax.

Estrilda caerulescens   Lavender Waxbill

SCIENTIFIC NAME *Estrilda* + *caerulescens*, to become blue, from Latin *caeruleus*, blue.

COMMON NAME Lavender, for the color of both the plumage and the bill. Waxbill, see *Estrilda astrild*.

Estrilda melpoda   Orange-cheeked Waxbill

SCIENTIFIC NAME *Estrilda* + *melpoda*, from Greek μελπωδος, *melpōdos*, singing songs.

COMMON NAME Orange-cheeked, descriptive. Waxbill, see *Estrilda astrild*.

Estrilda troglodytes   Black-rumped Waxbill

SCIENTIFIC NAME *Estrilda* + *troglodytes*, from Greek τρωγλοδυτες, *trōglo-dutes*, one who creeps into holes, a caveman, a wren.

COMMON NAME Black-rumped, for the short black tail. Waxbill, see *Estrilda astrild*.

Eudocimus albus   White Ibis

SCIENTIFIC NAME *Eudocimus*, from Greek ευδοκιμος, *eudokimos*, in good repute, honored, famous, glorious. Reference is not to the bird but to the fact that it was removed from the genus *Scolpax* by Johann Georg Wagler (1800–1832) and placed in the appropriate genus, where it was considered to be in an honored (correct) position + *albus*, Latin for white. Reference is to the plumage.

COMMON NAME White, for the overall color of the plumage. Ibis, from Greek ιβις, *ibis*, from the Egyptian name for this type of bird.

Eudocimus ruber   Scarlet Ibis

SCIENTIFIC NAME *Eudocimus* + *ruber*, Latin for red, including shades of orange. Reference is to the red plumage.

COMMON NAME Scarlet, for the overall red color of the plumage. Ibis, see *Eudocimus albus*.

Eugenes fulgens   Magnificent Hummingbird

SCIENTIFIC NAME *Eugenes*, from Greek ευγενης, *eugenēs*, for well born, noble in outward appearance. Reference is to the attractive colors of the plumage + *fulgens*, Latin for flashing, gleaming, glittering, resplendent. Reference is to the iridescent hues of the plumage.

COMMON NAME Magnificent, for the appearance. Hummingbird, for the buzzing hum of the wingbeats.

Euphagus carolinus   Rusty Blackbird

SCIENTIFIC NAME *Euphagus*, good glutton, from Greek ευ, *eu*, good, well, and φαγος, *phagos*, a glutton. Reference is to the wide variety of the diet and to the voracious appetite + *carolinus*, of the Carolina colonies, an area encompassing the southeastern United States, where the type specimen was obtained.

COMMON NAME Rusty, for the color of the nonbreeding plumage. Black-bird, for the male's body color in breeding plumage.

Euphagus cyanocephalus   Brewer's Blackbird

SCIENTIFIC NAME *Euphagus* + *cyanocephalus*, having a dark blue head, from Greek κυανος, *kuanos*, dark blue, and κεφαλη, *kephalē*, head. Reference is to the color of the male's head in breeding plumage.

COMMON NAME Brewer's, for Thomas Mayo Brewer (1814–1880), a physician, editor, and publisher. He collected for John James Audubon (1785–1851), who named this and other birds in his honor. Brewer wrote *North American Oology* (1857); only the first volume was ever published because of the high cost of reproducing the egg illustrations. Blackbird, for the male's body color.

Euplectes franciscanus   Orange Bishop

SCIENTIFIC NAME *Euplectes*, well plaited, from Greek ευ, *eu*, good, well, and πλεκτος, *plektos*, plaited, twisted. Reference is to the woven nests of some members of this genus + *franciscanus*, to be related to the Franciscans, from Latin *Franciscus*, Francis, for Saint Francis of Assisi (1182–1226), the founder of the Franciscan Order. Reference is to the scarlet on the male in breeding plumage, which was thought to resemble the robes of the Franciscans.

COMMON NAME Orange, a reference to the male's bright red breeding plumage. Bishop, the red color and pattern of the male's breeding plumage suggests a bishop's robe.

Euptilotis neoxenus   Eared Quetzal

SCIENTIFIC NAME *Euptilotis*, good feather ear, from Greek ευ, *eu*, good, well, πτιλον, *ptilon*, soft feathers or down under the true feathers, any feather or wing, and ωτις, *ōtis*, from ους, *ous*, ear. Reference is to the small, usually hidden, tufts of feathers that look like ears + *neoxenus*, a new stranger, from Greek νεο, *neo*, new, and ξενος, *xenos*, stranger, foreigner. Reference is thought to be to finding the type specimen in an unusual area, north of the range of most quetzals.

COMMON NAME Eared, for the feather tufts on the head. Quetzal, from Nahuatl Indian (Central America) *quetzalli*, long green feather.

Falcipennis canadensis   Spruce Grouse

SCIENTIFIC NAME *Falcipennis*, sickle winged, from Latin *falx*, an agricultural implement with a curved blade, hook, scythe, sickle, and *penna*, a wing. Reference is to the swept back wings in flight + *canadensis*, Latin for belonging to Canada. Reference is to the natural range.

COMMON NAME Spruce, for the habitat in spruce forests. Grouse, origin unknown but thought to come from French *griais*, speckled gray.

Falco columbarius   Merlin

SCIENTIFIC NAME *Falco*, Later Latin for falcon, from Latin *falx*, an agricultural implement with a curved blade, hook, scythe, sickle. Reference is to the hooked talons + *columbarius*, pertaining to pigeons or doves, from Latin *columba*, a pigeon or dove, and *-arius*, pertaining to. Strictly translated, *columbarius* means a pigeon keeper. Reference is to the prey.

COMMON NAME Merlin, from Old English *marlin*, which referred to a female falcon. In the United States this bird was formerly called the pigeon hawk.

Falco femoralis   Aplomado Falcon

SCIENTIFIC NAME *Falco* + *femoralis*, Late Latin for on the thigh. Reference is to the bright tawny thighs.

COMMON NAME Aplomado, Spanish for lead colored, leaden. Reference is to the lead-gray adult plumage. Falcon, from Latin *falx*, an agricultural implement with a curved blade, hook, scythe, sickle. Reference is to the hooked talons.

Falco mexicanus   Prairie Falcon

SCIENTIFIC NAME *Falco* + *mexicanus*, Latin for pertaining to Mexico, from Mexico. Reference is to the region of the type specimen.

COMMON NAME Prairie, for the habitat. Falcon, see *Falco femoralis*.

Falco peregrinus   Peregrine Falcon

SCIENTIFIC NAME *Falco* + *peregrinus*, Latin for foreign, alien, not native, exotic. Used to imply a wanderer from another place.

COMMON NAME Peregrine, see scientific name. Falcon, see *Falco femoralis*.

Falco rusticolus — Gyrfalcon

SCIENTIFIC NAME *Falco* + *rusticolus*, Latin for of or suited to the farm or country. Carl Linnaeus (1707–1778) named this bird and probably meant *rusticulus*, a diminutive of *rusticus*, a little rustic. In either case, reference is to the habitat.

COMMON NAME Gyrfalcon, vulture falcon. An unusually large number of translations and derivations have been attempted for this name. *The Oxford English Dictionary* (1989) has a long discussion of these derivations and concludes that the ultimate source is the Old High German *gir*, vulture. Falcon, see *Falco femoralis*.

Falco sparverius — American Kestrel

SCIENTIFIC NAME *Falco* + *sparverius*, New Latin for a sparrow-hawk; also spelled *sparvarius*, *sparaverius*, and *esparvarius*. In Early Modern English, *sparver* was a term for a sparrow-hawk, and *sparve* was a dialectical form of sparrow in Cornwall, England. Reference is to this falcon preying on sparrows and other small birds.

COMMON NAME American, to differentiate it from the Eurasian kestrel. Kestrel, from French *crecelle*, their name for this type of bird. *Crecelle* means a noisy bell, and the reference is thought to be to this bird's call.

Francolinus erckelii — Erckel's Francolin

SCIENTIFIC NAME *Francolinus*, from French *francolin*, in turn from Old Italian *francolino*, a little hen, a partridge + *erckelii*, for Theodor Erckel (1811–1897), a German taxidermist who collected birds in Africa under Wilhem Peter Eduard Ruppell (1794–1884).

COMMON NAME Erckel's, see scientific name. Francolin, see scientific name.

Francolinus francolinus — Black Francolin

SCIENTIFIC NAME *Francolinus* + *francolinus*.

COMMON NAME Black, for the male's black breast. Francolin, see *Francolinus erckelii*.

Francolinus pondicerianus — Gray Francolin

SCIENTIFIC NAME *Francolinus* + *pondicerianus*, Latin for pertaining to Pondichery, the former French India colony where the type specimen was described.

COMMON NAME Gray, a poor descriptive term because this bird is brown. Francolin, see *Francolinus erckelii.*

Fratercula arctica   Atlantic Puffin

SCIENTIFIC NAME *Fratercula,* little brother, friar, from Latin *fraterculus,* a little brother. Reference is to the hooded appearance of the head plumage, reminiscent of the hood a friar wears + *arctica,* from Greek αρκτιος, *ark-tios,* arctic, northern. Reference is to the natural range.

COMMON NAME Atlantic, for the natural range. Puffin, puff plus the diminutive *-in. The Oxford English Dictionary* (1989) states the origin is uncertain; other sources suggest puffy cheeks, puffy bill, and the puffy appearance of the adult.

Fratercula cirrhata   Tufted Puffin

SCIENTIFIC NAME *Fratercula* + *cirrhata,* curly headed, a misspelling of the Latin *cirratus, cirrata,* curly headed. The principle of priority allows the mistake to stand. Reference is to the curly tuft of feathers on the back of the head in breeding plumage.

COMMON NAME Tufted, see scientific name. Puffin, see *Fratercula arctica.*

Fratercula corniculata   Horned Puffin

SCIENTIFIC NAME *Fratercula* + *corniculata,* from Latin *corniculum,* a small horn, a small projection resembling a horn. Reference is to the small fleshy hornlike projections above the eyes.

COMMON NAME Horned, see scientific name. Puffin, see *Fratercula arctica.*

Fregata magnificens   Magnificent Frigatebird

SCIENTIFIC NAME *Fregata,* from Italian for frigate. Reference is to the light, swift, sailing flight like that of a frigate warship + *magnificens,* from Latin *magnificus,* magnificent, splendid, excellent. Reference here is to the size, this is the largest of the frigatebirds.

COMMON NAME Magnificent, see scientific name. Frigatebird, see scientific name.

Fregata minor   Great Frigatebird

SCIENTIFIC NAME *Fregata* + *minor,* Latin for smaller in size, height, extent, of the smaller kind. Reference is to it being smaller than *Fregata magnificens.*

COMMON NAME Great, for the size, larger than the least frigatebird. Frigatebird, see *Fregata magnificens*.

Fringilla montifringilla Brambling

SCIENTIFIC NAME *Fringilla*, Latin for a songbird, in turn from Greek φρυγιλος, *phrugilos*, the chaffinch + *montifringilla*, mountain chaffinch, from Latin *montis*, a mountain, and *fringilla*, the chaffinch. Reference is to the mountain breeding grounds.

COMMON NAME Brambling, little bramble or little blackberry. Most probably an erroneous reference to the habitat.

Fulica alai 'Alae Ke 'Oke 'O or Hawaiian Coot

SCIENTIFIC NAME *Fulica*, Latin for a waterfowl, in turn from Greek φαλαρις, *phalaris*, a coot + *alai*, Latinized form of Hawaiian, '*alae*, a coot or moorhen.

COMMON NAME 'Alae Ke 'Oke 'O, complete Hawaiian name for this bird. Hawaiian, endemic in the Hawaiian Island chain. Coot, from Middle English *coote*, their name for this type of bird.

Fulica americana American Coot

SCIENTIFIC NAME *Fulica* + *americana*, of America, to differentiate it from the European coot.

COMMON NAME American, see scientific name. Coot, see *Fulica alai*.

Fulmarus glacialis Northern Fulmar

SCIENTIFIC NAME *Fulmarus*, Latinized form of the Old Norse, *fulmar*, their name for this bird, from *ful*, foul, and *mar*, gull. Reference is to the foul smell of this bird + *glacialis*, Latin for characterized by ice, icy, frozen. Reference is to the natural range.

COMMON NAME Northern, for the natural range. Fulmar, see scientific name.

Gallinago gallinago Common Snipe

SCIENTIFIC NAME *Gallinago*, from Latin *gallina*, a hen. Reference is to the appearance + *gallinago*.

COMMON NAME Common, most common snipe in the range in Europe. Snipe, from Anglo-Saxon *snite*, their name for this type of bird.

Gallinula chloropus   Common Moorhen

SCIENTIFIC NAME *Gallinula*, little hen, from Latin *gallina*, hen, and the diminutive *-ula* + *chloropus*, green footed, from Greek χλωρος, *khlōros*, greenish yellow, pale green, any green color, and πος, *pos*, foot. Reference is to the pale greenish yellow legs and feet. A Hawaiian subspecies is named *sandvicensis*, of the Sandwich Islands, an old name for the Hawaiian Islands. They were named for John Montagu, fourth earl of Sandwich (1718–1792), the first lord of the British Admiralty.

COMMON NAME Common, abundant in its range. Moorhen, for the habitat. There is also a moorcock, but the common name of moorhen is used for both sexes because they are sexually monomorphic.

Gallus gallus   Red Junglefowl

SCIENTIFIC NAME *Gallus*, Latin for a farmyard cock + *gallus*.

COMMON NAME Red, a poor descriptor, the neck and back are orange-brown. Junglefowl, for the natural habitat.

Garrulax caerulatus   Gray-sided Laughingthrush

SCIENTIFIC NAME *Garrulax*, inclined to chatter, from Latin *garrulus*, talkative, loquacious, chattering, and *-ax*, inclining toward + *caerulatus*, a form of *caeruleatus*, colored with blue.

COMMON NAME Gray-sided, descriptive. Laughingthrush, for the rhythm of the song.

Garrulax canorus   Hwamei

SCIENTIFIC NAME *Garrulax* + *canorus*, Latin for having a resonant, sonorous singing voice.

COMMON NAME Hwamei, Hawaiian name for this bird.

Garrulax pectoralis   Greater Necklaced Laughingthrush

SCIENTIFIC NAME *Garrulax* + *pectoralis*, Latin for of or on the breast. Reference is to the black stripe across the breast.

COMMON NAME Greater, for the size. Necklaced, for the black stripe on the sides of the neck and across the breast. Laughingthrush, see *Garrulax caerulatus*.

Gavia adamsii   Yellow-billed Loon

SCIENTIFIC NAME *Gavia*, Latin for a seabird + *adamsii*, for Edward Adams (1824–1856), a British Navy surgeon, explorer, and naturalist. He made a major voyage on the HMS *Enterprise* (1850–1855) under Captain Collinson, during which he collected and sketched many specimens that he later presented to the British Museum.

COMMON NAME Yellow-billed, has a yellow bill that is especially obvious in the breeding plumage. Loon, a corruption of the Shetland *loom*, their name for a guillemot, a diver.

Gavia arctica   Arctic Loon

SCIENTIFIC NAME *Gavia* + *arctica*, from Greek αρκτιος, *arktios*, arctic, northern. Reference is to the natural range.

COMMON NAME Arctic, for the natural range. Loon, see *Gavia adamsii*.

Gavia immer   Common Loon

SCIENTIFIC NAME *Gavia* + *immer*, from Icelandic *himbrimi*, their name for the great northern diver.

COMMON NAME Common, most common loon in its range. Loon, see *Gavia adamsii*.

Gavia pacifica   Pacific Loon

SCIENTIFIC NAME *Gavia* + *pacifica*, for the Pacific Ocean, the U.S. range is along the Pacific Coast.

COMMON NAME Pacific, see scientific name. Loon, see *Gavia adamsii*.

Gavia stellata   Red-throated Loon

SCIENTIFIC NAME *Gavia* + *stellata*, Latin for adorned with a star, stars, or starlike markings. Reference is to the white dots on the dark back in the nonbreeding plumage.

COMMON NAME Red-throated, for the red throat in breeding plumage. Loon, see *Gavia adamsii*.

Geococcyx californianus   Greater Roadrunner

SCIENTIFIC NAME *Geococcyx*, earth cuckoo, from Greek γη, *gē*, earth, land, country, and κοκκυξ, *kokkux*, a cuckoo (see *Coccyzus americanus*)

Gavia immer, common loon

+ *californianus*, pertaining to California, from California. For the province of Alta California, Mexico, where the type specimen was described.

COMMON NAME Greater, for the size; it is larger than the lesser roadrunner, which shares a range with it in Mexico. Roadrunner, for its habit of running along roads, where it is most commonly sighted.

Geopelia striata   Zebra Dove

SCIENTIFIC NAME *Geopelia*, earth dove, from Greek γη, *gē*, earth, land, country, and πελεια, *peleia*, a dove or pigeon + *striata*, Modern Latin for striped, streaked. Reference is to the stripes on the sides and breast.

COMMON NAME Zebra, for the stripes on the sides and breast. Dove, from Anglo-Saxon *dufan*, to dive, for its irregular flight pattern.

Geothlypis poliocephala   Gray-crowned Yellowthroat

SCIENTIFIC NAME *Geothlypis*, earth finch, from Greek γη, *gē*, earth, land, country, and the obscure θλυπις, *thlupis*, a type of finch. This genus spends a lot of time on the ground + *poliocephala*, gray headed, from Greek πολιος, *polios*, gray, grizzled, and κεφαλη, *kephalē*, head. Reference is to the male's gray crown.

COMMON NAME Gray-crowned, descriptive. Yellowthroat, both sexes have yellow throats.

Geothlypis trichas   Common Yellowthroat

SCIENTIFIC NAME *Geothlypis* + *trichas*, from Greek τριχας, *trikhas*, the song-thrush.

COMMON NAME Common, most common in some parts of the range. Yellowthroat, see *Geothlypis poliocephala*.

Geotrygon chrysia   Key West Quail-Dove

SCIENTIFIC NAME *Geotrygon*, earth turtle dove, from Greek γη, *gē*, earth, land, country, and τρυγων, *trugōn*, the turtle dove. Reference is to the appearance and to its terrestrial habitat + *chrysia*, from Greek χρυσους, *khrusous*, golden.

COMMON NAME Key West, for the natural range. Quail-Dove, for the behavior, it lives on the ground like a quail.

Glaucidium brasilianum   Ferruginous Pygmy-Owl

SCIENTIFIC NAME *Glaucidium*, little little owl, from Greek γλαυξ, *glaux*, the little owl (*Athene noctua*), and the diminutive *-idium*, from Greek ιδιον, *idion*, smaller + *brasilianum*, Latinized term for pertaining to Brazil. Reference is to the country of origin of the type specimen.

COMMON NAME Ferruginous, from Latin *ferrugo*, iron rust. Reference is to the reddish brown of the plumage. Pygmy, for its small size. Owl, from Anglo-Saxon *ule*, owl, and from Latin *ululo*, to cry out.

Glaucidium gnoma   Northern Pygmy-Owl

SCIENTIFIC NAME *Glaucidium* + *gnoma*, from Greek γνωμη, *gnōmē*, means of knowing, intelligence, judgment, opinion. Reference is to the association of owls with knowledge and intelligence. *The Oxford English Dictionary* (1989) states that the connection of this word with the English *gnome* seems unlikely.

COMMON NAME Northern, for the range relative to that of the ferruginous pygmy-owl. Pygmy-owl, see *Glaucidium brasilianum*.

Gracula religiosa   Hill Myna

SCIENTIFIC NAME *Gracula*, Latin for the jackdaw and other crowlike birds. Reference is to the overall black color + *religiosa*, from Latin *religiosus*, full of religious scruples, sacred. Carl Linnaeus (1707–1778) named this bird, mistaking it for the common myna, which is sacred to the Hindus.

COMMON NAME Hill, for the habitat. Myna, from the Hindustani name for this bird, *maina*, a starling.

Grus americana   Whooping Crane

SCIENTIFIC NAME *Grus*, Latin for a large bird, a crane + *americana*, of America, for the natural range.

COMMON NAME Whooping, for the call. Crane, from Anglo-Saxon *cran*, their name for this type of bird.

Grus canadensis   Sandhill Crane

SCIENTIFIC NAME *Grus* + *canadensis*, Latin for belonging to Canada. Reference is to the natural range.

COMMON NAME Sandhill, small sandhills are the preferred site for the courtship dance. Crane, see *Grus americana*.

Gygis alba   White Tern

SCIENTIFIC NAME *Gygis*, from Greek γυγης, *gugēs*, a mythical bird, used by Dionysius of Halicarnassus in *de Avium* + *alba*, from Latin *albus*, white. Reference is to the body color.

COMMON NAME White, for the overall color of the plumage. Tern, from Old Norse *taerne*, their name for this type of bird.

Gymnogyps californianus   California Condor

SCIENTIFIC NAME *Gymnogyps*, naked vulture, from Greek γυμνος, *gumnos*, naked, unclad, and γυψ, *gups*, a vulture. Reference is to the featherless head and neck + *californianus*, Latin for pertaining to California, from California.

COMMON NAME California, for the natural range. Condor, from the Spanish *condor*, in turn from the Quechuan (Andes) word *cuntur*, the name for this type of bird.

Gymnorhinus cyanocephalus   Pinyon Jay

SCIENTIFIC NAME *Gymnorhinus*, naked beak, from Greek γυμνος, *gumnos*, naked, unclad, and ρινο, *rino*, nostrils. Reference is to the large exposed nostrils + *cyanocephalus*, dark blue headed, from Greek κυανος, *kuanos*, dark blue, and κεφαλη, *kephalē*, head. Reference is to the darker blue of the head than that of the body.

COMMON NAME Pinyon, for the pinyon pine habitat. Jay, from French *geai*, a jay. Origin is unknown, onomatopoeia of the call is a possibility.

Haematopus bachmani   Black Oystercatcher

SCIENTIFIC NAME *Haematopus*, blood foot, from Greek αιμα, *aima*, genitive αιματος, *aimatos*, blood, anything like blood, and πος, *pos*, foot. Reference is to the pink feet and legs + *bachmani*, John James Audubon (1785–1851) named this bird for Reverend John Bachman (1790–1874) of Charleston, South Carolina. The two families were close friends; Audubon's two sons married Bachman's daughters.

COMMON NAME Black, for the overall color of the plumage. Oystercatcher, part of the diet is shellfish.

Haematopus palliatus   American Oystercatcher

SCIENTIFIC NAME *Haematopus* + *palliatus*, wearing a pallium, a rectangular piece of material worn by Greek men draped over the body as an outer garment, a mantle or cloak. Reference is to the dark back and the white underparts, which give the impression of a cloak draped over this bird.

COMMON NAME American, for the natural range. This was the first oystercatcher named in the United States, and at the time it was thought to be the only one. Oystercatcher, see *Haematopus bachmani*.

Haliaeetus leucocephalus   Bald Eagle

SCIENTIFIC NAME *Haliaeetus*, Latin for a kind of eagle, perhaps the osprey, in turn from Greek αλιαετος, *aliaetos*, the sea eagle. The spelling should be *haliaetus*, the original mistake was made by Marie Jules Cesar Lelorgne de Savigny (1777–1851), a French botanist and zoologist, when separating this genus from the falcons. The principle of priority preserves the mistake + *leucocephalus*, white headed, from Greek λευκος, *leukos*, of color, white, and κεφαλη, *kephalē*, head. Reference is to the white head.

COMMON NAME Bald, from Middle English *balled*, shining, white. Its head appeared to be bald, as we now use the term, when compared to the dark body. Eagle, from French *aigle*, in turn from Latin *aquila*, an eagle.

Heliomaster constantii   Plain-capped Starthroat

SCIENTIFIC NAME *Heliomaster*, sun seeker, from Greek ηλιος, *ēlios*, the sun, and μαστηρ, *mastēr*, seeker, searcher + *constantii*, for C. Constant (1820–1905), a French taxidermist.

COMMON NAME Plain-capped, for the brown cap. Starthroat, for the male's bright red throat.

Helmitheros vermivorus   Worm-eating Warbler

SCIENTIFIC NAME *Helmitheros*, worm hunter, from Greek ελμινς, *elmins*, a worm, and θηραν, *thēran*, to hunt + *vermivorus*, worm eating, from Latin *vermis*, a worm, maggot, or other small creature of similar appearance, and *voro*, *vorare*, to swallow ravenously, devour. Reference is to the main diet of smooth caterpillars.

COMMON NAME Worm-eating, see scientific name. Warbler, for the trills and quavers of the song.

Hemignathus chloris   Oahu 'Amakihi

SCIENTIFIC NAME *Hemignathus*, half-jawed, from Greek ημι, *ēmi*, half, and γναθος, *gnathos*, jaw. Reference is to the mandible, which is shorter and thinner than the maxilla + *chloris*, the greenfinch, from Greek χλορις, *khloris*, the greenfinch. Reference is to the color of the plumage.

COMMON NAME Oahu, for the island of Oahu in the Hawaiian archipelago, the natural range. 'Amakihi, the Hawaiian name for this type of bird.

Hemignathus kauaiensis   Kauai 'Amakihi

SCIENTIFIC NAME *Hemignathus* + *kauaiensis*, Latin for belonging to Kauai. Reference is to the natural range on the island of Kauai in the Hawaiian archipelago.

COMMON NAME Kauai, see scientific name. 'Amakihi, see *Hemignathus chloris*.

Hemignathus lucidus   Nuku Pu 'U

SCIENTIFIC NAME *Hemignathus* + *lucidus*, Latin for splendid, glorious. When referring to sources of light, bright, shining, also refers to polished surfaces and white or lightly colored objects. Reference here is to the splendid appearance of this bird.

COMMON NAME Nuku Pu 'U, the Hawaiian name for this bird.

Hemignathus munroi 'Akiapola 'Au

SCIENTIFIC NAME *Hemignathus* + *munroi*, for George C. Munro (1866–1963), the American ornithologist who wrote *Birds of Hawaii* (1960).

COMMON NAME 'Akiapola 'Au, the Hawaiian name for this bird.

Hemignathus parvus 'Anianiau

SCIENTIFIC NAME *Hemignathus* + *parvus*, Latin for small in size or extent.

COMMON NAME 'Anianiau, the Hawaiian name for this bird.

Hemignathus virens Hawaii 'Amakihi

SCIENTIFIC NAME *Hemignathus* + *virens*, from Latin *vireo*, to be green.

COMMON NAME Hawaii, for the island of Hawaii, the natural range. 'Amakihi, the Hawaiian name for this type of bird.

Heteroscelus brevipes Gray-tailed Tattler

SCIENTIFIC NAME *Heteroscelus*, Latin for with uneven legs, used here to mean having different legs, from Greek ετεροσκελης, *eteroskelēs*, with uneven legs. Reference is to the scaled legs of this genus, which are different from the smoother legs of other sandpipers + *brevipes*, short footed, from Latin *brevis*, having a small spatial extent, short, and *pes*, the lowest part of the legs, the foot.

COMMON NAME Gray-tailed, descriptive. Tattler, for the call, which was thought to draw the attention of other birds to the presence of a hunter.

Heteroscelus incanus Wandering Tattler

SCIENTIFIC NAME *Heteroscelus* + *incanus*, Latin for quite gray, hoary. Reference is to the gray upperparts.

COMMON NAME Wandering, for its habit of ranging over a large area. Tattler, see *Heteroscelus brevipes*.

Himantopus mexicanus Black-necked Stilt

SCIENTIFIC NAME *Himantopus*, from Greek ιμαντοπους, *imantopous*, spindle shanked, a kind of waterbird, by extension one with very thin legs (*Oxford Greek-English Lexicon*, 1996). Most other references give "thong foot," from Greek ιμαντ, *imant*, a thong, and πους, *pous*, foot. The illusion is that the legs look like a thin leather thong + *mexicanus*, Latin for pertaining to Mexico, from Mexico. For the country where the type specimen was collected. The subspecies endemic to the Hawaiian Islands, *knudseni*, named for V. Knudsen (1822–1898), a Norwegian ornithologist who worked in Hawaii.

COMMON NAME Black-necked, for the black stripe on the back of the neck found on both sexes. Stilt, for the unusually long legs.

Himatione sanguinea   'Apapane

SCIENTIFIC NAME *Himatione*, from Greek ιματιον, *imation*, an outer garment, a cloak, an oblong piece of cloth that was wrapped round the body and fell to the feet or was worn to just cover the back and shoulders. The Spartan soldiers wore such a cloak that was red. Reference is to the red back and sides + *sanguinea*, from Latin *sanguineus*, consisting of blood, bloody, blood stained, colored like blood. Reference is to the red in the plumage.

COMMON NAME 'Apapane, the Hawaiian name for this bird.

Hirundo rustica   Barn Swallow

SCIENTIFIC NAME *Hirundo*, Latin for all swallows and various martins + *rustica*, Latin for of or suited to a farm or the country.

COMMON NAME Barn, for a common nesting site. Swallow, from Anglo-Saxon *swalewe*, their name for this type of bird.

Histrionicus histrionicus   Harlequin Duck

SCIENTIFIC NAME *Histrionicus*, Latin for of or connected with the theater. Reference is to the male's showy plumage patterns, which make him appear dressed up as if to go on the stage + *histrionicus*.

COMMON NAME Harlequin, for the patterns of the male's plumage, thought to resemble a harlequin of the stage. Duck, from Anglo-Saxon *duce*, a form of *ducan*, to duck or dive.

Hylocharis leucotis   White-eared Hummingbird

SCIENTIFIC NAME *Hylocharis*, forest beauty, from Greek υλη, *ulē*, a forest or woodland, and χαρις, *kharis*, outward grace or beauty + *leucotis*, white eared, from Greek λευκος, *leukos*, of color, white, and ους, *ous*, ear. Reference is to the bright white supercilium, which makes a stripe where an ear would be expected.

COMMON NAME White-eared, see scientific name. Hummingbird, for the buzzing hum of the wingbeats.

Hylocichla mustelina   Wood Thrush

SCIENTIFIC NAME *Hylocichla*, wood thrush, from Greek υλη, *ulē*, a forest or woodland, and κιχλε, *kikhle*, a thrush + *mustelina*, Latin for of or belonging to a weasel. Reference is to the chestnut and white plumage, like the colors of a weasel.

COMMON NAME Wood, for the habitat. Thrush, from Middle English *thrusch*, their name for this type of bird.

Icteria virens   Yellow-breasted Chat

SCIENTIFIC NAME *Icteria*, from Greek ικτερος, *ikteros*, jaundice, a yellowish green bird the sight of which would cure a jaundiced person, however, the bird would die. Reference here is to the yellowish green breast + *virens*, from Latin *vireo*, to be green. Reference is to the olive-green back.

COMMON NAME Yellow-breasted, both sexes have yellow breasts. Chat, most probably an abbreviation of chatter for the multitude of changing and constant calls.

Icterus bullockii   Bullock's Oriole

SCIENTIFIC NAME *Icterus*, from Greek ικτερος, *ikteros*, jaundice (see *Icteria virens*) + *bullockii*, for William Bullock (1775–1840), an English traveler and mine owner who had a private museum in London. He collected the type specimen in Mexico; William Swainson (1789–1855) named it in his honor.

COMMON NAME Bullock's, see scientific name. Oriole, from Modern Latin *oriolus*, golden, in turn from Latin *aureolus*, golden. The American orioles were so named because they looked like the European golden oriole.

Icterus cucullatus   Hooded Oriole

SCIENTIFIC NAME *Icterus* + *cucullatus*, to wear a *cuculla*, from Later Latin *cucullus*, a monk's cowl. Reference is to the yellowish orange hood, black face, and front of the neck, which reminds one of a monk's hood with the face sticking out.

COMMON NAME Hooded, see scientific name. Oriole, see *Icterus bullockii*.

Icterus bullockii, Bullock's oriole

Icterus galbula   Baltimore Oriole

SCIENTIFIC NAME *Icterus* + *galbula*, a small yellow bird, a diminutive of
the Latin *galbulus*, a yellow bird.

COMMON NAME Baltimore, named for George Calvert (c. 1580–1632),
the first baron Baltimore and the founder of Maryland. His black and
orange livery colors were the same as the colors on this bird. Oriole, see
Icterus bullockii.

Icterus graduacauda   Audubon's Oriole

SCIENTIFIC NAME *Icterus* + *graduacauda*, step tail, from Latin *gradus*, a
step, a stair, and *cauda*, tail. Reference is to the graduated tail.

COMMON NAME Audubon's, for John James Audubon (1785–1851), the
artist who illustrated *Birds of America* (1827–1838) and became the best-
known painter of American birds. Oriole, see *Icterus bullockii*.

Icterus gularis — Altamira Oriole

SCIENTIFIC NAME *Icterus + gularis*, Modern Latin for of the throat, from Latin *gula*, the throat. Reference is to the black throat.

COMMON NAME Altamira, the type specimen was collected in Altamira, Tamaulipas, Mexico. Oriole, see *Icterus bullockii*.

Icterus parisorum — Scott's Oriole

SCIENTIFIC NAME *Icterus + parisorum*, for the Paris brothers (fl. 1837), French dealers in natural history specimens.

COMMON NAME Scott's, for Winfield Scott (1786–1866), commanding general of the American forces in the Mexican War. When Darius Nash Couch (1822–1897) found this bird he named it *Icterus scottii*, with the common name of Scott's oriole. It was later discovered that Charles Bonaparte (1803–1857) had already named this bird *Icterus parisorum*.

Icterus pectoralis — Spot-breasted Oriole

SCIENTIFIC NAME *Icterus + pectoralis*, Latin for of or for the breast. Reference is to the black spots on the breast.

COMMON NAME Spot-breasted, descriptive. Oriole, see *Icterus bullockii*.

Icterus pustulatus — Streaked-backed Oriole

SCIENTIFIC NAME *Icterus + pustulatus*, Latin for covered with blisters or pustules. Reference is to the spotted streaks on the mantle.

COMMON NAME Streaked-backed, has streaks on the mantle. Oriole, see *Icterus bullockii*.

Icterus spurius — Orchard Oriole

SCIENTIFIC NAME *Icterus + spurius*, Latin for the son of an unknown father. This reflects the common name bastard Baltimore oriole once assigned to this bird. The female Baltimore oriole was thought to be the male of this species, so a name was assigned to imply a bird inferior but similar to the Baltimore oriole. When the mistake was discovered the objectionable common name was changed, but the principle of priority protected the scientific name.

COMMON NAME Orchard, for a favorite habitat. Oriole, see *Icterus bullockii*.

Ictinia mississippiensis   Mississippi Kite

SCIENTIFIC NAME *Ictinia*, from Greek ικτινος, *iktinos*, a kite + *mississippiensis*, Latin for belonging to Mississippi. Reference is to the state where the type specimen was collected.

COMMON NAME Mississippi, see scientific name. Kite, from Anglo-Saxon *cyta*, their name for this type of bird.

Ixobrychus exilis   Least Bittern

SCIENTIFIC NAME *Ixobrychus*, reed roarer. Gustaf Johan Billberg (1772-1844), the Swedish zoologist and botanist who named this bird, meant for the translation to be reed roarer, but he confused the Greek ιξος, *ixos*, mistletoe, mistletoe berry, or birdlime made from mistletoe berries, with ιξιας, *ixias*, a reedlike plant. Latin *brychus*, from Greek βρυχο, *brukho*, to eat noisily with belching, to roar or bellow. The principle of priority preserves the original intent. The name reed roarer was originally chosen because of a folklore belief that this bird stuck its bill into a hollow reed at the waterside and produced a bellowing sound by blowing into the reed + *exilis*, Latin for small or slender.

COMMON NAME Least, for the size; this is the smallest heron in the United States. Bittern, the many forms of this name in Old English became standardized as *bittern* in 1678, when Francis Willughby's (1635–1672) *Ornithologia* was published (see also *Botaurus lentiginosus*).

Ixoreus naevius   Varied Thrush

SCIENTIFIC NAME *Ixoreus*, belonging to mistletoe, from Greek ιξος, *ixos*, mistletoe, mistletoe berry, birdlime made from mistletoe berries, and the Latin -*orius*, belonging to. Reference is to this bird resembling the mistle thrush. Some sources suggest mistletoe mountain, from Greek ιξος, *ixos*, and ορεος, *oreos*, mountain + *naevius*, a form of the Latin *naeuus*, a discolored mark on the skin, mole, birthmark. Used to imply varied, for the markings of the plumage.

COMMON NAME Varied, for the varied markings of the plumage. Thrush, from Middle English *thrusch*, their name for this type of bird.

Jacana spinosa   Northern Jacana

SCIENTIFIC NAME *Jacana*, the Tupi Indian (upper Amazon Basin) name for this type of bird + *spinosa*, Latin for thorny, spiny, prickly. Reference is to the spur at the bend of the wing.

COMMON NAME Northern, for the natural range in Mexico. Jacana, see scientific name.

Junco hyemalis   Dark-eyed Junco

SCIENTIFIC NAME *Junco*, Medieval Latin for the reed bunting, which this genus resembles, in turn from Latin *iuncus*, a rush or similar plant + *hyemalis*, from Latin *hiemalis*, of or belonging to winter. In Sweden, where Carl Linnaeus (1707–1778) lived, it was known only as a winter visitor.

COMMON NAME Dark-eyed, to contrast this bird with the yellow-eyed junco. Junco, see scientific name.

Junco phaeonotus   Yellow-eyed Junco

SCIENTIFIC NAME *Junco* + *phaeonotus*, gray backed, from Greek φαιος, *phaios*, gray, of any color mixed of black and white, and νωτον, νωτος, *nōton, nōtos*, back. This is not a descriptively accurate name because the back is rufous.

COMMON NAME Yellow-eyed, has yellow irises. Junco, see *Junco hyemalis*.

Lagopus lagopus   Willow Ptarmigan

SCIENTIFIC NAME *Lagopus*, Latin for a ptarmigan, in turn from Greek λαγωπους, *lagōpous*, rough footed like a hare, from λαγως, *lagōs*, a hare, πους, *pous*, foot. Reference is to the feather-covered legs (see *Buteo lagopus*) + *lagopus*.

COMMON NAME Willow, willow buds are a favorite food. Ptarmigan, from Gaelic *tarmachan*, their name for this type of bird.

Lagopus leucurus   White-tailed Ptarmigan

SCIENTIFIC NAME *Lagopus* + *leucurus*, white tailed, from Greek λευκος, *leukos*, of color, white, and ουρα, *oura*, tail. According to the *Oxford Greek-English Lexicon* (1996), ουρα, *oura* should not be used for the tail of a bird but is restricted to other animals. Reference is to the white underside of the tail.

COMMON NAME White-tailed, for the white underside of the tail. Ptarmigan, see *Lagopus lagopus*.

Lagopus mutus   Rock Ptarmigan

SCIENTIFIC NAME *Lagopus* + *mutus*, Latin for animals that can only mutter, dumb creatures, uttering no cry. Reference is to the low call.

COMMON NAME Rock, for the habitat on rocky tundra. Ptarmigan, see *Lagopus lagopus*.

Lampornis clemenciae   Blue-throated Hummingbird

SCIENTIFIC NAME *Lampornis*, bright bird, from Greek λαμπος, *lampos*, bright, and ορνις, *ornis*, bird + *clemenciae*, for Clemence Lesson (fl. 1825), wife of René P. Lesson (1794–1849), a French naturalist who first described this bird.

COMMON NAME Blue-throated, for the male's bright blue throat. Hummingbird, for the buzzing hum of the wingbeats.

Lanius cristatus   Brown Shrike

SCIENTIFIC NAME *Lanius*, from Latin *lanio*, to butcher, to pull to pieces. Reference is to the method of feeding: the shrike will impale its prey on a thorn and pull off pieces to eat + *cristatus*, Latin for crested.

COMMON NAME Brown, for the overall color of the plumage. Shrike, from Old English *scric*, a thrush, or Anglo-Saxon *scric*, a shrieker.

Lanius excubitor   Northern Shrike

SCIENTIFIC NAME *Lanius* + *excubitor*, Latin for a watchman, guard, or sentinel. Carl Linnaeus (1707–1778) used this name because of the belief at the time that this bird watched out for hawks and warned little birds of their presence.

COMMON NAME Northern, for the natural range, north of that of the loggerhead shrike. Shrike, see *Lanius cristatus*.

Lanius ludovicianus   Loggerhead Shrike

SCIENTIFIC NAME *Lanius* + *ludovicianus*, pertaining to *Ludovicius*, Louis, in reference to Louis XIV (1638–1715), king of France. Used here to mean from Louisiana, for the Louisiana Territory, where the type specimen was collected.

COMMON NAME Loggerhead, for the head that is larger in proportion to the body than in most birds. Shrike, see *Lanius cristatus*.

Larus argentatus   Herring Gull

SCIENTIFIC NAME *Larus*, from Greek λαρος, *laros*, a ravenous seabird + *argentatus*, Latin for adorned with silver, silvered. Reference is to the color of the back and the tops of the wings.

Lanius ludovicianus, loggerhead shrike

COMMON NAME Herring, part of the diet is scavenged fish. Gull, from Celtic *gullan, gwylan, gwelan*, all names for this type of bird.

Larus atricilla   Laughing Gull

SCIENTIFIC NAME *Larus + atricilla*, black tail, from Latin *ater*, black, and Modern Latin *cilla*, a tail (but see *Bombycilla cedrorum*). Reference is to the black band at the end of the tail in the juvenile.

COMMON NAME Laughing, for the rhythm of the call. Gull, see *Larus argentatus*.

Larus cachinnans   Yellow-legged Gull

SCIENTIFIC NAME *Larus + cachinnans*, from Latin *cachinno*, to laugh, especially to laugh loudly or boisterously. Reference is to the call, which resembles human laughter.

COMMON NAME Yellow-legged, descriptive. Gull, see *Larus argentatus*.

Larus californicus   California Gull

SCIENTIFIC NAME *Larus + californicus*, of California, the state in which the type specimen was collected.

COMMON NAME California, see scientific name. Gull, see *Larus argentatus*.

Larus canus   Mew Gull

SCIENTIFIC NAME *Larus + canus*, Latin for white or gray haired. Reference is to the color of the plumage.

COMMON NAME Mew, from Old English *mew*, a gull. Gull, see *Larus argentatus*.

Larus crassirostris   Black-tailed Gull

SCIENTIFIC NAME *Larus + crassirostris*, thick billed, from Latin *crassus*, thick, and *rostris*, from Latin *rostrum*, the snout or muzzle of an animal, the beak or bill of a bird.

COMMON NAME Black-tailed, for the white-edged black tail. Gull, see *Larus argentatus*.

Larus delawarensis   Ring-billed Gull

SCIENTIFIC NAME *Larus + delawarensis*, Latin for belonging to Delaware. Reference is to the Delaware River below Philadelphia, where the type specimen was found.

COMMON NAME Ring-billed, for the black ring close to the tip of the bill. Gull, see *Larus argentatus*.

Larus dominicanus   Kelp Gull

SCIENTIFIC NAME *Larus + dominicanus*, pertaining to the Dominicans. Reference is to the black and white plumage, reminiscent of the black and white robes of the Dominican monks.

COMMON NAME Kelp, for the habit of feeding among intertidal kelp beds. Gull, see *Larus argentatus*.

Larus fuscus   Lesser Black-backed Gull

SCIENTIFIC NAME *Larus + fuscus*, Latin for dark colored, dusky. Reference is to the dark color of the back and tops of the wings.

COMMON NAME Lesser, smaller than the great black-backed gull. Black-backed, descriptive. Gull, see *Larus argentatus*.

Larus glaucescens   Glaucous-winged Gull

SCIENTIFIC NAME *Larus* + *glaucescens*, to become bluish gray. However, used here to mean somewhat like a glaucous gull, from *glaucus*, the old species name for the glaucous gull, and *-escens*, somewhat like.

COMMON NAME Glaucous-winged, bluish gray winged, from Latin *glaucus*, bluish gray, in turn from Greek γλαυκος, *glaukos*, bluish green, gray. Gull, see *Larus argentatus*.

Larus glaucoides   Iceland Gull

SCIENTIFIC NAME *Larus* + *glaucoides*, to resemble a glaucous, from *glaucus*, the old species name for the glaucous gull, and *-oides*, to be like, resemble.

COMMON NAME Iceland, for the breeding range and the collection site of the type specimen. Gull, see *Larus argentatus*.

Larus heermanni   Heermann's Gull

SCIENTIFIC NAME *Larus* + *heermanni*, for Adolphus Lewis Heermann (1818–1865), a U.S. Army surgeon who also worked as a naturalist and collector on the Pacific Railroad Surveys. He coined the term *oology* for the study of eggs.

COMMON NAME Heermann's, see scientific name. Gull, see *Larus argentatus*.

Larus livens   Yellow-footed Gull

SCIENTIFIC NAME *Larus* + *livens*, Latin for dull or grayish blue, the color of a bruise. Reference is to the color of the back and tops of the wings.

COMMON NAME Yellow-footed, has yellow legs and feet. Gull, see *Larus argentatus*.

Larus marinus   Great Black-backed Gull

SCIENTIFIC NAME *Larus* + *marinus*, Latin for of or belonging to the sea. Reference is to the natural habitat.

COMMON NAME Great, for the size, larger than the lesser black-backed gull. Black-backed, descriptive. Gull, see *Larus argentatus*.

Larus minutus   Little Gull

SCIENTIFIC NAME *Larus* + *minutus*, Latin for small in size or length, tiny.

COMMON NAME Little, for the size; this is the United States' smallest gull. Gull, see *Larus argentatus*.

Larus occidentalis   Western Gull

SCIENTIFIC NAME *Larus* + *occidentalis*, Latin for of or connected to the west, coming from the west, westerly. Reference is to the natural range along the western coast of the United States.

COMMON NAME Western, see scientific name. Gull, see *Larus argentatus*.

Larus philadelphia   Bonaparte's Gull

SCIENTIFIC NAME *Larus* + *philadelphia*, for Philadelphia, Pennsylvania, near where the type specimen was found.

COMMON NAME Bonaparte's, for Charles Lucien Jules Laurent Bonaparte (1803–1857), Prince of Canino and Musignano, a nephew of Napoleon Bonaparte, and a noted naturalist and ornithologist; considered the father of American systematic ornithology. Gull, see *Larus argentatus*.

Larus pipixcan   Franklin's Gull

SCIENTIFIC NAME *Larus* + *pipixcan*, an Aztec (Mexico) word for this type of gull, noted by Francisco Hernandez (1514–1578) in *Historia Avium Novae Hispaniae* (1615).

COMMON NAME Franklin's, for Sir John Franklin (1786–1847), a British naval officer and explorer who died while seeking the Northwest Passage. Gull, see *Larus argentatus*.

Larus ridibundus   Black-headed Gull

SCIENTIFIC NAME *Larus* + *ridibundus*, Latin for in a state of laughter. Reference is to the rhythm of the call, which resembles human laughter.

COMMON NAME Black-headed, has a black head in breeding plumage. Gull, see *Larus argentatus*.

Larus schistisagus   Slaty-backed Gull

SCIENTIFIC NAME *Larus* + *schistisagus*, slate cloak, from Later Latin *schistus*, slate, and Latin *sagum*, *sagus*, a coarse woolen cloak worn by soldiers.

Reference is to the slate color of the back and tops of the wings, about the area a cloak would fit.

COMMON NAME Slaty-backed, descriptive. Gull, see *Larus argentatus*.

Larus thayeri   Thayer's Gull

SCIENTIFIC NAME *Larus* + *thayeri*, for John Eliot Thayer (1862–1933), a patron of ornithology. His extensive collection of bird skins and his ornithological library are now in Harvard's Museum of Comparative Anatomy.

COMMON NAME Thayer's, see scientific name. Gull, see *Larus argentatus*.

Laterallus jamaicensis   Black Rail

SCIENTIFIC NAME *Laterallus*, hiding rail, from Latin *lateo*, to go into or be in hiding, and Modern Latin *rallus*, a rail. Reference is to the secretive behavior: this bird is more often heard than seen + *jamaicensis*, Latin for belonging to Jamaica. Reference is to the collection site of the type specimen.

COMMON NAME Black, for the overall color of the plumage. Rail, from Old French *raale*, to make a scraping noise. Reference is to the call.

Leiothrix lutea   Red-billed Leiothrix

SCIENTIFIC NAME *Leiothrix*, smooth hair, from Greek λειος, *leios*, smooth to the touch, and θριξ, *thrix*, hair. Reference is to the smooth appearance of the plumage + *lutea*, from Latin *luteus*, yellow, especially bright reddish or orange-yellow. Reference is to the yellow breast and wing bars.

COMMON NAME Red-billed, the distal part of the bill is red. Leiothrix, see scientific name.

Leptotila verreauxi   White-tipped Dove

SCIENTIFIC NAME *Leptotila*, thin feather, from Greek λεπτος, *leptos*, thin, fine, delicate, and πτιλον, *ptilon*, soft feathers or down under the true feathers, anything like a feather or wing. Reference is to the thin first primaries + *verreauxi*, for J. B. Edouard Verreaux (1810–1868) and Jules P. Verreaux (1807–1873), French brothers who were naturalists and collected in many countries.

COMMON NAME White-tipped, for the white corners of the tail. Dove, from Anglo-Saxon *dufan*, to dive, for its irregular flight pattern.

Leucosticte atrata Black Rosy-Finch

SCIENTIFIC NAME *Leucosticte*, dappled white, from Greek λευκος, *leukos*, of color, white, and στικος, *stikos*, spotted, dappled. Reference is to the dappled white of the plumage + *atrata*, Latin for darkened, blackened, dingy. Reference is to the overall color or the plumage.

COMMON NAME Black, for the predominant color of the plumage. Rosy, for the rose wings and belly. Finch, from Anglo-Saxon *finc*, their name for this bird, an imitation of the call. Other languages have similar names for the finch for the same reason.

Leucosticte australis Brown-capped Rosy-Finch

SCIENTIFIC NAME *Leucosticte* + *australis*, Latin for of the south wind, southern. Reference is to the natural range, which is the most southerly of the rosy-finches.

COMMON NAME Brown-capped, for the male's brown crown. Rosy-Finch, see *Leucosticte atrata*.

Leucosticte tephrocotis Gray-crowned Rosy-Finch

SCIENTIFIC NAME *Leucosticte* + *tephrocotis*, ash-colored back of the head, from Greek τεφρος, *tephros*, ash colored, and κοτις, *kotis*, the occiput, a form of κοττις, *kottis*, a Doric form of κεφαλη, *kephalē*, the head. Hippocrates used κοτις, *kotis*, to mean the occiput.

COMMON NAME Gray-crowned, for the male's gray crown. Rosy-Finch, see *Leucosticte atrata*.

Limnodromus griseus Short-billed Dowitcher

SCIENTIFIC NAME *Limnodromus*, marsh runner, from Greek λιμνη, *limnē*, a pool of standing water left by the sea or a river, a marshy lake, a marsh, and δρομος, *dromos*, refers to racing, speed, and running. Reference is to the habitat + *griseus*, Modern Latin for gray. Reference is to the non-breeding plumage.

COMMON NAME Short-billed, this species has a shorter bill than the long-billed dowitcher. Dowitcher, the Iroquois (New York State) name for this type of bird.

Limnodromus scolopaceus   Long-billed Dowitcher

SCIENTIFIC NAME *Limnodromus* + *scolpaceus*, from Greek σκολοπαξ, *skolopax*, a form of ασκαλωπας, *askalōpas*, used by Aristotle to mean a woodcock. Reference is to this bird resembling a woodcock.

COMMON NAME Long-billed, this species has a longer bill than the short-billed dowitcher. Dowitcher, see *Limnodromus griseus*.

Limnothlypis swainsonii   Swainson's Warbler

SCIENTIFIC NAME *Limnothlypis*, marsh finch, from Greek λιμνη, *limnē*, a pool of standing water left by the sea or a river, a marshy lake, a marsh, and θλυπις, *thlupis*, a kind of finch. Reference is to the habitat and appearance + *swainsonii*, for William Swainson (1789–1855), a British naturalist and artist. He published *Zoological Illustrations* (1820–1823) and was a strong advocate of the quinary system of taxonomy, a failed method of classifying plants and animals.

COMMON NAME Swainson's, see scientific name. Warbler, for the trills and quavers of the song.

Limosa fedoa   Marbled Godwit

SCIENTIFIC NAME *Limosa*, Latin for full of mud or mire, muddy. Reference is to the habitat + *fedoa*, given as a species name by Carl Linnaeus (1707–1778); it is thought to be a Latinized form of an English common name for godwit.

COMMON NAME Marbled, for the pattern of the plumage on the back. Godwit, of uncertain origin; a possibility is the Anglo-Saxon *god whit*, good creature.

Limosa haemastica   Hudsonian Godwit

SCIENTIFIC NAME *Limosa* + *haemastica*, from Greek αιματικος, *aimatikos*, of the blood. Reference is to the male's red breast in breeding plumage.

COMMON NAME Hudsonian, the type specimen came from the Hudson Bay area. Godwit, see *Limosa fedoa*.

Limosa lapponica   Bar-tailed Godwit

SCIENTIFIC NAME *Limosa* + *lapponica*, Latinized term for of Lapland, where the type specimen was found.

COMMON NAME Bar-tailed, has black and white bars on the tail. Godwit, see *Limosa fedoa*.

Limosa limosa — Black-tailed Godwit

SCIENTIFIC NAME *Limosa* + *limosa*.

COMMON NAME Black-tailed, has a black tail with white coverts. Godwit, see *Limosa fedoa*.

Lonchura malabarica — Indian Silverbill

SCIENTIFIC NAME *Lonchura*, to have a tail like a spearhead, from Greek λογχη, *logkhē*, a spearhead, and ουρα, *oura*, tail. According to the *Oxford Greek-English Lexicon* (1996), ουρα, *oura*, should not be used for the tail of a bird but is restricted to other animals + *malabarica*, for the Malabar Coast of India, where the type specimen was collected.

COMMON NAME Indian, for the natural range in India. Silverbill, descriptive.

Lonchura malacca — Tricolored Munia

SCIENTIFIC NAME *Lonchura* + *malacca*. for the town and district of Malacca, Malaya, where the type specimen was collected.

COMMON NAME Tricolored, for the slate blue bill, black head and underparts, and the reddish brown upperparts. Munia, an East Indian name for this bird.

Lonchura punctulata — Nutmeg Mannikin

SCIENTIFIC NAME *Lonchura* + *punctulata*, Modern Latin for spotted. Reference is to the pattern on the breast and sides.

COMMON NAME Nutmeg, for the predominant color of the male. Mannikin, from Dutch *manneken*, a little man, their name for this type of bird.

Lophodytes cucullatus — Hooded Merganser

SCIENTIFIC NAME *Lophodytes*, crested diver, from Greek λοφος, *lophos*, used by Homer for the crest or tuft on the heads of birds, whether of feathers or flesh, and δυτης, *dutēs*, a diver + *cucullatus*, Late Latin for hooded, from Latin *cucullus*, a covering for the head, a hood. Reference is to the appearance of the crest.

Lophodytes cucullatus, hooded merganser

COMMON NAME Hooded, see scientific name. Merganser, a diving goose, from Latin *mergo*, to plunge into a liquid, dip, dive, and *anser*, a goose.

Lophura leucomelanos Kalij Pheasant

SCIENTIFIC NAME *Lophura*, tail crest, from Greek λοφος, *lophos*, used by Homer for the crest or tuft on the heads of birds, whether of feathers or flesh, and ουρα, *oura*, tail. According to the *Oxford Greek-English Lexicon* (1996), ουρα, *oura* should not be used for the tail of a bird but is restricted to other animals. Reference is to the top of the tail sticking up like a crest + *leucomelanos*, white and black, from Greek λευκος, *leukos*, of color, white, and μελας, *melas*, black. Reference is to the colors of the plumage.

COMMON NAME Kalij, the Nepali (India) local name for this bird. Pheasant, from Greek φασιανος, *phasianos*, a pheasant. So named because these birds were introduced to Greece from the region of the River Phasis, which was their natural range.

Loxia curvirostra Red Crossbill

SCIENTIFIC NAME *Loxia*, from Greek λοξος, *loxos*, slanting, crosswise. Reference is to the crossed bill + *curvirostra*, curved beak, from Latin *curuus*, having a curved surface or outline, bent, crooked, and *rostrum*, the snout or muzzle of an animal, the beak or bill of a bird.

COMMON NAME Red, in reference to the male's head and body. Crossbill, the bill is crossed at the tip.

Loxia leucoptera   White-winged Crossbill

SCIENTIFIC NAME *Loxia* + *leucoptera*, white winged, from Greek λευκος, *leukos*, of color, white, and πετρον, *petron*, feather, bird's wing. Reference is to the white bars on the wings of both sexes.

COMMON NAME White-winged, see scientific name. Crossbill, see *Loxia curvirostra*.

Loxioides bailleui   Palila

SCIENTIFIC NAME *Loxioides*, to resemble a crossbill, from *Loxia*, the genus of the crossbills, and -*oides*, to resemble + *bailleui*, for Pierre Etienne Ballieu (1829–1900), a bird collector and the French consul to Hawaii, where this bird is endemic.

COMMON NAME Palila, the Hawaiian name for this bird.

Loxops caeruleirostris   'Akeke 'E

SCIENTIFIC NAME *Loxops*, to look like a crossbill, from *Loxia*, the genus of the crossbills, and Greek οψ, *ops*, eye, face, appearance + *caerulerostris*, blue beaked, from Latin *caeruleus*, blue or greenish blue, and *rostris*, billed, from Latin *rostrum*, the snout or muzzle of an animal, the beak or bill of a bird. Reference is to the bluish gray bill.

COMMON NAME 'Akeke 'E, the Hawaiian name for this bird.

Loxops coccineus   'Akepa

SCIENTIFIC NAME *Loxops* + *coccineus*, scarlet, from Latin *coccinus*, scarlet dyed, scarlet clothes, scarlet color, in turn from Greek κοκκινος, *kokkinos*, scarlet. Reference is to the color of the plumage.

COMMON NAME 'Akepa, the Hawaiian name for this bird.

Luscinia svecica   Bluethroat

SCIENTIFIC NAME *Luscinia*, Latin for nightingale + *svecica*, from Modern Latin *suecicus*, Swedish. Reference is to the natural range.

COMMON NAME Bluethroat, the male has a bright blue throat with a central rufous patch.

Melamprosops phaeosoma   Po 'Ouli

SCIENTIFIC NAME *Melamprosops*, black near the eyes or on the sides of the face, from Greek μελας, *melas*, black, and προς, *pros*, near, on the side of, and οψ, *ops*, the eye, the face, appearance + *phaeosoma*, dusky body, from Greek φαιος, *phaios*, gray, any mixture of black and white, dusky, and σωμα, *sōma*, body.

COMMON NAME Po 'Ouli, the Hawaiian name for this bird.

Melanerpes aurifrons   Golden-fronted Woodpecker

SCIENTIFIC NAME *Melanerpes*, black creeper, from Greek μελας, *melas*, black, and ερπειν, ερπο, *erpein, erpo*, to creep. Reference is to the behavior of creeping up tree trunks + *aurifrons*, gold forehead, from Latin *aurum*, gold as a metal or color, and *frons*, forehead, front. Reference is to the gold forehead.

COMMON NAME Golden-fronted, see scientific name. Woodpecker, descriptive of the feeding and nesting behavior.

Melanerpes carolinus   Red-bellied Woodpecker

SCIENTIFIC NAME *Melanerpes* + *carolinus*, of the Carolina colonies, an area encompassing the southeastern United States. Reference is to the natural range.

COMMON NAME Red-bellied, has a red spot on the belly. Woodpecker, see *Melanerpes aurifrons*.

Melanerpes erythrocephalus   Red-headed Woodpecker

SCIENTIFIC NAME *Melanerpes* + *erythrocephalus*, red headed, from Greek ερυθρος, *eruthros*, red, and κεφαλη, *kephalē*, head.

COMMON NAME Red-headed, descriptive. Woodpecker, see *Melanerpes aurifrons*.

Melanerpes formicivorus   Acorn Woodpecker

SCIENTIFIC NAME *Melanerpes* + *formicivorus*, ant eater, from Latin *formica*, an ant, and *voro*, to swallow ravenously, to devour. A small part of the diet is ants and other insects.

Melanerpes carolinus, red-bellied woodpecker

COMMON NAME Acorn, caches acorns in precisely pecked holes in tree trunks. Woodpecker, see *Melanerpes aurifrons*.

Melanerpes lewis   Lewis's Woodpecker

SCIENTIFIC NAME *Melanerpes* + *lewis*, for Meriwether Lewis (1774–1809) of the Lewis and Clark Expedition. Lewis collected the type specimen, and Alexander Wilson (1766–1813) named the bird in his honor.

COMMON NAME Lewis's, see scientific name. Woodpecker, see *Melanerpes aurifrons*.

Melanerpes uropygialis — Gila Woodpecker

SCIENTIFIC NAME *Melanerpes* + *uropygialis*, from Greek ουροπυγιον, *ouropugion*, a form of οππροπυγιον, *orr(h)opugion*, the rump of birds in which the tail feathers are set. Reference is to the barred rump.

COMMON NAME Gila, for the Gila River in Arizona, where the type specimen was collected. Woodpecker, see *Melanerpes aurifrons*.

Melanitta fusca — White-winged Scoter

SCIENTIFIC NAME *Melanitta*, black duck, from Greek μελας, *melas*, black, and νεττα, *netta*, a duck. When Heinrich Boie (1794–1827) Latinized this Greek word for duck, he misspelled the word. The principle of priority allows the mistake to stand + *fusca*, from Latin *fuscus*, dark colored, somber, dusky. Reference is to the overall color of the plumage.

COMMON NAME White-winged, both sexes have white wing-patches. Scoter, origin is unknown; the first printed reference as a common name was by Ray in *Collective Catalogue Birds* (1674).

Melanitta nigra — Black Scoter

SCIENTIFIC NAME *Melanitta* + *nigra*, from Latin *niger*, black. Reference is to the overall color of the male's plumage.

COMMON NAME Black, see scientific name. Scoter, see *Melanitta fusca*.

Melanitta perspicillata — Surf Scoter

SCIENTIFIC NAME *Melanitta* + *perspicillata*, from Modern Latin *perspicillatus*, spectacled. Reference is to the pattern on the bill, which makes it look like this bird has on a pair of pince-nez.

COMMON NAME Surf, for the habit of feeding in the surf. Scoter, see *Melanitta fusca*.

Meleagris gallopavo — Wild Turkey

SCIENTIFIC NAME *Meleagris*, from Greek μελεαγρις, *meleagris*, the guineafowl. Reference is to the plumage pattern and the body shape looking somewhat like that of the guineafowl + *gallopavo*, from Latin *gallus*, a farmyard cock, and *pavo*, a peacock. Reference is to the physical appearance.

COMMON NAME Wild, as opposed to domesticated fowl. Turkey, when Carl Linnaeus (1707–1778) named this genus, the guineafowl was being called a *turkey* in the mistaken belief that it came from Turkey. When the wild turkey was introduced to Europe from America, this name was attached to it because it resembled the guineafowl.

Melopsittacus undulatus   Budgerigar

SCIENTIFIC NAME *Melopsittacus*, song parrot, from Greek μελος, *melos*, song, and ψιττακος, *psittakos*, a parrot + *undulatus*, Latin for having a wavy form. Reference is to the plumage pattern on the back and tops of the wings.

COMMON NAME Budgerigar, the Australian name for this bird, most probably from *gijirriga*, the Kamilaroi (Aboriginal, New South Wales and southern Queensland) word for this bird.

Melospiza georgiana   Swamp Sparrow

SCIENTIFIC NAME *Melospiza*, song finch, from Greek μελος, *melos*, song, and σπιζα, *spiza*, the chaffinch + *georgiana*, of Georgia, the state where the type specimen was collected.

COMMON NAME Swamp, for the habitat. Sparrow, from Anglo-Saxon *spearwa*, to flutter. Originally used to denote any small bird.

Melospiza lincolnii   Lincoln's Sparrow

SCIENTIFIC NAME *Melospiza* + *lincolnii*, for Thomas Lincoln (1812–1883), who accompanied John James Audubon (1785–1851) on a trip to Labrador, where this bird was discovered. Audubon named it in his honor.

COMMON NAME Lincoln's, see scientific name. Sparrow, see *Melospiza georgiana*.

Melospiza melodia   Song Sparrow

SCIENTIFIC NAME *Melospiza* + *melodia*, Latin for a pleasant song.

COMMON NAME Song, for the pleasant song. Sparrow, see *Melospiza georgiana*.

Mergus merganser   Common Merganser

SCIENTIFIC NAME *Mergus*, Latin name given to several seabirds + *merganser*, a diving goose, from Latin *mergo*, to plunge into a liquid, dip, dive, and *anser*, a goose.

COMMON NAME Common, more abundant than the other mergansers in the United States. Merganser, see scientific name.

Mergus serrator   Red-breasted Merganser

SCIENTIFIC NAME *Mergus* + *serrator*, Latin for one who saws. Reference is to the serrated bill.

COMMON NAME Red-breasted, for the male's rufous breast in breeding plumage. Merganser, see *Mergus merganser*.

Micrathene whitneyi   Elf Owl

SCIENTIFIC NAME *Micrathene*, little *Athene*, from Greek μικρο, *mikro*, small, tiny, little, and the genus *Athene*, the burrowing owl. Reference is to this bird looking like a smaller version of the burrowing owl + *whitneyi*, for Joseph Dwight Whitney (1819–1896), an eminent geologist who worked on the geological surveys of several states. James G. Cooper (fl. 1860), son of William C. Cooper (1798–1864), discovered this owl and named it in honor of Whitney.

COMMON NAME Elf, for its small size and secretive behavior. Owl, from Anglo-Saxon *ule*, owl, and from Latin *ululo*, to cry out.

Mimus gundlachii   Bahama Mockingbird

SCIENTIFIC NAME *Mimus*, Latin for an actor in mimes, a mimic. Reference is to this bird copying the calls of the birds around it + *gundlachii*, for Juan Gundlach (1810–1896), the Cuban ornithologist who wrote *Catalogo de los Aves Cubanas* (1873).

COMMON NAME Bahama, for the natural range. Mockingbird, for its habit of copying the calls of the birds around it.

Mimus polyglottos   Northern Mockingbird

SCIENTIFIC NAME *Mimus* + *polyglottos*, many tongued, from Greek πολυγλωττος, *poluglōttos*, the Attic form of πολυγλωσσος, *poluglōssos*, many tongued. Reference is to its habit of copying the calls of the birds around it.

COMMON NAME Northern, for the habitat. Mockingbird, see *Mimus gundlachii*.

Mniotilta varia   Black-and-white Warbler

SCIENTIFIC NAME *Mniotilta*, moss plucker, from Greek μνιον, *mnion*, seaweed, moss, and τιλτος, *tiltos*, one who plucks, a gatherer. This name came from the belief that moss was consistently used in the nests + *varia*, from

Mimus polyglottos, northern mockingbird

Latin *varius*, having two or more contrasting colors, variegated, varied. Reference is to the black and white plumage.

COMMON NAME Black-and-white, for the colors of the plumage. Warbler, for the trills and quavers of the song.

Moho bishopi Bishop's 'O 'O

SCIENTIFIC NAME *Moho*, from the Hawaiian name '*o* '*o* used for this bird + *bishopi*, for Charles Reed Bishop (1822–1915), a native of New York State who traveled to Hawaii 1846 and eventually married into Hawaiian royalty.

COMMON NAME Bishop's, see scientific name. 'O 'O, the Hawaiian name for this bird.

Moho braccatus   Kauai 'O 'O or 'O 'O 'A 'A

SCIENTIFIC NAME *Moho* + *braccatus*, a form of Latin *bracatus*, wearing breeches or trousers. Reference is to the yellow feathers on the thighs, which contrast sharply with the black body.

COMMON NAME Kauai, for the island of Kauai in the Hawaiian archipelago. 'O 'O, the Hawaiian name for this bird. 'O 'O 'A 'A, another Hawaiian name for this bird, originally used for a now-extinct Hawaiian rail.

Molothrus aeneus   Bronzed Cowbird

SCIENTIFIC NAME *Molothrus*, from Greek μολοβρος, *molobros*, a greedy beggar. Reference is to the feeding behavior + *aeneus*, Latin for made of bronze, connected with bronze, bronze colored. Reference is to the metallic sheen of the feathers when reflecting light.

COMMON NAME Bronzed, see scientific name. Cowbird, for the habit of feeding around cattle.

Molothrus ater   Brown-headed Cowbird

SCIENTIFIC NAME *Molothrus* + *ater*, Latin for black, dark colored. Reference is to the body color.

COMMON NAME Brown-headed, descriptive. Cowbird, see *Molothrus aeneus*.

Molothrus bonariensis   Shiny Cowbird

SCIENTIFIC NAME *Molothrus* + *bonariensis*, belonging to Buenos Aires, Argentina, from *bonum*, any good thing or circumstance, *aer*, air, and *-ensis*, belonging to. Reference is to the natural range.

COMMON NAME Shiny, for the metallic sheen of the plumage. Cowbird, see *Molothrus aeneus*.

Morus bassanus   Northern Gannet

SCIENTIFIC NAME *Morus*, from Greek μωρος, *mōros*, dull, sluggish, stupid. Reference is to the ease with which these birds can be caught + *bassanus*, pertaining to Bass Rock at Firth of Forth, Scotland. Reference is to a breeding site.

COMMON NAME Northern, for the breeding range. Gannet, from Anglo-Saxon *ganot*, their name for this type of bird.

Motacilla alba   White Wagtail

SCIENTIFIC NAME *Motacilla*, little mover, from Latin *motacis*, mover, and the diminutive *-illa*. Because this name was assigned by the Roman scholar Varro to the wagtail and the Latin word *moto* means to move, to shake, early scholars mistakenly assumed that *-cilla* must mean tail. The *c* in *-cilla* properly belongs to the first part of the word derived from *motacis*, mover. Since the original mistake, the word *cilla* has been used in bird names to mean tail (see *Bombycilla cedrorum*) + *alba*, from Latin *albus*, white. Reference is to the predominantly white plumage.

COMMON NAME White, see scientific name. Wagtail, for the behavior of pumping the tail when standing on the ground.

Motacilla flava   Yellow Wagtail

SCIENTIFIC NAME *Motacilla* + *flava*, from Latin *flauus*, yellow, especially pale yellow or golden. Reference is to the color of the underparts.

COMMON NAME Yellow, see scientific name. Wagtail, see *Motacilla alba*.

Motacilla lugens   Black-backed Wagtail

SCIENTIFIC NAME *Motacilla* + *lugens*, from Latin *lugeo*, to mourn, grieve, lament. Reference is to the black, cloaklike pattern of the male in breeding plumage, which brings to mind a mourning cloak.

COMMON NAME Black-backed, for the male's breeding plumage. Wagtail, see *Motacilla alba*.

Myadestes myadestinus   Kamao

SCIENTIFIC NAME *Myadestes*, fly eater, from Greek μυα, *mua*, a form of μυια, *muia*, a fly, and εδεστης, *edestēs*, eater + *myadestinus*, from *Myadestes*, fly eater, and *-inus*, resembling.

COMMON NAME Kamao, the Hawaiian name for this bird.

Myadestes obscurus   'Oma 'O

SCIENTIFIC NAME *Myadestes* + *obscurus*, Latin for dim, dark, obscure, dark or dingy in color. Reference is to the color of the plumage.

COMMON NAME 'Oma 'O, the Hawaiian name for this bird.

Myadestes palmeri Puaiohi

SCIENTIFIC NAME *Myadestes* + *palmeri*, for Henry Palmer (fl. 1890s), an Australian collector who worked in the Hawaiian Islands.

COMMON NAME Puaiohi, the Hawaiian name for this bird.

Myadestes townsendi Townsend's Solitaire

SCIENTIFIC NAME *Myadestes* + *townsendi*, for John Kirk Townsend (1809–1851), an ornithologist from Philadelphia who traveled and collected birds in the western United States. He was the author of *Narrative of a Journey across the Rocky Mountains* (1839), in which he wrote descriptions of some of the new birds he found.

COMMON NAME Townsend's, see scientific name. Solitaire, for the secretive behavior.

Mycteria americana Wood Stork

SCIENTIFIC NAME *Mycteria*, from Greek μυκτηρ, *muktēr*, nostril, to sneer, an elephant's trunk. Reference is to the large bill of this bird + *americana*, of America. Reference is to the natural range.

COMMON NAME Wood, for the nesting site in the woods. Stork, from Old English *storc*, their name for this type of bird.

Myiarchus cinerascens Ash-throated Flycatcher

SCIENTIFIC NAME *Myiarchus*, fly ruler, from Greek μυια, *muia*, a fly, and αρχυς, *arkhus*, leader, chief, ruler + *cinerascens*, a form of Late Latin *cinerescens*, ashen, becoming ashy. Reference is to the color of the plumage.

COMMON NAME Ash-throated, descriptive. Flycatcher, for the habit of catching insects in the air.

Myiarchus crinitus Great Crested Flycatcher

SCIENTIFIC NAME *Myiarchus* + *crinitus*, Latin for having long hair. Reference is to the crest.

COMMON NAME Great Crested, one of the largest flycatchers with a crest. Flycatcher, see *Myiarchus cinerascens*.

Myiarchus sagrae   La Sagra's Flycatcher

SCIENTIFIC NAME *Myiarchus* + *sagrae*, for Ramon de la Sagra (1801–1871), a Cuban naturalist and author.

COMMON NAME La Sagra's, see scientific name. Flycatcher, see *Myiarchus cinerascens*.

Myiarchus tuberculifer   Dusky-capped Flycatcher

SCIENTIFIC NAME *Myiarchus* + *tuberculifer*, carrying a small protuberance, from Latin *tuberculum*, a small protuberance or excrescence, and -*fer*, from *fero*, carrying. Reference is to the small crest.

COMMON NAME Dusky-capped, for the dark gray crown. Flycatcher, see *Myiarchus cinerascens*.

Myiarchus tyrannulus   Brown-crested Flycatcher

SCIENTIFIC NAME *Myiarchus* + *tyrannulus*, a little *Tyrannus*, a diminutive of the genus *Tyrannus*. Reference is to the appearance.

COMMON NAME Brown-crested, descriptive. Flycatcher, see *Myiarchus cinerascens*.

Myioborus pictus   Painted Redstart

SCIENTIFIC NAME *Myioborus*, fly glutton, from Greek μυια, *muia*, a fly, and βορος, *boros*, a glutton + *pictus*, Latin for painted. Reference is to the plumage patterns.

COMMON NAME Painted, see scientific name. Redstart, from Anglo-Saxon *read*, red, and *steort*, tail. This name originated with the European redstart and was used for the American redstart; the painted redstart was so named because it resembled the other two birds, although it has no red in its tail.

Myiodynastes luteiventris   Sulphur-bellied Flycatcher

SCIENTIFIC NAME *Myiodynastes*, fly master, from Greek μυια, *muia*, a fly, and δυναστης, *dunastēs*, lord, master, ruler + *luteiventris*, yellow bellied, from Latin *luteus*, yellow, especially bright reddish or orange-yellow, and *venter*, the lower part of the torso, abdomen, belly.

COMMON NAME Sulphur-bellied, for the yellow belly. Flycatcher, for the habit of catching insects in the air.

Myiopsitta monachus — Monk Parakeet

SCIENTIFIC NAME *Myiopsitta*, fly parrot, from Greek μυια, *muia*, a fly, and ψιττακος, *psittakos*, a parrot. Insects make up part of the diet + *monachus*, Modern Latin for hooded as a monk, in turn from Greek μοναχος, *monakhos*, a monk. Reference is to the plumage pattern that resembles a green hood over a gray face, neck, and chest.

COMMON NAME Monk, see scientific name. Parakeet, Anglicized form of the French *perroquet*, another name for a parrot. Used in English to describe smaller types of parrots.

Nandayus nenday — Black-hooded Parakeet

SCIENTIFIC NAME *Nandayus*, Latinized from Guarani Indian (eastern lowlands of South America), *nenday*, their name for this bird + *nenday*.

COMMON NAME Black-hooded, head plumage looks like a black hood. Parakeet, see *Myiopsitta monachus*.

Netta rufina — Red-crested Pochard

SCIENTIFIC NAME *Netta*, from Greek νεττα, *netta*, duck + *rufina*, from *rufus*, red of various shades, tawny, and *-inus*, resembling. Reference is to the male's rufous head.

COMMON NAME Red-crested, for the male's rufous head. Pochard, from various French words (*pocher*, *poche*, *poach*) for this bird.

Nomonyx dominicus — Masked Duck

SCIENTIFIC NAME *Nomonyx*, to posses a claw, from Greek νομη, *nomē*, to have possession, and ονυξ, *onux*, talons, claws, nail. Reference is to the sharp downcurved tip of the bill, which looks like a claw + *domimicus*, for Santo Domingo (Hispaniola). Reference is to the natural range.

COMMON NAME Masked, for the black pattern on the male's face. Duck, from Anglo-Saxon *duce*, a form of *ducan*, to duck or dive.

Nucifraga columbiana — Clark's Nutcracker

SCIENTIFIC NAME *Nucifraga*, nut breaker, from Latin *nucis*, a nut, and *frango*, to break, shatter, smash. Reference is to the feeding habits + *columbiana*, for the Columbia River area, where the type specimen was collected.

COMMON NAME Clark's, for William Clark (1770–1838), of the Lewis and Clark Expedition. This bird was discovered on that expedition. Nutcracker, for the feeding habits.

Numenius americanus   Long-billed Curlew

SCIENTIFIC NAME *Numenius*, from Greek νουμηνια, *noumēnia*, the new moon. Reference is to the thin crescent shape of the bill + *americanus*, pertaining to America, from America. Reference is to the natural range.

COMMON NAME Long-billed, has the longest bill of all curlews. Curlew, from French *corlieu*, their name for this bird.

Numenius phaeopus   Whimbrel

SCIENTIFIC NAME *Numenius* + *phaeopus*, gray footed, from Greek φαιος, *phaios*, gray, any mixture of black and white, dusky, and πους, *pous*, foot.

COMMON NAME Whimbrel, little whimperer, from English *whine* or *whimper* and the diminutive *-rel*. Reference is to the call.

Numenius tahitiensis   Bristle-thighed Curlew

SCIENTIFIC NAME *Numenius* + *tahitiensis*, Latin for belonging to Tahiti. The type specimen was found on Tahiti.

COMMON NAME Bristle-thighed, has barbless feather shafts on the thighs that look like bristles. Curlew, see *Numenius americanus*.

Numida meleagris   Helmeted Guineafowl

SCIENTIFIC NAME *Numida*, Latin for a native of Numidia (Africa). Reference is to the natural range + *meleagris*, from Greek μελεαγρις, *meleagris*, the guineafowl, for the natural range in West Africa.

COMMON NAME Helmeted, for the prominent, hard crest. Guineafowl, see scientific name.

Nyctanassa violacea   Yellow-crowned Night-Heron

SCIENTIFIC NAME *Nyctanassa*, night queen, from Greek νυξ, νυκτος, *nux*, *nuktos*, night, and αναοοα, *anassa*, a queen or lady. Reference is to its beauty and nocturnal behavior + *violacea*, from Latin *viola*, the color of a violet. Reference is to the faint violet cast on the back and tops of the wings.

COMMON NAME Yellow-crowned, descriptive. Night, for its nocturnal behavior. Heron, from Old High German *haiger*, *heiger*, their name for this type of bird.

Nyctea scandiaca   Snowy Owl

SCIENTIFIC NAME *Nyctea*, from Greek νυκτιος, *nuktios*, of the night. Reference is to the nocturnal behavior + *scandiaca*, Modern Latin for of Scandinavia. Reference is to the natural range.

COMMON NAME Snowy, for the pure white winter plumage. Owl, from Anglo-Saxon *ule*, owl, and from Latin *ululo*, to cry out. Both words are onomatopoeic of the owl's call.

Nycticorax nycticorax   Black-crowned Night-Heron

SCIENTIFIC NAME *Nycticorax*, night raven, from Greek νυξ, νυκτος, *nux*, *nuktos*, night, and κοραξ, *korax*, a raven. Carl Linnaeus (1707–1778) originally used this name for the species only, and it was most likely suggested by the ravenlike call in the night. The long-eared owl was called νυκτι-κοραξ, *nuktikorax*, by the Greeks. These names do not seem to be related + *nycticorax*.

COMMON NAME Black-crowned, descriptive. Night-heron, see *Nyctanassa violacea*.

Nyctidromus albicollis   Common Pauraque

SCIENTIFIC NAME *Nyctidromus*, from Greek νυκτιδρομος, *nuktidromos*, running by night, from Greek νυξ, νυκτος, *nux*, *nuktos*, night, and δρομος, *dromos*, race, running. Reference is to the nocturnal habits + *albicollis*, white neck, from Latin *albus*, white, and *collum*, neck. Reference is to the white throat-patch.

COMMON NAME Common, abundant in its range. Pauraque, a Mexican name for this bird, an imitation of the Spanish rendering of its call.

Nymphicus hollandicus   Cockatiel

SCIENTIFIC NAME *Nymphicus*, Latin for to be like a nymph + *hollandicus*, of New Holland, the original name of the eastern half of Australia. This bird is endemic to Australia.

COMMON NAME Cockatiel, a little cockatoo, from the Dutch *kaketielje*, the name Dutch sailors called this bird, in turn most probably from *cacatilho*, a diminutive of the Portuguese *cacatu*, a cockatoo.

Oceanites oceanicus   Wilson's Storm-Petrel

SCIENTIFIC NAME *Oceanites*, from the Oceanids, the three thousand sea nymphs born to Oceanus and Tethys of Greek mythology. The direct translation is Ὠκεανῖτις, *Okeanitis*, daughter of the sea. Reference is to this bird being found at sea, sometimes resting on the water + *oceanicus*, of the ocean, from Latin *oceanus*, the ocean, in turn from Greek ὠκεανος, *okeanos*, the ocean.

COMMON NAME Wilson's, for Alexander Wilson (1766–1813), known as the father of American ornithology. He initiated the first series on birds of the eastern United States, *American Ornithology* (1808–1814). Storm, during a storm these birds fly leeward of waves for protection from the wind. If a ship were around in the storm, these birds may suddenly appear on its leeward side; therefore, they are commonly seen during storms. Petrel, little Peter, this bird pats the water with its feet when landing, which gives the appearance of walking on water. It was named for St. Peter, who was said to walk on water.

Oceanodroma castro   Band-rumped Storm-Petrel

SCIENTIFIC NAME *Oceanodroma*, ocean runner, from Greek ὠκεανος, *okeanos*, ocean, and δρομος, *dromos*, race, running. Reference is to the appearance of walking or running on the surface of the water when landing + *castro*, from *roque de Castro* (rook of Castro), the local name for this bird in the Deserta Islands, Madeira.

COMMON NAME Band-rumped, descriptive. Storm-Petrel, see *Oceanites oceanicus*.

Oceanodroma furcata   Fork-tailed Storm-Petrel

SCIENTIFIC NAME *Oceanodroma* + *furcata*, from Later Latin *furcatus*, shaped like a fork. Reference is to the forked tail.

COMMON NAME Fork-tailed, descriptive. Storm-Petrel, see *Oceanites oceanicus*.

Oceanodroma homochroa   Ashy Storm-Petrel

SCIENTIFIC NAME *Oceanodroma* + *homochroa*, from Greek ομοχρους, *omokhrous*, of one color. This bird has very subtle markings and appears to be just one color.

COMMON NAME Ashy, for the overall color of the plumage. Storm-Petrel, see *Oceanites oceanicus*.

Oceanodroma leucorhoa   Leach's Storm-Petrel

SCIENTIFIC NAME *Oceanodroma* + *leucorhoa*, white rump, from Greek λευκος, *leukos*, of color, white, and οππος, *orr(h)os*, the end of the sacrum, rump.

COMMON NAME Leach's, for William Elford Leach (1790–1836), an English medical doctor who worked at the British Museum. He reclassified the conch and insect collections and was a world authority on crustacea. He acquired the type specimen of this bird at a sale of William Bullock's (1775–1840) collection. Storm-Petrel, see *Oceanites oceanicus*.

Oceanodroma melania   Black Storm-Petrel

SCIENTIFIC NAME *Oceanodroma* + *melania*, from Greek μελανια, *melania*, blackness. Reference is to the overall color.

COMMON NAME Black, for the overall color of the plumage. Storm-Petrel, see *Oceanites oceanicus*.

Oceanodroma microsoma   Least Storm-Petrel

SCIENTIFIC NAME *Oceanodroma* + *microsoma*, from Greek μικρος, *mikros*, small, little, tiny, and σωμα, *sōma*, body.

COMMON NAME Least, for the size; this is the United States' smallest storm-petrel. Storm-Petrel, see *Oceanites oceanicus*.

Oenanthe oenanthe   Northern Wheatear

SCIENTIFIC NAME *Oenanthe*, from Greek οινανθη, *oinanthē*, a bird, the wheatear + *oenanthe*.

COMMON NAME Northern, for the natural range. Wheatear, from a local English name for this bird, *whiteeres*, white ass, for the white rump.

Oporornis agilis   Connecticut Warbler

SCIENTIFIC NAME *Oporornis*, autumn bird, from Greek οπωρα, *opōra*, autumn, and οπνις, *ornis*, bird. Because of its migratory pattern, in the United States this bird is seen more in the fall + *agilis*, Latin for that which moves or can be moved easily, nimble, swift, agile, alert, quick, active. Reference is to the ease that it moves through trees and brush.

COMMON NAME Connecticut, for the locality of the type specimen. Warbler, for the trills and quavers of the song.

Oporornis formosus   Kentucky Warbler

SCIENTIFIC NAME *Oporornis* + *formosus*, Latin for having a fine appearance or form, handsome, beautiful.

COMMON NAME Kentucky, abundant in this state. Warbler, see *Oporornis agilis*.

Oporornis philadelphia   Mourning Warbler

SCIENTIFIC NAME *Oporornis* + *philadelphia*, the type specimen was found near Philadelphia, Pennsylvania.

COMMON NAME Mourning, for the black chest, suggesting mourning clothes. Warbler, see *Oporornis agilis*.

Oporornis tolmiei   MacGillivray's Warbler

SCIENTIFIC NAME *Oporornis* + *tolmiei*, for William Fraser Tolmie (1818–1886), a physician who worked for the Hudson Bay Company. John Kirk Townsend (1809–1851) named this bird in his honor.

COMMON NAME MacGillivray's, for Wiliam MacGillivray (1796–1852), author of the five-volume *History of British Birds* (1837–1852) who originated the classification of birds based on their anatomy. John James Audubon (1785–1851) named this bird in his honor, assigning MacGillivray both the species and common names. It was later discovered that John Kirk Townsend (1809–1851) had described this bird earlier and gave the species name of *tolmiei*. Warbler, see *Oporornis agilis*

Oreomystis bairdi   'Akikiki

SCIENTIFIC NAME *Oreomystis*, mountain mystic, from Greek ορος, *oros*, mountain, hill, and μυστις, *mustis*, a feminine form of μυστης, *mustēs*, one who is initiated into the mysteries, mystical doctrine, or divine worship + *bairdi*, for Spencer Fullerton Baird (1823–1887), secretary of the Smithsonian Institution and author of *Catalogue of North American Mammals* (1857) and *Catalogue of North American Birds* (1868).

COMMON NAME 'Akikiki, the Hawaiian name for this bird.

Oreomystis mana   Hawaii Creeper

SCIENTIFIC NAME *Oreomystis* + *mana*, named by Alexander Wilson (1766–1813); most probably a local Hawaiian name.

COMMON NAME Hawaii, for the island of Hawaii. Creeper, for its habit of creeping up and down tree trunks.

Oreortyx pictus Mountain Quail

SCIENTIFIC NAME *Oreortyx*, mountain quail, from Greek ορος, *oros*, mountain, hill, and ορτυξ, *ortux*, quail. Reference is to the habitat + *pictus*, Latin for painted, for the colorful plumage.

COMMON NAME Mountain, for the habitat. Quail, from Old French *quaille*, quail, imitative of the call of the European species.

Oreoscoptes montanus Sage Thrasher

SCIENTIFIC NAME *Oreoscoptes*, mountain mocker, from Greek ορος, *oros*, mountain, hill, and σκωπτω, *skōptō*, to mock, jeer, scoff at. Reference is to its habit of mimicking the calls of other birds in the region + *montanus*, Latin for of or belonging to the mountains.

COMMON NAME Sage, for the habitat. Thrasher, from English *thrusher*, like a thrush.

Ortalis vetula Plain Chachalaca

SCIENTIFIC NAME *Ortalis*, from Greek ορταλις, *ortalis*, fowl, chick + *vetula*, Latin for an elderly woman. Reference is to the shrill call.

COMMON NAME Plain, for the dull, unmarked body plumage. Chachalaca, the Nahuatl Indian (Central America) name for this bird, imitative of the call.

Otus asio Eastern Screech-Owl

SCIENTIFIC NAME *Otus*, from Greek ωτος, *ōtos*, a horned or eared owl + *asio*, a form of Latin *axio*, the little horned owl.

COMMON NAME Eastern, for the natural range in the United States. Screech, for the call. Owl, from Anglo-Saxon *ule*, owl, and from Latin *ululo*, to cry out.

Otus flammeolus Flammulated Owl

SCIENTIFIC NAME *Otus* + *flammeolus*, little flame, little flame-colored thing, diminutive of the Latin *flammeus*, flaming, flame colored. Reference is to the red phase of this dichromatic species.

COMMON NAME Flammulated, see scientific name. Owl, see *Otus asio*.

Otus kennicotti Western Screech-Owl

SCIENTIFIC NAME *Otus* + *kennicotti*, for Robert Kennicott (1835–1866), a founder of the Chicago Academy of Sciences.

COMMON NAME Western, for the natural range in the United States. Screech-Owl, see *Otus asio*.

Otus trichopsis Whiskered Screech-Owl

SCIENTIFIC NAME *Otus* + *trichopsis*, hair face or hairy appearance, from Greek θριξ, *thrix*, hair, and οψις, *opsis*, aspect, appearance, face. Reference is to the facial bristles, which are longer than those of other screech-owls.

COMMON NAME Whiskered, see scientific name. Screech-Owl, see *Otus asio*.

Oxyura jamaicensis Ruddy Duck

SCIENTIFIC NAME *Oxyura*, sharp tailed, from Greek οξυς, *oxus*, sharp, keen, brought to a point, and ουρα, *oura*, tail. According to the *Oxford Greek-English Lexicon* (1996), ουρα, ουρος, *oura ouros*, should not be used for the tail of a bird but is restricted to other animals + *jamaicensis*, Latin for belonging to Jamaica. Reference is to the location of the type specimen.

COMMON NAME Ruddy, for the male's reddish breeding plumage. Duck, from Anglo-Saxon *duce*, a form of *ducan*, to duck or dive.

Pachyramphus aglaiae Rose-throated Becard

SCIENTIFIC NAME *Pachyramphus*, thick billed, from Greek παχυς, *pakhus*, thick, and ραμφος, *ramphos*, the crooked beak of birds of prey, generally any beak or bill + *aglaiae*, for Aglaea (Aglaia), the youngest of the three Charities or Graces. She represented radiance or brilliance. Reference is to the appearance of this bird.

COMMON NAME Rose-throated, for the male's rose throat-patch. Becard, big beak, from French *bec*, beak, and High German *hart*, bold, hardy.

Padda oryzivora Java Sparrow

SCIENTIFIC NAME *Padda*, a local word in Java for rice, the preferred food of this bird + *oryzivora*, rice eater, from Latin *oryza*, rice, in turn from Greek ορυζα, *oruza*, rice, and *uoro*, to swallow ravenously, devour.

COMMON NAME Java, for the natural range. Sparrow, from Anglo-Saxon *spearwa*, to flutter. Originally used to denote any small bird.

Pagophila eburnea {Ivory Gull}

SCIENTIFIC NAME *Pagophila*, frost lover, from Greek παγος, *pagos*, here meaning frost, and φιλος, *philos*, beloved, dear, loving. Reference is to the natural range in the far north + *eburnea*, Latin for made of ivory, ivory colored.

COMMON NAME Ivory, for the overall color of the plumage. Gull, from Celtic *gullan, gwylan, gwelan*, all names for this type of bird.

Palmeria dolei {'Akohekohe}

SCIENTIFIC NAME *Palmeria*, for Henry Palmer (fl. 1893), an Australian collector who worked in the Hawaiian Islands + *dolei*, for Sanford Ballard Dole (1844–1926), president of Hawaii (1893–1898).

COMMON NAME 'Akohekohe, the Hawaiian name for this bird.

Pandion haliaetus {Osprey}

SCIENTIFIC NAME *Pandion*, a mythological king of Athens. Marie Jules Cesar Lelorgne de Savigny (1777–1851), assigned the osprey to a new genus, removing it from the original *Falco*, where it had been placed by Carl Linnaeus (1707–1778). He took the name from the myth of Pandion, which he either did not read or misunderstood. Pandion's two daughters, Procne and Philomela, were both wives (through the usual deceptions) of Tereus, the king of Thrace. After the sisters discover the deception, they cooked and served Tereus his only son, an infant, whose mother was Procne. All of this made the gods so angry that the three were changed into birds. Procne was changed into a swallow, Philomela into a nightingale, and Tereus into a hawk or hoopoe, which continually chases the other two. Pandion was not involved in all of this and was not changed into anything. Tereus would have been a better choice for this genus name + *haliaetus*, from Latin *haliaetos*, a sea eagle, here spelled correctly (see *Haliaeetus leucocephalus*).

COMMON NAME Osprey, from Latin *ossifragus*, from *os*, bone, and *frangere*, to break. The Old Roman name *ossifragus* referred to the lammergrier (*Gypaetus barbatus*), a large vulture that drops bones and turtles from the air to break them up. This name was transferred to the osprey around the sixteenth century.

Pandion haliaetus, osprey

Parabuteo unicinctus   Harris's Hawk

SCIENTIFIC NAME *Parabuteo*, like a *Buteo*, from Greek παρα, *para*, beside, like, near, and the Latin genus *Buteo*. Reference is to the appearance + *unicinctus*, once girdled, from Latin *unus*, one, single, and *cinctus*, fastened round with a girdle. Reference is to the white circle of feathers at the base of the tail.

COMMON NAME Harris's, for Edward Harris (1799–1863), a patron of John James Audubon (1785–1851) who accompanied Audubon on some collecting trips. Hawk, from Anglo-Saxon *hafoc*, hawk, their name for this type of bird.

Paroaria capitata   Yellow-billed Cardinal

SCIENTIFIC NAME *Paroaria*, from the Tupi Indian (upper Amazon Basin) name for this bird + *capitata*, from Latin *capitatus*, having or forming a head. Reference is to the conspicuous red head.

COMMON NAME Yellow-billed, descriptive. Cardinal, so named because the red color of the male's head was thought to resemble the red robes of a Roman Catholic cardinal.

Paroaria coronata   Red-crested Cardinal

SCIENTIFIC NAME *Paroaria* + *coronata*, crowned, from Latin *coronatus*, adorned with wreaths, garlanded, crowned. Reference is to the prominent red crest.

COMMON NAME Red-crested, descriptive. Cardinal, see *Paroaria capitata*.

Paroreomyza flammea   Kakawahie

SCIENTIFIC NAME *Paroreomyza*, like an *Oreomyza*, from Greek παρα, *para*, beside, like, near, and the genus *Oreomyza*, the mountain honey-eaters. Reference is to the appearance + *flammea*, from Latin *flammeus*, fiery, flame colored.

COMMON NAME Kakawahie, the Hawaiian name for this bird.

Paroreomyza maculata   Oahu 'Alauahio

SCIENTIFIC NAME *Paroreomyza* + *maculata*, from Latin *maculosus*, variegated, spotted, striped. Reference is most probably to the female's wing-bars.

COMMON NAME Oahu, for the island of Oahu in the Hawaiian archipelago, the bird's natural range. 'Alauahio, the Hawaiian name for this bird.

Paroreomyza montana   Maui 'Alauahio

SCIENTIFIC NAME *Paroreomyza* + *montana*, Latin for of or belonging to
the mountains. Reference is to the natural range.

COMMON NAME Maui, for the island of Maui in the Hawaiian archipelago, the natural range. 'Alauahio, see *Paroreomyza maculata*.

Parula americana   Northern Parula

SCIENTIFIC NAME *Parula*, little titmouse, from the genus *Parus*, the old
genus for the titmouse, and the diminutive *-ula*. Reference is to the size +
americana, of America. Reference is to the natural range in the United
States.

COMMON NAME Northern, for the natural range, which is north of that of
the tropical parula. Parula, see scientific name.

Parula pitiayumi   Tropical Parula

SCIENTIFIC NAME *Parula* + *pitiayumi*, the Guarani Indian (eastern lowlands of South America) name for this bird.

COMMON NAME Tropical, for the natural range in South America. Parula,
see *Parula americana*.

Passer domesticus   House Sparrow

SCIENTIFIC NAME *Passer*, Latin for a small bird, often used to mean a sparrow + *domesticus*, Latin for of or belonging to the home or house. Reference is to the habit of nesting in or near human dwellings.

COMMON NAME House, see scientific name. Sparrow, from Anglo-Saxon
spearwa, to flutter. Originally used to denote any small bird.

Passer montanus   Eurasian Tree Sparrow

SCIENTIFIC NAME *Passer* + *montanus*, Latin for of or belonging to the
mountains. This is a poor species name because the habitat is not limited
to or even mainly in the mountains.

COMMON NAME Eurasian, for the region of the natural range. Sparrow, see
Passer domesticus.

Passerculus sandwichensis Savannah Sparrow

SCIENTIFIC NAME *Passerculus*, little sparrow, from Latin *passer*, a small bird, often used to mean a sparrow, and the diminutive *-culus*. Reference is to the size being smaller than a *Passer* + *sandwichensis*, for Sandwich Bay, Labrador, where the type specimen was found.

COMMON NAME Savannah, for Savannah, Georgia. The common name was given by Alexander Wilson (1766–1813), who collected a specimen in Savannah. Sparrow, from Anglo-Saxon *spearwa*, to flutter.

Passerella iliaca Fox Sparrow

SCIENTIFIC NAME *Passerella*, little sparrow, from Latin *passer*, a small bird, often used to mean a sparrow, and the diminutive *-ella*. This name is a strange choice because members of this genus are some of the largest sparrows + *iliaca*, relating to the flanks, from Latin *ilia*, the side of the body from the hips to the groin. Reference is to the rufous streaks in this area.

COMMON NAME Fox, for the rufous color of the plumage, which resembles a fox. Sparrow, from Anglo-Saxon *spearwa*, to flutter.

Passerina amoena Lazuli Bunting

SCIENTIFIC NAME *Passerina*, Latin for of sparrows, sparrowlike + *amoena*, Latin for pleasing to the senses, beautiful, attractive, charming. Reference is to the beautifully colored plumage of the male in breeding colors.

COMMON NAME Lazuli, from Medieval Latin *lazulus*, azure, for the male's breeding plumage. Bunting, the origin of this word is unknown, but *The Oxford English Dictionary* (1989) suggests the Scandinavian *buntin*, short and thick, plump.

Passerina caerulea Blue Grosbeak

SCIENTIFIC NAME *Passerina* + *caerulea*, Latin for blue or greenish blue. Reference is to the male's striking blue body.

COMMON NAME Blue, for the body color of the male. Grosbeak, large beak, from French *grosbec*, *gros*, large, and *bec*, beak.

Passerina ciris Painted Bunting

SCIENTIFIC NAME *Passerina* + *ciris*, from Greek κιρις, *kiris*, a bird of Greek mythology. Scylla, daughter of Nisus, king of Megara, betrayed her father and her people to King Minos of Crete, who had besieged their city. One form of the myth has Nisus possessing a purple lock of hair that served as a protection of both his life and the fate of the kingdom. Scylla cut off this lock while her father was sleeping and delivered it to Minos, to whom she had become enthralled while watching him from the walls of her besieged city. Megara was then defeated. Minos, however, was morally outraged by Scylla's behavior and he refused to take her in (although this did not stop him from accepting the lock of hair, the information of the city's new vulnerability, or taking his new advantage for victory). In attempting to swim after Mino's ship when he was leaving (or after being lashed to the rudder as punishment), Scylla drowned and was changed by the gods into a kiris. Her father was changed into a sea eagle and constantly pursued her. The name was supposedly chosen because of the male bird's purple head. In that case, the species name should honor Nisus, not Scylla.

COMMON NAME Painted, for the beautiful colors of the male's plumage, which appear to have been painted on. Bunting, see *Passerina amoena*.

Passerina cyanea   Indigo Bunting

SCIENTIFIC NAME *Passerina* + *cyanea*, from Greek κυανεος, *kuaneos*, dark blue. Reference is to the overall color of the male in breeding plumage

COMMON NAME Indigo, see scientific name. Bunting, see *Passerina amoena*.

Passerina versicolor   Varied Bunting

SCIENTIFIC NAME *Passerina* + *versicolor*, Latin for having colors that change in time or angle of view, variegated. Reference is to the male's plumage pattern.

COMMON NAME Varied, for the male's different shades of color. Bunting, see *Passerina amoena*.

Pavo cristatus   Common Peafowl

SCIENTIFIC NAME *Pavo*, Latin for peacock + *cristatus*, Latin for with a crest. Reference is to the fan-shaped crest on the crown.

COMMON NAME Common, abundant in its range. Peafowl, the *pea* in this name originated from *tokei*, the local name for this bird in Ceylon. It was then corrupted in a series of steps through Arabic, Persian, Greek, Latin, French, and then Old English to *pawe*, and finally *pea*.

Pelagodroma marina   White-faced Storm-Petrel

SCIENTIFIC NAME *Pelagodroma*, sea runner, from Greek πελαγος, *pelagos*, the seas, especially the high sea or open sea, and δρομος, *dromos*, race, running. Reference is to the appearance of walking or running on the surface of the water when landing + *marina*, from *marinus*, Latin for of or belonging to the sea, marine. Reference is to the natural range.

COMMON NAME White-faced, descriptive. Storm, during a storm these birds fly leeward of waves for protection from the wind. If a ship were around in the storm, these birds may suddenly appear on its leeward side; therefore, they are commonly seen during storms. Petrel, little Peter, this bird pats the water with its feet when landing, which gives the appearance of walking on water. It was named for St. Peter, who was said to walk on water.

Pelecanus erythrorhynchos   American White Pelican

SCIENTIFIC NAME *Pelecanus*, from Greek πελεκαν, *pelekan*, a pelican + *erythrorhynchos*, red or yolk-colored beak, from Greek ερυθρος, *eruthros*, red, the color of an egg yolk, and ρυγχος, *rugkhos*, the snout or muzzle of an animal, the beak or bill of a bird. Reference is to the orange bill.

COMMON NAME American, for the natural range. White, the plumage appears completely white with the wings folded. Pelican, see scientific name.

Pelecanus occidentalis   Brown Pelican

SCIENTIFIC NAME *Pelecanus* + *occidentalis*, Latin for of or connected to the west, western. Reference is to it being a New World species, that is, west of Europe.

COMMON NAME Brown, for the predominant body color. Pelican, see *Pelecanus erythrorhynchos*.

Perdix perdix   Gray Partridge

SCIENTIFIC NAME *Perdix*, Latin for a partridge, in turn from Greek περδιξ, *perdix*, a partridge + *perdix*.

COMMON NAME Gray, for the overall color of the plumage. Partridge, from Latin *perdix*, a partridge, in turn from Greek περδιξ, *perdix*, a partridge.

Perisoreus canadensis   Gray Jay

SCIENTIFIC NAME *Perisoreus*, from Greek περισωρευυς, *perisōreōus*, to heap up all around. Reference is most probably to the hoarding behavior of this bird + *canadensis*, Latin for belonging to Canada. Reference is to the natural range.

COMMON NAME Gray, for the overall color of the plumage. Jay, from French *geai*, a jay. Origin is unknown, onomatopoeia of the call is a possibility.

Petrochelidon fulva   Cave Swallow

SCIENTIFIC NAME *Petrochelidon*, rock swallow, from Greek πετρος, *petros*, stone, rock, and χελιδων, *khelidōn*, a swallow. Reference is to the nesting sites among rocks and caves + *fulva*, from Latin *fuluus*, brown, ranging between dull yellowish brown and reddish brown, tawny. Reference is to the color of the breast, throat, and face.

COMMON NAME Cave, for the common nesting site. Swallow, from Anglo-Saxon *swalewe*, their name for this type of bird.

Petrochelidon pyrrhonota   Cliff Swallow

SCIENTIFIC NAME *Petrochelidon* + *pyrrhonota*, flame-colored back, from Greek πυρρος, *purr(h)os*, flame colored, and νοτων, *notōn*, back. Reference is to the rufous rump.

COMMON NAME Cliff, for the common nesting site. Swallow, see *Petrochelidon fulva*.

Peucedramus taeniatus   Olive Warbler

SCIENTIFIC NAME *Peucedramus*, pine runner, from Greek πευκη, *peukē*, a pine, and δρομος, *dromos*, race, running. Reference is to the behavior in its preferred habitat, pine trees + *taeniatus*, possessing a stripe, from Latin *taenia*, a ribbon, band, string, stripe, and *-atus*, possessing. Reference is to the male's black eye stripe.

COMMON NAME Olive, for the female's olive-gray head and neck. Warbler, for the trills and quavers of the song.

Phaethon aethereus   Red-billed Tropicbird

SCIENTIFIC NAME *Phaethon*, for the Greek mythological character Phaethōn the son of Helios and Clymene. When he became a young man, he was told who his father was. He traveled to the palace of Helios in the east and asked his father for a gift. Helios granted Phaethōn anything he wished for, and Phaethōn asked to drive the chariot that carried the sun across the sky for just one day. He was unable to handle the immortal horses,

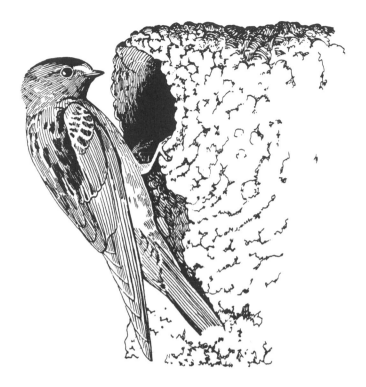

Petrochelidon pyrrhonota, cliff swallow

and the chariot careened toward the earth and was about to set the world on fire. Zeus killed Phaethōn with a thunderbolt, sending the chariot back on its path. Reference is to the belief that this bird followed the path of the sun + *aethereus*, from Greek αεθεριος, *aetherios*, high in the air. Reference is to its flight habits.

COMMON NAME Red-billed, descriptive. Tropicbird, for the natural range in the tropical regions of the Pacific.

Phaethon lepturus dorotheae   White-tailed Tropicbird

SCIENTIFIC NAME *Phaethon* + *lepturus*, thin tailed, from Greek λεπτος, *leptos*, fine, small, thin, and ουρα, *oura*, tail. According to the *Oxford Greek-English Lexicon* (1996), ουρα, *oura* should not be used for the tail of a bird but is restricted to other animals. Reference is to the long, thin tail. In the Hawaiian Islands, there is the subspecies *dorotheae*, for Dorothy

White (fl. 1916), the daughter of Henry White (1860–1927), an Australian naturalist.

COMMON NAME White-tailed, descriptive. Tropicbird, see *Phaethon aethereus*.

Phaethon rubricauda rothschildi   Red-tailed Tropicbird

SCIENTIFIC NAME *Phaethon* + *rubricauda*, red tailed, from Latin *ruber*, red, and *cauda*, tail. Reference is to the two central red tail feathers, which are longer than the others. In the Hawaiian Islands, there is the subspecies *rothschildi*, for Lionel Walter, second baron Rothschild of Tring (1868–1937), an English ornithologist and author.

COMMON NAME Red-tailed, see scientific name. Tropicbird, see *Phaethon aethereus*.

Phainopepla nitens   Phainopepla

SCIENTIFIC NAME *Phainopepla*, shining robe, from Greek φαεινος, *phaeinos*, shining, radiant, and πεπλος, *peplos*, any woven cloth, curtain, a man's cloak or robe. Reference is to the male's shiny black plumage + *nitens*, Latin for shining, bright, radiant. Reference is the same as the genus.

COMMON NAME Phainopepla, see scientific name.

Phalacrocorax auritus   Double-crested Cormorant

SCIENTIFIC NAME *Phalacrocorax*, Latin for cormorant, in turn from Greek φαλακρος, *phalakros*, bald headed, and κοραξ, *korax*, a crow. Reference is to the white head and black body of the European species + *auritus*, Latin for eared. Reference is to the crest just behind the eyes.

COMMON NAME Double-crested, for the small crests just behind the eyes. Cormorant, from French *cormoran*, their name for this type of bird, in turn from Latin *coruus*, crow, and *marinus*, of or belonging to the sea.

Phalacrocorax brasilianus   Neotropic Cormorant

SCIENTIFIC NAME *Phalacrocorax* + *brasilianus*, Latin for pertaining to Brazil, from Brazil. Reference is to the natural range.

COMMON NAME Neotropic, the region of Central and South America and the West Indies. Reference is to the natural range. Cormorant, see *Phalacrocorax auritus*.

Phalacrocorax carbo Great Cormorant

SCIENTIFIC NAME *Phalacrocorax* + *carbo*, Latin for a piece of charcoal. Reference is to the color of the plumage.

COMMON NAME Great, for the size; this is the largest cormorant in the United States. Cormorant, see *Phalacrocorax auritus*.

Phalacrocorax pelagicus Pelagic Cormorant

SCIENTIFIC NAME *Phalacrocorax* + *pelagicus*, from Greek πελαγος, *pelagos*, the sea, the open sea. Reference is to the habitat.

COMMON NAME Pelagic, see scientific name. Cormorant, see *Phalacrocorax auritus*.

Phalacrocorax penicillatus Brandt's Cormorant

SCIENTIFIC NAME *Phalacrocorax* + *penicillatus*, possessing a paint brush, from Latin *penicillus*, a paint brush, and *-atus*, possessing. Reference is to the tufts of feathers on the head in breeding plumage.

COMMON NAME Brandt's, for Johann Friedrich von Brandt (1802–1879), a German zoologist who became director of the Zoological Museum in St. Petersburg, Russia. He published many papers in various scientific areas and led two expeditions to Siberia. Cormorant, see *Phalacrocorax auritus*.

Phalacrocorax urile Red-faced Cormorant

SCIENTIFIC NAME *Phalacrocorax* + *urile*, most probably a Latinized formation for the Kurile Islands, Japan (now Kuril Islands, Russia). These birds were believed to range in that region sometime in the past.

COMMON NAME Red-faced, descriptive. Cormorant, see *Phalacrocorax auritus*.

Phalaenoptilus nuttallii Common Poorwill

SCIENTIFIC NAME *Phalaenoptilus*, moth feathered, from Greek φαλαινα, *phalaina*, a form of φαλλαινα, *phallaina*, a whale, any devouring creature, a moth (Rhodian form), and πτιλον, *ptilon*, soft feathers or down under the true feathers, anything like a feather or wing. Reference is to the soft feathers + *nuttallii*, for Thomas Nuttall (1786–1859), the curator of the Botanical Gardens at Harvard and author of *A Manual of the Ornithology of the United States and Canada* (1832).

COMMON NAME Common, more numerous than other nightjars. Poor-will, onomatopoeic of the call.

Phalaropus fulicarius   Red Phalarope

SCIENTIFIC NAME *Phalaropus*, coot footed, from Greek φαλαρις, *phalaris*, a coot, and πους, *pous*, foot. Reference is to the lobed toes like those of a coot + *fulicarius*, relating to a coot, from Latin *fulica*, a coot, and -*arius*, relating to. Again the reference is to the feet.

COMMON NAME Red, for the underparts in breeding plumage, especially the female's. Phalarope, see scientific name.

Phalaropus lobatus   Red-necked Phalarope

SCIENTIFIC NAME *Phalaropus* + *lobatus*, lobed, Latinized from Greek λοβος, *lobos*, lobe of the ear, liver, or lung; pod. Reference is to the lobes on the feet.

COMMON NAME Red-necked, for the red neck in breeding plumage, especially on the female. Phalarope, see *Phalaropus fulicarius*.

Phalaropus tricolor   Wilson's Phalarope

SCIENTIFIC NAME *Phalaropus* + *tricolor*, Latin for having three colors. Reference is to the colors of the female in breeding plumage: buff breast, black face and neck stripe, and gray crown and back.

COMMON NAME Wilson's, for Alexander Wilson (1766–1813), known as the father of American ornithology. He initiated the first series on birds of the eastern United States, *American Ornithology* (1808–1814). Phalarope, see *Phalaropus fulicarius*.

Phasianus colchicus   Ring-necked Pheasant

SCIENTIFIC NAME *Phasianus*, from Greek φασιανος, *phasianos*, a pheasant. Named for the River Phasis, the region from which these birds were first brought back to Greece + *colchicus*, Latinized form of Colchis, an ancient country located on the banks of the Black Sea in the region that is now the Republic of Georgia; the site of the River Phasis.

COMMON NAME Ring-necked, the male has a white ring around the neck. Pheasant, see scientific name.

Phasianus versicolor   Japanese Green Pheasant

SCIENTIFIC NAME *Phasianus* + *versicolor*, Latin for having colors that change in time or from the angle of view, variegated. Reference is to the plumage.

COMMON NAME Japanese, for the natural range. Green, for the predominant body color. Pheasant, see *Phasianus colchicus*.

Pheucticus chrysopeplus   Yellow Grosbeak

SCIENTIFIC NAME *Pheucticus*, from Greek φευκτικος, *pheuktikos*, inclined to avoid, shy. Reference is to the secretive behavior + *chrysopeplus*, golden robed, from Greek χρυσος, *khrusos*, gold, and πεπλος, *peplos*, any woven cloth, upper garment, robe. Reference is to the yellow body color.

COMMON NAME Yellow, for the overall color of the plumage. Grosbeak, large beak, from French *grosbec*, *gros*, large, and *bec*, beak.

Pheucticus ludovicianus   Rose-breasted Grosbeak

SCIENTIFIC NAME *Pheucticus* + *ludovicianus*, pertaining to *Ludovicius*, Louis, in reference to Louis XIV (1638–1715), king of France. Used here to mean from Louisiana, where the type specimen was collected.

COMMON NAME Rose-breasted, for the rose-colored patch on the male's breast in breeding plumage. Grosbeak, see *Pheucticus chrysopeplus*.

Pheucticus melanocephalus   Black-headed Grosbeak

SCIENTIFIC NAME *Pheucticus* + *melanocephalus*, black headed, from Greek μελας, *melas*, black, and κεφαλη, *kephale*, head. Reference is to the black head of the male in breeding plumage.

COMMON NAME Black-headed, see scientific name. Grosbeak, see *Pheucticus chrysopeplus*.

Philomachus pugnax   Ruff

SCIENTIFIC NAME *Philomachus*, from Greek φιλομαχος, *philomakhos*, loving to fight, warlike, from φιλος, *philos*, loving, and μαχη, *makhe*, battle, combat. Reference is to the males' fighting behavior during breeding season + *pugnax*, Latin for eager to fight, combative.

COMMON NAME Ruff, a contraction of *ruffle*, the fluffing up of feathers when threatening or bluffing. The male has a large ruff of feathers on the neck that he displays over his head.

Pheucticus melanocephalus, black-headed grosbeak

Phoebastria albatrus Short-tailed Albatross

SCIENTIFIC NAME *Phoebastria*, from Greek φοιβαστρια, *phoibastria*, a prophetess. Reference is to the old belief among seamen that an albatross was the embodiment of the soul of a dead sailor and that seeing one was an omen + *albatrus*, Latinized form of albatross.

COMMON NAME Short-tailed, descriptive but not a good field mark; the tail of this species looks the same length as the other species of albatrosses. Albatross, English name based on the Portuguese *alcatras*, the frigatebird; the change from *alca-* to *alba-* is thought to be a reference to the white color of some albatrosses in contrast to the black color of the frigatebirds.

Phoebastria immutabilis Laysan Albatross

SCIENTIFIC NAME *Phoebastria* + *immutabilis*, in this case, Latin for unchangeable. Reference is to the juvenile and the adult plumage appearing very much the same.

COMMON NAME Laysan, for the island of Laysan in the Hawaiian archipelago, where the type specimen was collected. Albatross, see *Phoebastria albatrus*.

Phoebastria nigripes Black-footed Albatross

SCIENTIFIC NAME *Phoebastria* + *nigripes*, black footed, from Latin *niger*, black, and *pes*, foot.

COMMON NAME Black-footed, descriptive. Albatross, see *Phoebastria albatrus*.

Phoeniconaias minor Lesser Flamingo

SCIENTIFIC NAME *Phoeniconaias*, crimson water nymph, from Greek φοι-νιξ, *phoinix*, purple or crimson, so named because the Greeks first obtained this dye color from the Phoenicians, and Ναις, *Nais*, a river or spring nymph + *minor*, Latin for smaller in size, height, extent, of the smaller kind. This bird is smaller than the other flamingos.

COMMON NAME Lesser, for the size; this is the United States' smallest flamingo. Flamingo, from Spanish *flamenco* or Portuguese *flamingo*, both are based on the Latin *flamma*, a flame. Reference is to the red plumage.

Phoenicoparrus andinus Andean Flamingo

SCIENTIFIC NAME *Phoenicoparrus*, crimson *Parra*, from Greek φοινιξ, *phoinix*, purple or crimson (see *Phoeniconaias minor*), and the old genus name for the jacana, *Parra*. Both the flamingo and the jacana are waterbirds + *andinus*, belonging to the Andes, from the Andes. Reference is to the natural range.

COMMON NAME Andean, see scientific name. Flamingo, see *Phoeniconaias minor*.

Phoenicoparrus jamesi Puna Flamingo

SCIENTIFIC NAME *Phoenicoparrus* + *jamesi*, for H. Berkeley James (1846–1892), a British businessman and naturalist who lived in Chile.

COMMON NAME Puna, for the natural range on the Isla de Puna, Ecuador. Flamingo, see *Phoeniconaias minor*.

Phoenicopterus chilensis Chilean Flamingo

SCIENTIFIC NAME *Phoenicopterus*, crimson winged, from Greek φοινιξ, *phoinix*, purple or crimson (see *Phoeniconaias minor*), and πτερον, *pteron*, feather, bird's wing + *chilensis*, Latin for belonging to Chile. Reference is to the natural range.

COMMON NAME Chilean, for the natural range in Chile. Flamingo, see *Phoeniconaias minor*.

Phoenicopterus ruber roseus   Greater Flamingo (Eurasian)

SCIENTIFIC NAME *Phoenicopterus* + *ruber*, Latin for red. Reference is to the pink legs and the pink along the wing edge + *roseus*, Latin for made of roses, rose colored. Reference is the same as for *ruber*.

COMMON NAME Greater, for the size; this species is the largest flamingo in the United States. Flamingo, see *Phoeniconaias minor*. Eurasian, for the natural range.

Phoenicopterus ruber ruber   Greater Flamingo (American)

SCIENTIFIC NAME *Phoenicopterus* + *ruber*, Latin for red. Reference is to the overall color + *ruber*.

COMMON NAME Greater, for the size; this species is the largest flamingo in the United States. Flamingo, see *Phoeniconaias minor*. American, for the natural range.

Phylloscopus borealis   Arctic Warbler

SCIENTIFIC NAME *Phylloscopus*, leaf watcher, from Greek φυλλον, *phullon*, leaf, leaves, foliage, and σκοπος, *skopos*, one that watches, one that looks after things. Reference is to the feeding habit of looking for insects on leaves + *borealis*, of the north, from Latin *boreus*, northern. Reference is to the natural range in Siberia.

COMMON NAME Arctic, for the natural range. Warbler, for the trills and quavers of the song.

Phylloscopus fuscatus   Dusky Warbler

SCIENTIFIC NAME *Phylloscopus* + *fuscatus*, Latin for to become dark. Reference is to the dusky plumage.

COMMON NAME Dusky, descriptive. Warbler, see *Phylloscopus borealis*.

Pica hudsonia   Black-billed Magpie

SCIENTIFIC NAME *Pica*, Latin for a jay or magpie + *hudsonia*, for the region that was controlled by the Hudson Bay Company in Canada. Reference is to the natural range.

Pica hudsonia, black-billed magpie

COMMON NAME Black-billed, descriptive. Magpie, the *mag* part, all sources agree, is a pet name for Margaret, the *pie* is most commonly listed as imitative of the call. The Old French name for this bird was *pie* or *maggot-pie*, *maggot* from Old French *Margot*, a pet name for Marguerite (Margaret).

Pica nuttalli   Yellow-billed Magpie

SCIENTIFIC NAME *Pica* + *nuttalli*, for Thomas Nuttall (1786–1859), curator of the Botanical Gardens at Harvard and author of *A Manual of the Ornithology of the United States and Canada* (1832).

COMMON NAME Yellow-billed, descriptive. Magpie, see *Pica hudsonia*.

Picoides albolarvatus   White-headed Woodpecker

SCIENTIFIC NAME *Picoides*, to resemble the great black woodpecker, from Latin *picus*, the great black woodpecker, and *-oides*, to resemble + *albolarvatus*, white masked, from Latin *albus*, white, and *larvatus*, a horrific mask, one possessed by evil spirits. Reference is to the white face, which contrasts sharply with the black body.

COMMON NAME White-headed, descriptive. Woodpecker, for the feeding and nesting behavior.

Picoides arcticus   Black-backed Woodpecker

SCIENTIFIC NAME *Picoides* + *arcticus*, from Greek αρκτικος, *arktikos*, near the bear (reference is to the constellation of the Great Bear in the northern sky), arctic, northern. Reference is to the natural range.

COMMON NAME Black-backed, descriptive. Woodpecker, see *Picoides albolarvatus*.

Picoides arizonae   Arizona Woodpecker

SCIENTIFIC NAME *Picoides* + *arizonae*, of Arizona, for the natural range in the Territory of Arizona, now the state of Arizona.

COMMON NAME Arizona, see scientific name. Woodpecker, see *Picoides albolarvatus*.

Picoides borealis   Red-cockaded Woodpecker

SCIENTIFIC NAME *Picoides* + *borealis*, of the north, from Latin *boreus*, northern. It was given this name because Louis Pierre Vieillot (1748–1831), who did not collect the specimen but was presented it for description, erroneously thought the bird came from the northern United States. Its range, however, is limited to the southeastern United States. The principle of priority allows this mistake to stand.

COMMON NAME Red-cockaded, for the small red patch at the upper edge of its white auriculars that makes it appear to be wearing a cockade, a ribbon or rosette worn on the hat as a badge of office or party. Woodpecker, see *Picoides albolarvatus*.

Picoides nuttallii   Nuttall's Woodpecker

SCIENTIFIC NAME *Picoides* + *nuttallii*, for Thomas Nuttall (1786–1859), curator of the Botanical Gardens at Harvard and author of *A Manual of the Ornithology of the United States and Canada* (1832).

COMMON NAME Nuttall's, see scientific name. Woodpecker, see *Picoides albolarvatus.*

Picoides pubescens   Downy Woodpecker

SCIENTIFIC NAME *Picoides + pubescens*, from Latin *pubescere*, to grow hair on the body at puberty, to become downy. Reference is to the bristles that cover the nostrils, which are shorter and appear softer than those of the hairy woodpecker.

COMMON NAME Downy, see scientific name. Woodpecker, see *Picoides albolarvatus.*

Picoides scalaris   Ladder-backed Woodpecker

SCIENTIFIC NAME *Picoides + scalaris*, Latin for of or relating to a ladder. Reference is to the striped pattern on the back that resembles the rungs of a ladder.

COMMON NAME Ladder-backed, see scientific name. Woodpecker, see *Picoides albolarvatus.*

Picoides tridactylus   Three-toed Woodpecker

SCIENTIFIC NAME *Picoides + tridactylus*, three toed, from Greek τριδακτυλιαιος, *tridaktuliaios*, having three fingers or toes, from τρι, *tri*, three, and δακτυλος, *daktulos*, finger or toe.

COMMON NAME Three-toed, descriptive. Woodpecker, see *Picoides albolarvatus.*

Picoides villosus   Hairy Woodpecker

SCIENTIFIC NAME *Picoides + villosus*, Latin for shaggy or hairy. Reference is to the bristles covering the nostrils.

COMMON NAME Hairy, see scientific name. Woodpecker, see *Picoides albolarvatus.*

Pinicola enucleator   Pine Grosbeak

SCIENTIFIC NAME *Pinicola*, to live in a pine tree, from Latin *pinus*, a pine tree, and *-cola*, inhabitant. Reference is to the favored habitat + *enucleator*, from Latin *enucleare*, to take the stones out of fruit. Reference is to the feeding behavior of extracting the seeds from pine cones.

COMMON NAME Pine, for the favored habitat and food. Grosbeak, large beak, from French *grosbec*, *gros*, large, and *bec*, beak.

Picoides scalaris, ladder-backed woodpecker

Pipilo aberti   Abert's Towhee

SCIENTIFIC NAME *Pipilo*, from Latin *pipo*, to chirp, cheep, peep, twitter + *aberti*, for James William Abert (1820–1897), a U.S. Army officer who collected birds for Spencer Fullerton Baird (1823–1887).

COMMON NAME Abert's, see scientific name. Towhee, imitative of the call.

Pipilo chlorurus   Green-tailed Towhee

SCIENTIFIC NAME *Pipilo* + *chlorurus*, green tailed, from Greek χλωρος, *khlōros*, greenish yellow, pale green, yellow, pallid, and ουρα, *oura*, tail.

According to the *Oxford Greek-English Lexicon* (1996), ουρα, ουρος, *oura ouros*, should not be used for the tail of a bird but is restricted to other animals.

COMMON NAME Green-tailed, has a yellowish green tail. Towhee, see *Pipilo aberti*.

Pipilo crissalis   California Towhee

SCIENTIFIC NAME *Pipilo* + *crissalis*, of the vent, Latinized form of crissum, the area around the vent including the undertail coverts. The crissum of this bird is a conspicuous orange.

COMMON NAME California, for the natural range. Towhee, see *Pipilo aberti*.

Pipilo erythrophthalmus   Eastern Towhee

SCIENTIFIC NAME *Pipilo* + *erythrophthalmus*, red eyed, from Greek ερυθρος, *eruthros*, red, and οφθαλμος, *ophthalmos*, eye. There are two forms of the male: a red-eyed and a white-eyed form.

COMMON NAME Eastern, for the natural range in the United States. Towhee, see *Pipilo aberti*.

Pipilo fuscus   Canyon Towhee

SCIENTIFIC NAME *Pipilo* + *fuscus*, Latin for dark colored, dusky. Reference is to the overall body color.

COMMON NAME Canyon, for the habitat. Towhee, see *Pipilo aberti*.

Pipilo maculatus   Spotted Towhee

SCIENTIFIC NAME *Pipilo* + *maculatus*, Latin for spotted. Reference is to the white spots on the wings.

COMMON NAME Spotted, see scientific name. Towhee, see *Pipilo aberti*.

Piranga bidentata   Flame-colored Tanager

SCIENTIFIC NAME *Piranga*, the Tupi Indian (upper Amazon Basin) name for a small bird, not specific or limited to this genus + *bidentata*, having two teeth, from Latin *bi*, two, and *dentatus*, provided with teeth. Reference is to the notches in the maxilla.

COMMON NAME Flame-colored, for the male's bright orange head and breast. Tanager, from the Tupi Indian (upper Amazon Basin) *tangara*, their name for this type of bird.

Piranga flava   Hepatic Tanager

SCIENTIFIC NAME *Piranga* + *flava*, Latin for yellow, golden. Reference is to the color of the female. The type bird for this species was probably a female, and the name was assigned before the bright red male was discovered.

COMMON NAME Hepatic, liver-red, from Latin *hepaticus*, of the liver, in this case the color of liver. Reference is to the red color of the male. Tanager, see *Piranga bidentata*.

Piranga ludoviciana   Western Tanager

SCIENTIFIC NAME *Piranga* + *ludoviciana*, from *Ludovicius*, Louis, in reference to Louis XIV (1638–1715), king of France. Used here to mean from the region of the Louisiana Purchase, in reference to the natural range.

COMMON NAME Western, for the natural range in the western United States. Tanager, see *Piranga bidentata*.

Piranga olivacea   Scarlet Tanager

SCIENTIFIC NAME *Piranga* + *olivacea*, Modern Latin for olive-colored, from Latin *oliva*, olive. Reference is to the color of the female. The summer tanager already had the species name *rubra* (red); to avoid confusion, the color of the female was chosen for the epithet of this species.

COMMON NAME Scarlet, for the bright red body of the male in breeding plumage. Tanager, see *Piranga bidentata*.

Piranga rubra   Summer Tanager

SCIENTIFIC NAME *Piranga* + *rubra*, Latin for red. Reference is to the male's completely red plumage.

COMMON NAME Summer, for its migratory habits; this bird is seen in the United States only during the summer. The original common name was summer red bird to differentiate it from the cardinal, then called the red bird, which was a year-round resident. Tanager, see *Piranga bidentata*.

Pitangus sulphuratus   Great Kiskadee

SCIENTIFIC NAME *Pitangus*, the Tupi Indian (upper Amazon Basin) name for this bird + *sulphuratus*, Latin for possessing sulfur. Reference is to the yellow underparts.

COMMON NAME Great, for the size; it is the largest in the genus. Kiskadee, imitative of the call.

Platalea ajaja Roseate Spoonbill

SCIENTIFIC NAME *Platalea*, Latin for spoonbill + *ajaja*, Tupi Indian (upper Amazon Basin) name for this bird.

COMMON NAME Roseate, for the rosy pink plumage. Spoonbill, descriptive of the shape of the bill.

Plectrophenax hyperboreus McKay's Bunting

SCIENTIFIC NAME *Plectrophenax*, something to strike a cheat with, from Greek πληκτρον, *plēktron*, anything to strike with, spear point, cock's spur, and φεναξ, *phenax*, a cheat, quack, impostor. The principle of priority preserves this nonsensical name. The original genus name was *Plectophanes*, from Greek πληκτρον, *plēktron*, and φαινω, *phainō*, to show, make appear. To show a cock's spur was the original intent, with reference to the long hind claw. While removing the snow bunting (*Plectrophenax* [*Emberiza*] *nivalis*) from the genus *Emberiza*, Leonhard Stejneger (1851–1943) changed or simply misspelled the genus *Plectophanes* to *Plectrophenax*, in which he placed this bird + *hyperboreus*, Latin for of the far north, polar, from Greek Υπερβορεοι, *Yperboreoi*, a people supposed to live in the extreme north. Reference is to the natural range.

COMMON NAME McKay's, for Charles Leslie McKay (d. 1883), a member of the signal corps who collected birds in Alaska. Bunting, the origin of this word is unknown, but *The Oxford English Dictionary* (1989) suggests the Scandinavian *buntin*, short and thick, plump.

Plectrophenax nivalis Snow Bunting

SCIENTIFIC NAME *Plectrophenax* + *nivalis*, Latin for snowy, wintry. Reference is to the winter range in the United States and the white head and underparts of the male in breeding plumage.

COMMON NAME Snow, see scientific name. Bunting, see *Plectrophenax hyperboreus*.

Plegadis chihi White-faced Ibis

SCIENTIFIC NAME *Plegadis*, from Greek πληγας, *plēgas*, the same as δρεπανον, *drepanon*, a sickle, scythe, curved sword. Reference is to the curved bill + *chihi*, imitative of the call.

COMMON NAME White-faced, for the white band on the face in breeding plumage. Ibis, from Greek ιβις, *ibis*, from the Egyptian name for this type of bird.

Plegadis falcinellus Glossy Ibis

SCIENTIFIC NAME *Plegadis* + *falcinellus*, a little sickle, from Latin *falx*, sickle, and the diminutive *-ellus*. Reference is to the shape of the bill.

COMMON NAME Glossy, for the appearance of the plumage. Ibis, see *Plegadis chihi*.

Pluvialis apricaria European Golden-Plover

SCIENTIFIC NAME *Pluvialis*, Latin for consisting of rain, produced by rain, associated with rain, rainy. There is no good evidence as to why this name was chosen + *apricaria*, from Latin *apricus*, warmed by the sunshine, basking. Reference is to the gold color on this bird.

COMMON NAME European, for the natural range. Golden, for the gold spots on the plumage. Plover, from Old French *plovier*, their name for this type of bird, in turn from Latin *pluuius*, see scientific name.

Pluvialis dominica American Golden-Plover

SCIENTIFIC NAME *Pluvialis* + *dominica*, for Santo Domingo (Hispaniola), where the type specimen was collected.

COMMON NAME American, for the natural range. Golden-Plover, see *Pluvialis apricaria*.

Pluvialis fulva Pacific Golden-Plover

SCIENTIFIC NAME *Pluvialis* + *fulva*, Latin for brown, ranging between dull yellow and a reddish brown, tawny. Reference is to the tawny spots on the plumage.

COMMON NAME Pacific, for the natural range along the U.S. Pacific coast. Golden-Plover, see *Pluvialis apricaria*.

Pluvialis squatarola Black-bellied Plover

SCIENTIFIC NAME *Pluvialis* + *squatarola*, the Venetian name for this bird.
COMMON NAME Black-bellied, descriptive. Plover, see *Pluvialis apricaria*.

Podiceps auritus Horned Grebe

SCIENTIFIC NAME *Podiceps*, a contraction of the Modern Latin *podicipes*, rump footed, from Latin *podex*, the anal orifice, and *pes*, the foot. Reference is to the position of the feet when swimming; they extend to the rear and appear to be coming out of the rump. Interestingly, if this word was not a contraction, it would strictly translate as rump headed (that is, from *podex* and *ceps*) + *auritus*, Latin for provided with ears, eared. Reference is to the feather tufts on the head.

COMMON NAME Horned, for the feather tufts on the head. Grebe, the French name for this type of bird.

Podiceps grisegena   Red-necked Grebe

SCIENTIFIC NAME *Podiceps* + *grisegena*, gray cheeked, from Medieval Latin *griseus*, gray, and Latin *gena*, cheek. Reference is to the gray cheeks seen in breeding plumage.

COMMON NAME Red-necked, for the red neck in breeding plumage. Grebe, see *Podiceps auritus*.

Podiceps nigricollis   Eared Grebe

SCIENTIFIC NAME *Podiceps* + *nigricollis*, black necked, from Latin *niger*, black, and the Modern Latin -*collis*, necked, from Latin *collum*, the neck. Reference is to the black neck of both sexes in breeding plumage.

COMMON NAME Eared, for the wispy yellow plumes behind the eyes in a position where external ears would be located. Grebe, see *Podiceps auritus*.

Podilymbus podiceps   Pied-billed Grebe

SCIENTIFIC NAME *Podilymbus*, this word was formed by combining two genus names, *Podiceps* and *Colymbus*. *Podiceps* is a genus of grebes, and *Colymbus* was an old genus name for grebes and loons. Grebe-grebe is the intended meaning + *podiceps*, a contraction of the Modern Latin *podicipes*, rump footed, from Latin *podex*, the anal orifice, and *pes*, the foot. Reference is to the position of the feet when swimming; they extend to the rear and appear to be coming out of the rump.

COMMON NAME Pied-billed, for the black and white bill of both sexes in breeding colors. Grebe, the French name for this type of bird.

Poecile atricapilla   Black-capped Chickadee

SCIENTIFIC NAME *Poecile*, from Greek ποικιλος, *poikilos*, many colored, spotted, pied, dappled. Pied is meant here, for the black and white colors of the plumage + *atricapilla*, from *ater*, black, and *capillus*, the hair of the head. Reference is to the black crown.

COMMON NAME Black-capped, descriptive. Chickadee, onomatopoeic of the call.

Poecile carolinensis   Carolina Chickadee

SCIENTIFIC NAME *Poecile* + *carolinensis*, Latin for belonging to Carolina. Reference is to the state of South Carolina, where the type specimen was found.

COMMON NAME Carolina, see scientific name. Chickadee, see *Poecile atricapilla*.

Poecile cincta   Gray-headed Chickadee

SCIENTIFIC NAME *Poecile* + *cincta*, Latin for girdled, the means of girding up clothes at the waist, a crown or garland. All sources translate this as girdled; those that comment note what a bad name it is because this bird is not banded. Pieter Boddaert (1730–1795) assigned this species name without explanation. In my opinion, he meant crowned, for the grayish brown cap.

COMMON NAME Gray-headed, for the grayish brown cap. Chickadee, see *Poecile atricapilla*.

Poecile gambeli   Mountain Chickadee

SCIENTIFIC NAME *Poecile* + *gambeli*, for William Gambel (1819–1849), an ornithologist and adventurer who spent several years in California and who collected the type specimen.

COMMON NAME Mountain, for the natural range in the Rocky Mountains. Chickadee, see *Poecile atricapilla*.

Poecile hudsonica   Boreal Chickadee

SCIENTIFIC NAME *Poecile* + *hudsonica*, of the Hudson Bay area, where the type specimen was collected.

COMMON NAME Boreal, for the natural range in the north. Chickadee, see *Poecile atricapilla*.

Poecile rufescens   Chestnut-backed Chickadee

SCIENTIFIC NAME *Poecile* + *rufescens*, somewhat red, from Latin *rufus*, red of various shades, tawny, and *-escens*, somewhat like. Reference is to the reddish back and sides.

COMMON NAME Chestnut-backed, descriptive. Chickadee, see *Poecile atricapilla*.

Poecile sclateri — Mexican Chickadee

SCIENTIFIC NAME *Poecile* + *sclateri*, for Philip Lutley Sclater (1829–1913), an English ornithologist, fellow of the Royal Society, and Secretary of the Zoological Society of London. He wrote several volumes of the *Catalogue of Birds of the British Museum*.

COMMON NAME Mexican, for the natural range. Chickadee, see *Poecile atricapilla*.

Polioptila caerulea — Blue-gray Gnatcatcher

SCIENTIFIC NAME *Polioptila*, gray feather, from Greek πολιος, *polios*, gray, and πτιλον, *ptilon*, soft feathers under the true feathers, down, anything like a feather or wing. Reference is to the overall color + *caerulea*, Latin for blue or greenish blue. Reference is to the pale bluish gray back.

COMMON NAME Blue-gray, for the overall color of the plumage. Gnatcatcher, for the habit of catching tiny insects in the air.

Polioptila californica — California Gnatcatcher

SCIENTIFIC NAME *Polioptila* + *californica*, of California. Reference is to the natural range.

COMMON NAME California, for the natural range. Gnatcatcher, see *Polioptila caerulea*.

Polioptila melanura — Black-tailed Gnatcatcher

SCIENTIFIC NAME *Polioptila* + *melanura*, black tailed, from Greek μελας, *melas*, black, and ουρα, *oura*, tail. According to the *Oxford Greek-English Lexicon* (1996), ουρα, *oura* should not be used for the tail of birds, but is restricted to other animals. Reference is to the black tail in breeding plumage of both sexes.

COMMON NAME Black-tailed, see scientific name. Gnatcatcher, see *Polioptila caerulea*.

Polioptila nigriceps — Black-capped Gnatcatcher

SCIENTIFIC NAME *Polioptila* + *nigriceps*, black headed, from Latin *niger*, black, and -*ceps*, headed, from Greek κεφαλη, *kephalē*, head. Reference is to the black cap of the male in breeding plumage.

COMMON NAME Black-capped, see scientific name. Gnatcatcher, see *Polioptila caerulea*.

Polioptila caerulea, blue-gray gnatcatcher

Polysticta stelleri   Steller's Eider

SCIENTIFIC NAME *Polysticta*, from Greek πολυστικτος, *polustiktos*, much spotted. The male does have a prominent black spot on each side in breeding plumage, but neither sex has many spots + *stelleri*, for Georg Wilhelm Steller (1709–1746), a German botanist and medical doctor who accompanied Vitus Bering (1680–1741) on his 1740 expedition to Alaska. Steller collected the type specimen of this eider on that trip.

COMMON NAME Steller's, see scientific name. Eider, from Icelandic *aedr*, their name for this type of bird.

Pooecetes gramineus   Vesper Sparrow

SCIENTIFIC NAME *Pooecetes*, grass dwelling, from Greek ποη, *poē*, grass, and οικητης, *oikētēs*, dweller. Reference is to the habitat + *gramineus*, Latin for covered with grass, grassy.

COMMON NAME Vesper, Latin for the evening. Reference is to this bird's habit of singing in the evening. Sparrow, from Anglo-Saxon *spearwa*, to flutter. Originally used to denote any small bird.

Porphyrio martinica   Purple Gallinule

SCIENTIFIC NAME *Porphyrio*, Latin for the purple coot or water hen, in turn from Greek πορφυριων, *porphuriōn*, of the same meaning. The root word is Greek πορφυριος, πορφυρεος, *porphurios, porphureos*, purple, among many other meanings. Reference is to the purple head and underparts + *martinica*, of Martinique, where the type specimen was collected.

COMMON NAME Purple, for the color of the head and underparts. Gallinule, from Latin *gallinula*, a little hen.

Porphyrio porphyrio   Purple Swamphen

SCIENTIFIC NAME *Porphyrio* + *porphyrio*.

COMMON NAME Purple, for the overall color of the plumage. Swamphen, for the habitat and the appearance.

Porzana carolina   Sora

SCIENTIFIC NAME *Porzana*, from *sporzana*, the Venetian name for this bird + *carolina*, of Carolina. Reference is to the natural range in the Carolina colonies, an area encompassing the southeastern United States.

COMMON NAME Sora, an American Indian name for this bird.

Procelsterna cerulea   Blue-gray Noddy

SCIENTIFIC NAME *Procelsterna*, a combination of the genera *Procellaria* and *Sterna*. *Procellaria*, relating to a storm, from Latin *procella*, a violent wind, storm, gale, and *-arius*, relating to. Some storm-petrels belong to this genus. *Sterna*, from Old English *stern*, a tern. Reference is to the appearance + *cerulea*, Latin for blue or greenish blue. Reference is to the overall pale blue plumage.

COMMON NAME Blue-gray, see scientific name. Noddy, a fool or simpleton. Reference is to the behavior of this bird, which is not fearful around humans and is thus easily caught and eaten.

Progne subis   Purple Martin

SCIENTIFIC NAME *Progne*, for Progne (Procne) of Greek mythology, who was turned into a swallow (see *Pandion haliaetus*) + *subis*, Latin word used by Pliny to describe a bird that broke eagles eggs. It is unknown why this unusual species name was assigned to the purple martin.

COMMON NAME Purple, for the overall color of the plumage. Martin, from French *martin*, little Mars, a pet name and their name for this bird.

Protonotaria citrea   Prothonotary Warbler

SCIENTIFIC NAME *Protonotaria*, from Late Latin *protonotarius*, a Vatican notary who wore a yellow robe. Reference is to the yellow head and body + *citrea*, from Latin *citrus*, the citron or lemon tree, in turn from Greek κεδρος, *kedros*, of the same meaning. Reference is to the lemon yellow on this bird.

COMMON NAME Prothonotary, see scientific name. Warbler, for the trills and quavers of the song

Psaltriparus minimus   Bushtit

SCIENTIFIC NAME *Psaltriparus*, a combination of the genera *Psaltria* and *Parus*. *Psaltria*, from Greek ψαλτρια, *psaltria*, a female harp player. Reference is to the song. *Parus*, Latin for the titmouse, from Icelandic *tittr*, anything small, and Anglo-Saxon *mase*, a small bird. *Psaltriparus* is a reference to this bird's call and small size + *minimus*, Latin for the smallest.

COMMON NAME Bush, for the habitat. Tit, a small bird, a contraction of titmouse (see scientific name).

Pseudonestor xanthophrys   Maui Parrotbill

SCIENTIFIC NAME *Pseudonestor*, false *Nester*, from Greek ψευδος, *pseudos*, false, lie, and the genus *Nestor*, which contains the Kaka parrot. In Greek mythology, Nestor was the king of Pylos at the time of the siege of Troy. As a Greek hero, he symbolized long life and wisdom. Reference is to the gray head of the Kaka, which implies long life and wisdom. *Pseudonestor* was selected as the name for this bird because it has a bill that resembles a parrot's beak but it is not a parrot + *xanthophrys*, yellow eyebrow, from Greek ξανθος, *xanthos*, yellow, and οφρυς, *ophrus*, eyebrow. Reference is to the yellow supercilium.

COMMON NAME Maui, for the natural range on the island of Maui in the Hawaiian archipelago. Parrotbill, the bill resembles that of a parrot.

Psittacula krameri   Rose-ringed Parakeet

SCIENTIFIC NAME *Psittacula*, little parrot, from the genus *Psittacus* and the Latin diminutive *-ula*. *Psittacus* is Latin for parrot, in turn from Greek ψιττακος, *psittakos*, a parrot. Reference is to the appearance + *krameri*, for W. H. Kramer (d. 1765), an Austrian zoologist and author.

COMMON NAME Rose-ringed, for the rose-colored half collar on the sides and back of the male's neck. Parakeet, Anglicized form of the French *perroquet*, another name for a parrot. Used in English to describe smaller types of parrots.

Psittirostra psittacea 'O 'U

SCIENTIFIC NAME *Psittirostra*, parrot beak, from Latin *psittacus*, a parrot, in turn from Greek ψιττακος, *psittakos*, a parrot, and Latin *rostrum*, the snout or muzzle of an animal, the beak or bill of a bird. Reference is to the shape of the beak, which has a downcurved maxilla and resembles that of a parrot + *psittacea*, somewhat like a parrot, from Latin *psittacus*, a parrot, and -*acens*, similar to. Again the reference is to the beak.

COMMON NAME 'O 'U, the Hawaiian name for this bird.

Pterocles exustus Chestnut-bellied Sandgrouse

SCIENTIFIC NAME *Pterocles*, endowed with wings, from Greek πτερον, *pteron*, feather, bird's wing, and -κλες, -*kles*, endowed with, known for. Reference is to the long primary feathers, as explained by Coenraad Jacob Temminck (1778–1858), who assigned the name + *exustus*, Latin for burnt, scorched. Reference is to the color and pattern of the plumage.

COMMON NAME Chestnut-bellied, descriptive of the male. Sand, for the habitat. Grouse, origin unknown but thought to come from French *griais*, speckled gray.

Pterodroma arminjoniana Herald Petrel

SCIENTIFIC NAME *Pterodroma*, wing runner, from Greek πτερον, *pteron*, feather, wing of a bird, and δρομος, *dromos*, race, running. Reference is to the swift, erratic flight + *arminjoniana*, for Vittorio Arminjon (1830–1897), an Italian vice admiral who circumnavigated the globe in 1865. The type specimen was collected on that trip.

COMMON NAME Herald, from the sailor's belief that this bird brought an omen or message. Petrel, little Peter, this bird pats the water with its feet when landing, which gives the appearance of walking on water. It was named for St. Peter, who was said to walk on water.

Pterodroma cahow
Bermuda Petrel

SCIENTIFIC NAME *Pterodroma* + *cahow*, a name given by early settlers in Bermuda that is onomatopoeic of the call.

COMMON NAME Bermuda, for the natural range. Petrel, see *Pterodroma arminjoniana*.

Pterodroma cervicalis
White-necked Petrel

SCIENTIFIC NAME *Pterodroma* + *cervicalis*, Latin for of the neck. Reference is to the white hind collar.

COMMON NAME White-necked, see scientific name. Petrel, see *Pterodroma arminjoniana*.

Pterodroma cookii
Cook's Petrel

SCIENTIFIC NAME *Pterodroma* + *cookii*, for James Cook (1728–1779), an English naval captain and explorer. This bird was named by George Robert Gray (1808–1872). Gray was from New Zealand, where this bird breeds and the type specimen was found. The name probably celebrates Cook's visit to New Zealand during his 1768–1771 voyage on the *Endeavour*.

COMMON NAME Cook's, see scientific name. Petrel, see *Pterodroma arminjoniana*.

Pterodroma feae
Fea's Petrel

SCIENTIFIC NAME *Pterodroma* + *feae*, for Leonardo Fea (1852–1903), an Italian ornithologist.

COMMON NAME Fea's, see scientific name. Petrel, see *Pterodroma arminjoniana*.

Pterodroma hasitata
Black-capped Petrel

SCIENTIFIC NAME *Pterodroma* + *hasitata*, a misspelling of *haesitata*, Latin for to be undecided over a course of action. The indecision in this case was whether this bird was a distinct species.

COMMON NAME Black-capped, descriptive but not a good field mark because other petrels also have black caps. Petrel, see *Pterodroma arminjoniana*.

Pterodroma hypoleuca   Bonin Petrel

SCIENTIFIC NAME *Pterodroma* + *hypoleuca*, white below, from Greek υπο, *upo*, from under, below, beneath, and λευκος, *leukos*, of color, white. Reference is to the white underparts.

COMMON NAME Bonin, for the natural range in the Bonin Islands, Japan. Petrel, see *Pterodroma arminjoniana*.

Pterodroma inexpectata   Mottled Petrel

SCIENTIFIC NAME *Pterodroma* + *inexpectata*, a form of *inexspectatus*, not expected, unforeseen. Reference is to the scarcity of this bird.

COMMON NAME Mottled, for the pattern of the plumage. Petrel, see *Pterodroma arminjoniana*.

Pterodroma longirostris   Stejneger's Petrel

SCIENTIFIC NAME *Pterodroma* + *longirostris*, long billed, from Latin *longus*, long, and *rostris*, billed, from *rostrum*, the snout or muzzle of an animal, the beak or bill of a bird.

COMMON NAME Stejneger's, for Leonhard Stejneger (1851–1943), a Norwegian ornithologist who lived in the United States. Petrel, see *Pterodroma arminjoniana*.

Pterodroma nigripennis   Black-winged Petrel

SCIENTIFIC NAME *Pterodroma* + *nigripennis*, black winged, from Latin *niger*, black, and *penna*, wing, feather. Reference is to the black band on the underwing.

COMMON NAME Black-winged, see scientific name. Petrel, see *Pterodroma arminjoniana*.

Pterodroma phaeopygia   Galapagos Petrel

SCIENTIFIC NAME *Pterodroma* + *phaeopygia*, gray rumped, from Greek φαιος, *phaios*, gray, any mixture of black and white, dusky, and πυγεων, *pugeōn*, rump, buttocks.

COMMON NAME Galapagos, for the natural range. Petrel, see *Pterodroma arminjoniana*.

Pterodroma sandwichensis Hawaiian Petrel

SCIENTIFIC NAME *Pterodroma* + *sandwichensis*, of the Sandwich Islands, an old name for the Hawaiian Islands, named for John Montagu, fourth earl of Sandwich (1718–1792), First Lord of the British Admiralty.

COMMON NAME Hawaiian, for the natural range. Petrel, see *Pterodroma arminjoniana*.

Pterodroma ultima Murphy's Petrel

SCIENTIFIC NAME *Pterodroma* + *ultima*, Latin for most distant, inhabiting the remotest of most distant parts. Reference is to the range over the Pacific Ocean.

COMMON NAME Murphy's, for Robert Cushman Murphy (1887–1973), an American ornithologist and the author of *Oceanic Birds of South America* (1936). Petrel, see *Pterodroma arminjoniana*.

Ptychoramphus aleuticus Cassin's Auklet

SCIENTIFIC NAME *Ptychoramphus*, folded beak, from Greek πτυξ, πτυχη, *ptux*, *ptukhē*, anything in folds, a fold, and ραμφος, *ramphos*, literally the crooked beaks of birds of prey, used generally for any beak or bill. Reference is to the ridges on the beak + *aleuticus*, for the range in the Aleutian Islands, Alaska.

COMMON NAME Cassin's, for John Cassin (1813–1869), a Philadelphia ornithologist with a broad knowledge of the birds of the world. Auklet, a little auk, from Old Norse *alka*, their name for several different northern birds.

Puffinus bulleri Buller's Shearwater

SCIENTIFIC NAME *Puffinus*, an English word applied in the seventeenth century to the razorbill, shearwater, and puffin. The genus name *Puffinus* is now used for the shearwaters, and the common name puffin is used for the genus *Fratercula* + *bulleri*, for Sir Walter Lawry Buller (1838–1906), a New Zealand lawyer; he became an authority on birds and wrote *A History of the Birds of New Zealand* (1873).

COMMON NAME Buller's, see scientific name. Shearwater, for the flight pattern close to the water.

Puffinus carneipes — Flesh-footed Shearwater

SCIENTIFIC NAME *Puffinus* + *carneipes*, flesh footed, from Latin *carnis*, an old nominative form of *caro*, flesh, and *pes*, foot. Reference is to the pink feet.

COMMON NAME Flesh-footed, see scientific name. Shearwater, see *Puffinus bulleri*.

Puffinus creatopus — Pink-footed Shearwater

SCIENTIFIC NAME *Puffinus* + *creatopus*, flesh footed, from Greek κρεας, *kreas*, flesh, dressed meat, and πους, *pous*, foot. Reference is to the pink feet, seen in flight against a mottled gray tail.

COMMON NAME Pink-footed, see scientific name. Shearwater, see *Puffinus bulleri*.

Puffinus gravis — Greater Shearwater

SCIENTIFIC NAME *Puffinus* + *gravis*, Latin for heavy, weighty. Reference is to this bird being heavier than the other shearwaters.

COMMON NAME Greater, for its bulk, not its length or wingspan. Shearwater, see *Puffinus bulleri*.

Puffinus griseus — Sooty Shearwater

SCIENTIFIC NAME *Puffinus* + *griseus*, a Latinized form of the English word *grey*. Reference is to the gray underside of the wings.

COMMON NAME Sooty, for the overall color of the plumage. Shearwater, see *Puffinus bulleri*.

Puffinus lherminieri — Audubon's Shearwater

SCIENTIFIC NAME *Puffinus* + *lherminieri*, for Felix Louis l'Herminier (1779–1833), a French naturalist whose father was exiled to the French colony of Guadeloupe in the West Indies. He wrote a seminal paper on the development and structure of the sternum of birds, which was widely accepted in Europe. In 1829 he was welcomed back to France and given the title of Royal Naturalist.

COMMON NAME Audubon's, for John James Audubon (1785–1851), the artist who illustrated *Birds of America* (1827–1838) and became the best-known painter of American birds. Shearwater, see *Puffinus bulleri*.

Puffinus nativitatis   Christmas Shearwater

SCIENTIFIC NAME *Puffinus* + *nativitatis*, Latin for birth or origin. Reference here is to the birth of Christ; the type specimens were collected on Christmas Island.

COMMON NAME Christmas, for the natural range on Christmas Island. Shearwater, see *Puffinus bulleri*.

Puffinus newelli   Newell's Shearwater or 'A 'O

SCIENTIFIC NAME *Puffinus* + *newelli*, for Matthias Newell (1854–1939), a missionary to Hawaii.

COMMON NAME Newel's, see scientific name. Shearwater, see *Puffinus bulleri*. 'A 'O, the Hawaiian name for this bird.

Puffinus opisthomelas   Black-vented Shearwater

SCIENTIFIC NAME *Puffinus* + *opisthomelas*, black rear, from Greek οπιο-θεν, *opisthen*, hinder parts, rear, back, and μελας, *melas*, black. Reference is to the dark undertail coverts.

COMMON NAME Black-vented, see scientific name. Shearwater, see *Puffinus bulleri*.

Puffinus pacificus   Wedge-tailed Shearwater

SCIENTIFIC NAME *Puffinus* + *pacificus*, Latin for of the Pacific Ocean.

COMMON NAME Wedge-tailed, descriptive of the tail when fanned. Shearwater, see *Puffinus bulleri*.

Puffinus puffinus   Manx Shearwater

SCIENTIFIC NAME *Puffinus* + *puffinus*.

COMMON NAME Manx, for the Isle of Man, where it was found in abundance in the late 1700s. Shearwater, see *Puffinus bulleri*.

Puffinus tenuirostris   Short-tailed Shearwater

SCIENTIFIC NAME *Puffinus* + *tenuirostris*, thin billed, from Latin *tenuis*, finely drawn, slender, thin, and *rostris*, billed, from Latin *rostrum*, the snout or muzzle of an animal, the beak or bill of a bird.

COMMON NAME Short-tailed, a poor descriptor; the tail is not obviously shorter that the other shearwaters. Shearwater, see *Puffinus bulleri*.

Pycnonotus cafer — Red-vented Bulbul

SCIENTIFIC NAME *Pycnonotus*, thick backed, from Greek πυκνος, *puknos*, a word of many meanings, here used to mean thick, and νωτον, *nōton*, back. Reference is to the thick feathers on the back + *cafer*, of South Africa, Latinized from the Arabic, *kafir*, an infidel. Reference is to the natural range.

COMMON NAME Red-vented, has red undertail coverts. Bulbul, the Persian name for this bird, imitative of the call.

Pycnonotus jocosus — Red-whiskered Bulbul

SCIENTIFIC NAME *Pycnonotus* + *jocosus*, from Latin *iocosus*, full of fun, joking, laughable. Reference is to the red cheeks of this bird, supposedly a sign of merriment.

COMMON NAME Red-whiskered, for the red cheek-patches. Bulbul, see *Pycnonotus cafer*.

Pyrocephalus rubinus — Vermilion Flycatcher

SCIENTIFIC NAME *Pyrocephalus*, fire headed, from Greek πυρ, *pur*, genitive πυρος, *puros*, fire, and κεφαλη, *kephalē*, head. Reference is to the male's bright red head + *rubinus*, Medieval Latin from French *rubin*, a ruby. Reference is to the male's red head and body.

COMMON NAME Vermilion, for the male's red head and body. Flycatcher, for the habit of catching insects in the air.

Quiscalus major — Boat-tailed Grackle

SCIENTIFIC NAME *Quiscalus*, from New Latin *quiscalis*, a quail. It is not known why this name was chosen for this genus + *major*, from Latin *maior*, greater in size, of the larger sort. This bird is larger than the common grackle but smaller than the great-tailed grackle. At the time it was named, the great-tailed grackle had not been described.

COMMON NAME Boat-tailed, for the shape of the tail in flight, the center of the tail is depressed and resembles the keel of a boat. Grackle, from Latin *graculus*, a jackdaw and other crowlike birds; the word is onomatopoeic of the birds' calls. Reference is to the appearance, which somewhat resembles a crow.

Quiscalus major, boat-tailed grackle

Quiscalus mexicanus   Great-tailed Grackle

SCIENTIFIC NAME *Quiscalus + mexicanus*, pertaining to Mexico, from Mexico. Reference is to the natural range.

COMMON NAME Great-tailed, for the large tail. Grackle, see *Quiscalus major*.

Quiscalus quiscula   Common Grackle

SCIENTIFIC NAME *Quiscalus + quiscula*.

COMMON NAME Common, abundant in its range. Grackle, see *Quiscalus major*.

Rallus elegans   King Rail

SCIENTIFIC NAME *Rallus*, Medieval Latin for a rail + *elegans*, Latin for tastefully attractive, graceful, elegant. Reference is to the appearance.

COMMON NAME King, for its fine appearance. Rail, from French *rale*, a rail.

Rallus limicola   Virginia Rail

SCIENTIFIC NAME *Rallus* + *limicola*, to live in mud, from Latin *limus*, mud, mire, slime, and *-cola*, to inhabit. Reference is to its marsh habitat.

COMMON NAME Virginia, from the region of the type specimen; the natural range covers the entire United States. Rail, from French *rale*, a rail.

Rallus longirostris   Clapper Rail

SCIENTIFIC NAME *Rallus* + *longirostris*, long billed, from Latin *longus*, long, and *rostris*, billed, from *rostrum*, the snout or muzzle of an animal, the beak or bill of a bird.

COMMON NAME Clapper, for the call, which sounds like clapping hands. Rail, from French *rale*, a rail.

Recurvirostra americana   American Avocet

SCIENTIFIC NAME *Recurvirostra*, recurved bill, from Latin *recuruo*, to bend back, cause to turn back on itself, and *rostrum*, the snout or muzzle of an animal, the beak or bill of a bird. Reference is to the long upturned bill + *americana*, of America, for the natural range and to differentiate it from the European species.

COMMON NAME American, see scientific name. Avocet, from French *avocette* and Italian *avosetta*, their names for this type of bird.

Regulus calendula   Ruby-crowned Kinglet

SCIENTIFIC NAME *Regulus*, Latin for a king ruling over a small territory, a king's son, a little king. Reference is to the small size and the ruby-colored crown + *calendula*, little lark, a diminutive of the Greek καλανδρος, *kalandros*, a kind of lark, the Calandra lark. Reference is to the loud song of this small bird, which was compared to that of a lark.

COMMON NAME Ruby-crowned, descriptive of the male. Kinglet, little king, for the size and the ruby crown.

Regulus satrapa   Golden-crowned Kinglet

SCIENTIFIC NAME *Regulus* + *satrapa*, Latin for a Persian provincial governor, in turn from Greek σατραπης, *satrapēs*, of the same meaning. Reference is to the gold crown of both sexes.

COMMON NAME Golden-crowned, descriptive. Kinglet, see *Regulus calendula*.

Rhodostethia rosea   Ross's Gull

SCIENTIFIC NAME *Rhodostethia*, rose breasted, from Greek ροδον, *rodon*, rose, and στηθος, *stēthos*, the breast. Reference is to the pink suffusion over the underparts; this color depends on the diet + *rosea*, Latin for made of roses, rose colored (used to cover a wide range of reds). Reference is to the pink underparts.

COMMON NAME Ross's, for Sir James Clark Ross (1800–1862), a Scottish polar explorer and British naval officer who is credited with the discovery of the magnetic north pole. Gull, from Celtic *gullan*, *gwylan*, *gwelan*, all names for this type of bird.

Rhodothraupis celaeno   Crimson-collared Grosbeak

SCIENTIFIC NAME *Rhodothraupis*, rose tanager, from Greek ροδον, *rodon*, rose, and the genus *Thraupis*, a South American tanager. Reference is to the rose on the male and to the general body shape + *celaeno*, there are several women in Greek mythology with the name Celaeno, three of them have an association with birds or with this bird in particular. The most famous is Celaeno, daughter of Atlas and Pleione; she was one of the Pleiades, which were changed into doves before becoming stars. Another was one of the Harpies, which were half bird and half maiden. The third was Celaeno the Amazon. The natural range of the genus *Thraupis* includes the Amazon region.

COMMON NAME Crimson-collared, for the male's red collar. Grosbeak, large beak, from French *grosbec*, *gros*, large, and *bec*, beak.

Rhynchopsitta pachyrhyncha   Thick-billed Parrot

SCIENTIFIC NAME *Rhynchopsitta*, parrot billed, from Greek ρυγχος, *rugkhos*, the snout or muzzle of an animal, the beak or bill of a bird, and ψιττακος, *psittakos*, a parrot + *pachyrhyncha*, thick billed, from Greek παχος, *pakhos*, thick, and ρυγχος, *rugkhos*. Reference is to the heavy bill.

COMMON NAME Thick-billed, see scientific name. Parrot, little Peter, from French *perrot*, a diminutive of Pierre (Peter), a pet name for this type of bird.

Ridgwayia pinicola   Aztec Thrush

SCIENTIFIC NAME *Ridgwayia*, for Robert Ridgway (1850–1929), an American ornithologist who wrote *The Birds of North and Middle America* (1901–1919) + *pinicola*, to live in a pine tree, from Latin *pinus*, a pine tree, and *-cola*, to inhabit. Reference is to the habitat in mountain pines.

COMMON NAME Aztec, for the natural range in Mexico. Thrush, from Middle English *thrusch*, their name for this type of bird.

Riparia riparia   Bank Swallow

SCIENTIFIC NAME *Riparia*, Latin for of or associated with banks. Reference is to the nesting sites in stream banks + *riparia*.

COMMON NAME Bank, see scientific name. Swallow, from Anglo-Saxon *swalewe*, their name for this type of bird.

Rissa brevirostris   Red-legged Kittiwake

SCIENTIFIC NAME *Rissa*, Latinized form of the Icelandic *rita*, their name for this type of bird + *brevirostris*, short beaked, from Latin *breuis*, short, and *rostrum*, the snout or muzzle of an animal, the beak or bill of a bird.

COMMON NAME Red-legged, for the coral-red legs. Kittiwake, imitative of the call.

Rissa tridactyla   Black-legged Kittiwake

SCIENTIFIC NAME *Rissa* + *tridactyla*, having three toes, from Greek τρι-δακτυλιαιος, *tridaktuliaios*, having three fingers or toes, from τρι, *tri*, three, and δακτυλος, *daktulos*, finger or toe.

COMMON NAME Black-legged, descriptive. Kittiwake, imitative of the call.

Rostrhamus sociabilis   Snail Kite

SCIENTIFIC NAME *Rostrhamus*, hooked bill, from Latin *rostrum*, the snout or muzzle of an animal, the beak or bill of a bird, and *hamus*, a hook. Reference is to the sharply hooked bill + *sociabilis*, Latin for easily joined in partnership, close, intimate. Reference is to the behavior of nesting in colonies.

COMMON NAME Snail, for the limited diet of snails of the genus *Pomacea*. Kite, from Anglo-Saxon *cyta*, their name for this type of bird. The kite that is flown on a string was so named because it appeared to hang in the air like the bird appears to do in flight.

Rynchops niger   Black Skimmer

SCIENTIFIC NAME *Rynchops*, beak-face, from Greek ρυγχος, *rugkhos*, the snout or muzzle of an animal, the beak or bill of a bird, and οψ, *ops*, face, eye, appearance. Reference is to the large bill, which seems to fill the face at its base + *niger*, Latin for black. Reference is to the black upperparts.

COMMON NAME Black, see scientific name. Skimmer, for the feeding habit of skimming the water with the mandible.

Salpinctes obsoletus Rock Wren

SCIENTIFIC NAME *Salpinctes*, from Greek σαλπιγκτης, *salpigktēs*, a trumpeter. Reference is to the call + *obsoletus*, Latin for shabby, dingy, dirty. Reference is to the dull grayish brown plumage.

COMMON NAME Rock, for the habitat. Wren, from Anglo-Saxon *wraenna*, their name for this type of bird.

Sayornis nigricans Black Phoebe

SCIENTIFIC NAME *Sayornis*, Say's bird, for Thomas Say (1787–1834), an American naturalist and a founding member of the Philadelphia Academy of Natural History. He wrote the three-volume *American Entomology* (1824–1828) and the six-volume *American Conchology* (1830–1834), as well as the report on birds for Stephen H. Long's expedition to the Rocky Mountains (1819–1820). The last part of the word is from the Greek ορνις, *ornis*, a bird + *nigricans*, Latin for shading into black, verging on black. Reference is to the dark upperparts.

COMMON NAME Black, see scientific name. Phoebe, one of the Greek Titans; later Greek writers identify her with the moon goddess. The other major opinion is that this name is imitative of the call.

Sayornis phoebe Eastern Phoebe

SCIENTIFIC NAME *Sayornis* + *phoebe*, see *Sayornis nigricans*.

COMMON NAME Eastern, for the natural range in the United States. Phoebe, see *Sayornis nigricans*.

Sayornis saya Say's Phoebe

SCIENTIFIC NAME *Sayornis* + *saya*, for Thomas Say (1787–1834), see *Sayornis nigricans*.

COMMON NAME Say's, see scientific name. Phoebe, see *Sayornis nigricans*.

Scolopax minor American Woodcock

SCIENTIFIC NAME *Scolopax*, a form of the Greek ασκαλωπας, *askalōpas*, the woodcock + *minor*, Latin for smaller in size, height, or extent. Refers to the size relative to the Eurasian woodcock.

COMMON NAME American, for the natural range and to differentiate it from the Eurasian woodcock. Woodcock, from Anglo-Saxon *wudu-cocc*, a woods cock, for the habitat and appearance.

Seiurus aurocapillus   Ovenbird

SCIENTIFIC NAME *Seiurus*, to wag the tail, from Greek σειω, *seiō*, to shake, move to and fro, and ουρα, *oura*, tail. According to the *Oxford Greek-English Lexicon* (1996), ουρα, *oura* should not be used for the tail of birds, but is restricted to other animals. Reference is to its habit of quickly jerking the tail upright and then slowly letting it down + *aurocapillus*, golden headed, from Latin *aurum*, gold, both as a metal and as a yellowish color, and *capillus*, the hair of the head. Reference is to the narrow orange crown.

COMMON NAME Ovenbird, for the shape of the nest, which resembles a small domed oven.

Seiurus motacilla   Louisiana Waterthrush

SCIENTIFIC NAME *Seiurus* + *motacilla*, Latin for a little mover, wagtail. (see *Motacilla alba*).

COMMON NAME Louisiana, for the region of the type specimen. Waterthrush, this bird is found around streams and ponds and has breast streaks that make it look like a thrush.

Seiurus noveboracensis   Northern Waterthrush

SCIENTIFIC NAME *Seiurus* + *noveboracensis*, belonging to New York, from Latin *nouus*, new, *Eboracum*, the Roman name for the city of York, England, and *-ensis*, belonging to. The type specimen was found in New York State.

COMMON NAME Northern, for the breeding range. Waterthrush, see *Seiurus motacilla*.

Selasphorus platycercus   Broad-tailed Hummingbird

SCIENTIFIC NAME *Selasphorus*, to bear a flame, from Greek σελας, *selas*, light, brightness, flame, and φορος, *phoros*, bearing. The males of this genus have iridescent gorgets that make them appear to be carrying a flame on their throats + *platycercus*, broad tailed, from Greek πλατυς, *platus*, wide, broad, and κερκος, *kerkos*, tail of an animal; this word should not be used for birds but is restricted to other sorts of animals.

COMMON NAME Broad-tailed, descriptive. Hummingbird, for the buzzing hum of the wingbeats.

Selasphorus rufus
Rufous Hummingbird

SCIENTIFIC NAME *Selasphorus* + *rufus*, Latin for red of various shades, tawny. Reference is to the overall color of the male's plumage.

COMMON NAME Rufous, see scientific name. Hummingbird, see *Selasphorus platycercus*.

Selasphorus sasin
Allen's Hummingbird

SCIENTIFIC NAME *Selasphorus* + *sasin*, the Nootka Indian (Pacific Northwest coast) name for this bird.

COMMON NAME Allen's, for Charles Andrew Allen (1841–1930), an amateur ornithologist and collector. He collected what was thought to be the type specimen of this bird in 1877 and sent it to Henry Wetherbee Henshaw (1850–1930), who named the species in honor of Allen. It was later discovered that this bird had been described in 1830 by René P. Lesson (1794–1849) and given the species name of *sasin*. Allen lost the scientific name but retained the common name. Hummingbird, see *Selasphorus platycercus*.

Serinus mozambicus
Yellow-fronted Canary

SCIENTIFIC NAME *Serinus*, from French *serin*, a canary + *mozambicus*, of Mozambique. Reference is to the natural range.

COMMON NAME Yellow-fronted, for the yellow forehead and breast. Canary, for the Canary Islands, from which this type of bird was first brought to Europe.

Setophaga ruticilla
American Redstart

SCIENTIFIC NAME *Setophaga*, moth eater, from Greek σης, σητος, *sēs*, *sētos*, a moth, and φαγειν, *phagein*, eat, devour + *ruticilla*, red tailed, from Latin *rutilus*, a warm or glowing red, and -*cilla*, thought by William Swainson (1789–1855) to mean tail (see *Bombycilla cedrorum*). Reference is to the male's orange-red tail.

COMMON NAME American, for the natural range and to distinguish it from the European redstart. Redstart, from Anglo-Saxon *read*, red, and *steort*, tail.

Sialia currucoides Mountain Bluebird

SCIENTIFIC NAME *Sialia*, from Greek οιαλις, *sialis*, a kind of bird; Athenaeus used this word for a bird without further elaboration + *currucoides*, to look like a lesser whitethroat (*Sylvia curruca*), from the species epithet *curruca*, and Greek -οιδες, -*oides*, that which is seen, form, shape, resembling.

COMMON NAME Mountain, for the breeding range. Bluebird, for the predominant color.

Sialia mexicana Western Bluebird

SCIENTIFIC NAME *Sialia* + *mexicana*, of Mexico. Reference is to the region of the type specimen.

COMMON NAME Western, for the natural range in the United States. Bluebird, see *Sialia currucoides*.

Sialia sialis Eastern Bluebird

SCIENTIFIC NAME *Sialia* + *sialis*.

COMMON NAME Eastern, for the natural range in the United States. Bluebird, see *Sialia currucoides*.

Sicalis flaveola Saffron Finch

SCIENTIFIC NAME *Sicalis*, a form of Greek ουκαλις, *sukalis*, the black-capped and other warblers. Reference is to this bird resembling a warbler + *flaveola*, little yellow, from Latin *flauus*, yellow, especially pale yellow or golden, and the diminutive -*ola*. This is a small, pale yellow bird.

COMMON NAME Saffron, for the overall color of the plumage. Finch, from Anglo-Saxon *finc*, their name for this bird, an imitation of the call. Other languages have similar names for the finch for the same reason.

Sitta canadensis Red-breasted Nuthatch

SCIENTIFIC NAME *Sitta*, from Greek οιττη, *sittē*, a nuthatch, originally used by Aristotle for a bird that pecked on a tree + *canadensis*, Latin for belonging to Canada. Reference is to the year-round range.

COMMON NAME Red-breasted, for the male's orange breast; the female's orange breast is much paler. Nuthatch, a corruption of *nuthack*, in reference to the feeding behavior of wedging a nut in tree bark and pecking at it until it breaks open.

Sitta carolinensis   White-breasted Nuthatch

SCIENTIFIC NAME *Sitta* + *carolinensis*, Latin for belonging to the Carolinas. Reference is to the Carolina colonies, an area encompassing the southeastern United States, where it was first found.

COMMON NAME White-breasted, both sexes have white breasts. Nuthatch, see *Sitta canadensis*.

Sitta pusilla   Brown-headed Nuthatch

SCIENTIFIC NAME *Sitta* + *pusilla*, Latin for very small, tiny, wee.

COMMON NAME Brown-headed, both sexes have brown heads. Nuthatch, see *Sitta canadensis*.

Sitta pygmaea   Pygmy Nuthatch

SCIENTIFIC NAME *Sitta* + *pygmaea*, from Latin *Pygmae*, in turn from Greek Πυγμαιοι, *Pugmaioi*, a mythological race of dwarfs on the upper Nile who were attacked each year by migrating cranes. The root word is πυγμη, *pugmē*, the distance from the elbows to the knuckles. This was representative of the height of the Pygmies. Reference is to the small size of this bird; it is the United States' smallest nuthatch.

COMMON NAME Pygmy, see scientific name. Nuthatch, see *Sitta canadensis*.

Somateria fischeri   Spectacled Eider

SCIENTIFIC NAME *Somateria*, body wool, from Greek σωμα, *sōma*, body, and εριον, *erion*, wool. Reference is to the thick down. It lines its nest with this down, and this was once collected for commercial use + *fischeri*, for Johann Gotthelf Fischer von Waldheim (1771–1853), a German physician, paleontologist, geologist, and zoologist. He lived in Russia most of his life and founded the Natural History Society of Moscow.

COMMON NAME Spectacled, for the plumage pattern around the eyes that make this bird appear to be wearing glasses. Eider, from Icelandic and Old Norse *aedr*, their name for this type of bird.

Somateria mollissima   Common Eider

SCIENTIFIC NAME *Somateria* + *mollissima*, softest, the Latin superlative of *mollis*, soft. Reference is to the down.

COMMON NAME Common, abundant in its range. Eider, see *Somateria fischeri*.

Sitta pusilla, brown-headed nuthatch

Somateria spectabilis   King Eider

SCIENTIFIC NAME *Somateria + spectabilis*, Latin for able to be seen or looked at, outstanding in appearance. Reference is to the male's showy colors.

COMMON NAME King, for the protruding bright orange area of the forehead, which suggests a golden crown. Eider, see *Somateria fischeri*.

Sphyrapicus nuchalis   Red-naped Sapsucker

SCIENTIFIC NAME *Sphyrapicus*, hammer woodpecker, from Greek σφυρα, *sphura*, a hammer, and Latin *picus*, a woodpecker, specifically the great black woodpecker + *nuchalis*, Modern Latin for *nuchal*, the nape of the neck. Reference is to the red nape of both sexes.

COMMON NAME Red-naped, both sexes have red napes. Sapsucker, for the feeding habit of pecking holes in trees and drinking the sap.

Sphyrapicus ruber   Red-breasted Sapsucker

SCIENTIFIC NAME *Sphyrapicus* + *ruber*, Latin for red, including some shades of orange. Reference is to the red head and breast.

COMMON NAME Red-breasted, descriptive. Sapsucker, see *Sphyrapicus nuchalis*.

Sphyrapicus thyroideus   Williamson's Sapsucker

SCIENTIFIC NAME *Sphyrapicus* + *thyroideus*, resembling a shield, from Greek θυρεος, *thureos*, an oblong shield, and -οιδες, *-oides*, that which is seen, form, shape, resembling. Reference is to the black patch on the female's breast, which resembles a shield.

COMMON NAME Williamson's, for Robert Stockton Williamson (1824–1882), the U.S. Army officer in charge of the Pacific Railroad Survey in northern California and Oregon. The survey's surgeon collected several woodpeckers thought to be new to science; in 1857 he named the species for Williamson. In 1851 John Cassin (1813–1869) had collected and named a sapsucker species, *thyroideus*. It was later discovered that these woodpeckers all belonged to the same species, even though they are quite different in appearance–the specimens collected by the surgeon were all males and those collected by Cassin were all females. When the birds were later found nesting together, the error was recognized. The principle of priority gave the scientific name to *thyroideus*, but Williamson kept the common name. Sapsucker, see *Sphyrapicus nuchalis*.

Sphyrapicus varius   Yellow-bellied Sapsucker

SCIENTIFIC NAME *Sphyrapicus* + *varius*, Latin for having two or more contrasting colors, variegated. Reference is to the extensive white barring on the black back and wings.

COMMON NAME Yellow-bellied, descriptive. Sapsucker, see *Sphyrapicus nuchalis*.

Spindalis zena   Western Spindalis

SCIENTIFIC NAME *Spindalis*, from Greek σπινδαλος, *spindalos*, an Indian bird akin to the ατταγας, *attagas*, the francolin, of the genus *Tetrao*. *Tetrao* is from Greek τετραων, *tetraōn*, a pheasant, a grouse. Although this name was assigned without comment, a possible reference is to the colors of this bird resembling those of a pheasant + *zena*, from Greek ζηνη, *zēnē*, the goldfinch. Reference is to the color pattern.

COMMON NAME Western, for its natural range in the Bahamas. Spindalis, from the genus name.

Spiza americana   Dickcissel

SCIENTIFIC NAME *Spiza*, from Greek σπιζα, *spiza*, the chaffinch, a finch + *americana*, of America, for the natural range.

COMMON NAME Dickcissel, imitative of the call.

Spizella arborea   American Tree Sparrow

SCIENTIFIC NAME *Spizella*, a little finch, from Greek σπιζα, *spiza*, the chaffinch, a finch, and the Latin diminutive *-ella* + *arborea*, Latin for of or belonging to trees. Reference is to the habitat.

COMMON NAME American, for the natural range. Tree, for the habitat. Sparrow, from Anglo-Saxon *spearwa*, to flutter. Originally used to denote any small bird.

Spizella atrogularis   Black-chinned Sparrow

SCIENTIFIC NAME *Spizella* + *atrogularis*, black throated, from Latin *ater*, black, and Modern Latin *gularis*, throated, from Latin *gula*, throat.

COMMON NAME Black-chinned, for the black chin and throat. Sparrow, see *Spizella arborea*.

Spizella breweri   Brewer's Sparrow

SCIENTIFIC NAME *Spizella* + *breweri*, for Thomas Mayo Brewer (1814–1880), a physician, editor, and publisher. He collected specimens for John James Audubon (1785–1851), who named this and other birds in his honor. Brewer wrote *North American Oology* (1857), only the first volume of which was ever published because of the high cost of reproducing the egg illustrations.

COMMON NAME Brewer's, see scientific name. Sparrow, see *Spizella arborea*.

Spizella pallida   Clay-colored Sparrow

SCIENTIFIC NAME *Spizella* + *pallida*, Latin for pale, colorless, pallid. Reference is to the lackluster plumage.

COMMON NAME Clay-colored, for the buff color of the nonbreeding plumage. Sparrow, see *Spizella arborea.*

Spizella passerina Chipping Sparrow

SCIENTIFIC NAME *Spizella* + *passerina*, Latin for of or for sparrows.

COMMON NAME Chipping, for the song of short, clipped notes. Sparrow, see *Spizella arborea.*

Spizella pusilla Field Sparrow

SCIENTIFIC NAME *Spizella* + *pusilla*, Latin for very small, tiny, wee.

COMMON NAME Field, for the habitat. Sparrow, see *Spizella arborea.*

Sporophila torqueola White-collared Seedeater

SCIENTIFIC NAME *Sporophila*, seed loving, from Greek σπορος, *sporos*, seed, and φιλος, *philos*, beloved, dear, loving. Reference is to the diet + *torqueola*, from Latin *toques*, a collar of twisted metal, a marking resembling a collar. Reference is to the buff-white partial collar.

COMMON NAME White-collared, the partial collar can sometimes appear white. Seedeater, for the diet.

Stelgidopteryx serripennis Northern Rough-winged Swallow

SCIENTIFIC NAME *Stelgidopteryx*, scraper wing, from Greek στελγις, *stelgis*, a scraper, and πτερυξ, *pterux*, the wing of a bird. Reference is to the recurved hooks on the first primary + *serripennis*, saw winged, from Latin *serra*, a saw, and *penna*, a wing. Reference is the same as for the genus.

COMMON NAME Northern, for the breeding range. Rough-winged, see the scientific name. Swallow, from Anglo-Saxon *swalewe*, their name for this type of bird.

Stellula calliope Calliope Hummingbird

SCIENTIFIC NAME *Stellula*, a little star, from Latin *stella*, star, and the diminutive *-ula*. Reference is to the bright plumage and small size. This is the smallest bird in the United States + *calliope*, the muse of epic poetry. Classically nine in number, the Muses were goddesses of the arts, history, and astronomy. They were all beautiful, as is this little bird.

COMMON NAME Calliope, see scientific name. Hummingbird, for the buzzing hum of the wingbeats.

Stercorarius longicaudus Long-tailed Jaeger

SCIENTIFIC NAME *Stercorarius*, Latin for connected with dung. Reference is to the scavenging feeding habits + *longicaudus*, long tailed, from Latin *longus*, long, and *cauda*, tail.

COMMON NAME Long-tailed, descriptive. Jaeger, from German *jager*, a hunter. This word originally was applied to hunters along the Rhine, who were also plunderers and robbers. Jaegers do hunt independently but spend a good deal of time chasing other seabirds and stealing their food.

Stercorarius maccormicki South Polar Skua

SCIENTIFIC NAME *Stercorarius* + *maccormicki*, for Robert McCormick (1800–1890), a surgeon in the British Navy, an explorer, and the surgeon for the British Antarctic Expedition (1839–1843).

COMMON NAME South Polar, for the breeding range in the Antarctic. Skua, a name adopted by Hoier (c. 1604) from the Faeroese (Faeroe Islands) *skugvur*, their name for this type of bird.

Stercorarius parasiticus Parasitic Jaeger

SCIENTIFIC NAME *Stercorarius* + *parasiticus*, Latin for of or characteristic of a parasite. Reference is to the habit of stealing food from other birds, a behavior shared by all jaegers.

COMMON NAME Parasitic, see scientific name. Jaeger, see *Stercorarius longicaudus*.

Stercorarius pomarinus Pomarine Jaeger

SCIENTIFIC NAME *Stercorarius* + *pomarinus*, nose lid, from Greek πωμα, πωματο, *pōma*, *pōmato*, a lid or cover, and ρυγχος, *rugkhos*, the snout or muzzle of an animal, the beak or bill of a bird, also ρις, ριν, *ris*, *rin*, a beak. This Latinized word was coined and misspelled by Coenraad Jacob Temminck (1778–1858). The correct spelling would be *pomatorhinus*, from the same elements. Reference is to the cover over the nostrils, which develops during breeding season.

COMMON NAME Pomarine, see scientific name. Jaeger, see *Stercorarius longicaudus*.

Stercorarius skua Great Skua

SCIENTIFIC NAME *Stercorarius* + *skua*, a name adopted by Hoier (c. 1604) from the Faeroese (Faeroe Islands) *skugvur*, their name for this type of bird.

COMMON NAME Great, for the size; this is the United States' largest skua. Skua, see scientific name.

Sterna albifrons   Little Tern

SCIENTIFIC NAME *Sterna*, Latinized by Turner (1544) from the Old English *stern* or *starn*, a tern + *albifrons*, white forehead, from Latin *albus*, white, and *frons*, the forehead, front.

COMMON NAME Little, for the small size. Tern, from Norwegian *terna*, Danish *terne*, and Old English *stern* or *starn*, their names for this type of bird.

Sterna aleutica   Aleutian Tern

SCIENTIFIC NAME *Sterna* + *aleutica*, of the Aleutian Islands, Alaska. Reference is to the breeding range.

COMMON NAME Aleutian, see scientific name. Tern, see *Sterna albifrons*.

Sterna anaethetus   Bridled Tern

SCIENTIFIC NAME *Sterna* + *anaethetus*, from Greek αναισθητος, *anaisthētos*, without perception or common sense, stupid. Reference is to the nesting birds being easily caught by sailors, who ate them.

COMMON NAME Bridled, for the black stripe that runs from the base of the bill through the eye and to the back of the crown. The illusion is that of a bridle. Tern, see *Sterna albifrons*.

Sterna antillarum   Least Tern

SCIENTIFIC NAME *Sterna* + *antillarum*, of the Lesser Antilles. Reference is to the site of the type specimen.

COMMON NAME Least, for the size; this is the United States' smallest tern. Tern, see *Sterna albifrons*.

Sterna bergii   Great Crested Tern

SCIENTIFIC NAME *Sterna* + *bergii*, for C. H. Bergius (1790–1818), a German naturalist.

COMMON NAME Great, for the size. Crested, descriptive. Tern, see *Sterna albifrons*.

Sterna caspia   Caspian Tern

SCIENTIFIC NAME *Sterna + caspia*, of the Caspian Sea. Reference is to the region of the type specimen.

COMMON NAME Caspian, see scientific name. Tern, see *Sterna albifrons*.

Sterna dougallii   Roseate Tern

SCIENTIFIC NAME *Sterna + dougallii*, George Montagu (1753–1815) named this bird in honor of a "Dr. M'Dougall," who collected the type specimen in 1812. The most likely candidate is Dr. Patrick MacDougall (1770–1817) of Glasgow, Scotland. This was the region of the type specimen, and he was the only MacDougall, M'Dougall, or McDougall practicing medicine in Glasgow in 1812.

COMMON NAME Roseate, for the faint pink breast, usually seen in breeding plumage. Tern, see *Sterna albifrons*.

Sterna elegans   Elegant Tern

SCIENTIFIC NAME *Sterna + elegans*, Latin for tastefully attractive, graceful, elegant. Reference is to the appearance of the breeding plumage.

COMMON NAME Elegant, see scientific name. Tern, see *Sterna albifrons*.

Sterna forsteri   Forster's Tern

SCIENTIFIC NAME *Sterna + forsteri*, for Johann Reinhold Forster (1729–1798), a German naturalist who accompanied Captain Cook on the 1772 circumnavigation of the world. Forster published the first book on American fauna, *A Catalogue of the Animals of North America* (1771).

COMMON NAME Forster's, see scientific name. Tern, see *Sterna albifrons*.

Sterna fuscata   Sooty Tern

SCIENTIFIC NAME *Sterna + fuscata*, from Latin *fuscus*, dark colored, dusky. Reference is to the dark plumage.

COMMON NAME Sooty, for the dark plumage. Tern, see *Sterna albifrons*.

Sterna hirundo   Common Tern

SCIENTIFIC NAME *Sterna + hirundo*, Latin for a swallow, a martin. An old common name for terns was sea swallow, for the forked tail and swept-back wings that resembled those of a swallow.

COMMON NAME Common, abundant in its range. Tern, see *Sterna albi-frons*.

Sterna lunata   Gray-backed Tern

SCIENTIFIC NAME *Sterna* + *lunata*, Latin for crescent shaped. Reference is to the outline of the swept-back wings in flight.

COMMON NAME Gray-backed, descriptive. Tern, see *Sterna albifrons*.

Sterna maxima   Royal Tern

SCIENTIFIC NAME *Sterna* + *maxima*, from Latin *maximus*, largest. Although this tern is larger than most other terns, the largest is the Caspian tern.

COMMON NAME Royal, for the impressive size. Tern, see *Sterna albifrons*.

Sterna nilotica   Gull-billed Tern

SCIENTIFIC NAME *Sterna* + *nilotica*, Latin for of or belonging to the Nile River. Reference is to the region of the type specimen.

COMMON NAME Gull-billed, the bill is thick and less pointed that that of other terns, more like that of a gull. Tern, see *Sterna albifrons*.

Sterna paradisaea   Arctic Tern

SCIENTIFIC NAME *Sterna* + *paradisaea*, Late Latin for paradise, originally from Old Persian *pairidaeza*, a park. This Persian word was used by translators of the Bible from Hebrew into Greek for the Garden of Eden; later it came to mean heaven or paradise. This bird was named by Erik Pontoppidan (1698–1764), the Bishop of Bergen, using the type specimen collected on Christmas Island.

COMMON NAME Arctic, for the breeding range. Tern, see *Sterna albifrons*.

Sterna sandvicensis   Sandwich Tern

SCIENTIFIC NAME *Sterna* + *sandvicensis*, Latin for belonging to Sandwich, Kent, England. Reference is to the region of the type specimen.

COMMON NAME Sandwich, see scientific name. Tern, see *Sterna albifrons*.

Streptopelia chinensis   Spotted Dove

SCIENTIFIC NAME *Streptopelia*, from Greek στρεπτος, *streptos*, twisted, a shirt of chain mail, a collar of twisted or linked metal, and πελεια, *peleia*, a dove or pigeon. Reference is to the black and white partial collar on the neck of the Eurasian collared-dove, the first of this genus to be named. The name also fits this dove well: it has spotted areas on the neck that resemble a chain-mail collar + *chinensis*, Latin for belonging to China. This bird was introduced to southern California; its natural range is China.

COMMON NAME Spotted, for the spots on the neck. Dove, from Anglo-Saxon *dufan*, to dive, for its irregular flight pattern.

Streptopelia decaocto   Eurasian Collared-Dove

SCIENTIFIC NAME *Streptopelia* + *decaocto*, eighteen, from Greek δεκα, *deka*, ten, and οκτω, *oktō*, eight. This name comes from a Greek folktale about a servant girl who was paid only eighteen pieces a year for her work. She prayed to the gods to release her from this situation and to let everyone know how poorly she was being treated. The gods answered her prayers by turning her into a dove that called "decaocto." This species name was derived from this story, even though this dove's call does not sound like the one described.

COMMON NAME Eurasian, for the natural range. Collared, for the black and white partial collar. Dove, see *Streptopelia chinensis*.

Streptopelia risoria   Ringed Turtle-Dove

SCIENTIFIC NAME *Streptopelia* + *risoria*, from Latin *risoris*, one who laughs. Reference is to the call.

COMMON NAME Ringed, for the black and white partial collar. Turtle, from Latin *turtur*, a turtle-dove, onomatopoeic of the call. Dove, see *Streptopelia chinensis*.

Strix nebulosa   Great Gray Owl

SCIENTIFIC NAME *Strix*, Latin for a kind of owl, in turn from Greek στριξ, *strix*, an owl + *nebulosa*, characterized by or subject to mists or clouds, cloudy. Reference is to the pattern and color of the plumage, resembling that of a dark cloud.

COMMON NAME Great, for the size; this is the United States' longest owl. Gray, for the overall color of the plumage. Owl, from Anglo-Saxon *ule*, owl, and from Latin *ululo*, to cry out. Both words are onomatopoeic of the owl's call.

Strix occidentalis   Spotted Owl

SCIENTIFIC NAME *Strix* + *occidentalis*, Latin for of or connected with the west, coming from the west, western. Reference is to the natural range in the United States.

COMMON NAME Spotted, has white spots on the plumage. Owl, see *Strix nebulosa*.

Strix varia   Barred Owl

SCIENTIFIC NAME *Strix* + *varia*, Latin for of many different colors, variegated. Reference is to the variegated pattern of the plumage.

COMMON NAME Barred, for the striped pattern of the plumage, best seen on the underparts. Owl, see *Strix nebulosa*.

Sturnella magna   Eastern Meadowlark

SCIENTIFIC NAME *Sturnella*, a little starling, from Latin *sturnus*, a starling, and the diminutive *-ella*. This genus is actually larger than the starling + *magna*, Latin for great in size, big.

COMMON NAME Eastern, for the natural range in the United States. Meadow, for the habitat. Lark, from Middle English, a contraction of *lavercock*, the name for lark. This bird was called a lark because of its song, but it is in the blackbird family.

Sturnella neglecta   Western Meadowlark

SCIENTIFIC NAME *Sturnella* + *neglecta*, Latin for neglected. This species looks so much like the eastern meadowlark that it was not placed in a separate species until about a hundred years after the description of *Sturnella magna*. (There are subtle marking differences but marked contrast in the songs of these two species.) John James Audubon (1785–1851) chose this species name to point out how long this separate species had been overlooked.

COMMON NAME Western, for the natural range in the United States. Meadowlark, see *Sturnella magna*.

Sturnus vulgaris — European Starling

SCIENTIFIC NAME *Sturnus*, Latin for starling + *vulgaris*, Latin for commonly found, ordinary.

COMMON NAME European, for the natural range. Starling, from Old English *staerline*, from *staer*, the original word for starling, and the diminutive *-line*. The suffix was probably added as a form of pet name.

Sula dactylatra — Masked Booby

SCIENTIFIC NAME *Sula*, the Icelandic name for this type of bird; it also means a foolish person. Reference is to the birds being easily caught and their awkward movement on land + *dactylatra*, black finger, from Greek δακτυλος, *daktulos*, a finger or toe, and Latin *ater*, black. Reference is to the black remiges, which resemble fingers–not the toes, which are yellow to olive-gray.

COMMON NAME Masked, for the black markings around the eyes. Booby, from Spanish and Portuguese *bobo*, for a dolt or buffoon. Reference is the same as the genus name.

Sula leucogaster — Brown Booby

SCIENTIFIC NAME *Sula* + *leucogaster*, white belly, from Greek λευκος, *leukos*, of color, white, and γαστηρ, *gastēr*, belly.

COMMON NAME Brown, for the color of the upperparts. Booby, see *Sula dactylatra*.

Sula nebouxii — Blue-footed Booby

SCIENTIFIC NAME *Sula* + *nebouxii*, for Adolphe Simon Neboux (1806–?), a French surgeon and naturalist who collected natural history specimens and served as surgeon on the Pacific voyage of the *Venus* (1836–1839).

COMMON NAME Blue-footed, has bright blue feet and legs. Booby, see *Sula dactylatra*.

Sula sula — Red-footed Booby

SCIENTIFIC NAME *Sula* + *sula*.

COMMON NAME Red-footed, has bright red feet and legs. Booby, see *Sula dactylatra*.

Surnia ulula   Northern Hawk Owl

SCIENTIFIC NAME *Surnia*, Latinized word coined by A. M. C. Dumeril (1774–1860), a French zoologist, probably from Greek ουρνιον, *surnion*, a bird of ill omen + *ulula*, Latin for an owl, imitative of the call.

COMMON NAME Northern, for the natural range. Hawk, for the appearance, perching posture, and the hawklike behavior of hunting in the daytime. Owl, from Anglo-Saxon *ule*, owl, and from Latin *ululo*, to cry out.

Synthliboramphus antiquus   Ancient Murrelet

SCIENTIFIC NAME *Synthliboramphus*, compressed beak, from Greek συνθ-λιβω, *sunthlibō*, press together, compress, and ραμφος, *ramphos*, literally the crooked beak of a bird of prey, generally any beak or bill. Reference is to the laterally compressed bill + *antiquus*, Latin for ancient, old. Reference is to the gray feathers on the head in breeding plumage, giving the impression of old age.

COMMON NAME Ancient, see scientific name. Murrelet, diminutive of the English *murre*, a type of auk, guillemot, or puffin, depending on the geographic region in which the word is used.

Synthliboramphus craveri   Craveri's Murrelet

SCIENTIFIC NAME *Synthliboramphus* + *craveri*, for Frederico Craveri (1815–1890), an Italian scientist who studied in several fields. He collected the type specimen off Baja California, Mexico.

COMMON NAME Craveri's, see scientific name. Murrelet, see *Synthliboramphus antiquus*.

Synthliboramphus hypoleucus   Xantus's Murrelet

SCIENTIFIC NAME *Synthliboramphus* + *hypoleucus*, white below, from Greek υπο, *upo*, from under, below, and λευκος, *leukos*, of color, white. Reference is to the white underparts.

COMMON NAME Xantus's, for John Xantus (1825–1894), also known as Louis de Versy and Lajos Janosz Xantus de Versy. He collected birds in the United States and Mexico and returned to his native Hungary to be curator of the Zoological Garden of Budapest. Murrelet, see *Synthliboramphus antiquus*.

Tachybaptus dominicus — Least Grebe

SCIENTIFIC NAME *Tachybaptus*, quick dipped, from Greek ταχυς, *takhus*, swift, fleet, quick, and βαπτω, *baptō*, to dip. Reference is to the behavior of quickly dipping beneath the water surface + *dominicus*, of Santo Domingo (Hispaniola), for the natural range.

COMMON NAME Least, for the size; this is the United States' smallest grebe. Grebe, from French *grebe*, a crest of feathers on a bird's head, a comb.

Tachycineta bicolor — Tree Swallow

SCIENTIFIC NAME *Tachycineta*, swift mover, from Greek ταχυς, *takhus*, swift, fleet, quick, and κινεω, *kineō*, set in motion, move. Reference is to the speed of the flight + *bicolor*, Latin for having two colors. Reference is to the sharply contrasting colors of the upper- and underparts.

COMMON NAME Tree, for the nesting sites in holes in trees. Swallow, from Anglo-Saxon *swalewe*, their name for this type of bird.

Tachycineta cyaneoviridis — Bahama Swallow

SCIENTIFIC NAME *Tachycineta* + *cyaneoviridis*, dark blue and green, from Latin *cyaneus*, dark blue, in turn from Greek κυανεος, *kuaneos*, dark blue, and Latin *viridis*, green. Reference is to the blue wings and the green back.

COMMON NAME Bahama, for the natural range. Swallow, see *Tachycineta bicolor*.

Tachycineta thalassina — Violet-green Swallow

SCIENTIFIC NAME *Tachycineta* + *thalassina*, Latin for resembling the sea in color. Reference is to the color of the underparts.

COMMON NAME Violet-green, for the color of the underparts. Swallow, see *Tachycineta bicolor*.

Tadorna ferruginea — Ruddy Shelduck

SCIENTIFIC NAME *Tadorna*, from French *tadorne*, their name for the common shelduck + *ferruginea*, Latin for rusty. Reference is to the overall brownish orange color.

COMMON NAME Ruddy, for the overall color of the plumage. Shelduck, from Old English *sheld*, for variegated, parti-colored. Reference is to the colors and patterns of the plumage. Duck, from Anglo-Saxon *duce*, a form of *ducan*, to duck or dive.

Tadorna tadorna   Common Shelduck

SCIENTIFIC NAME *Tadorna + tadorna*.

COMMON NAME Common, abundant in its range. Shelduck, see *Tadorna ferruginea*.

Telespiza cantans   Laysan Finch

SCIENTIFIC NAME *Telespiza*, far finch, from Greek τηλε, *tēle*, at a distance, far off, and σπιζα, *spiza*, the chaffinch, a finch. Reference is to the natural range on the remote island of Laysan in the Hawaiian archipelago + *cantans*, Latin for singing.

COMMON NAME Laysan, for the natural range. Finch, from Anglo-Saxon *finc*, their name for this bird, an imitation of the call. Other languages have similar names for the finch for the same reason.

Telespiza ultima   Nihoa Finch

SCIENTIFIC NAME *Telespiza + ultima*, Latin for most distant, farthest away. Reference is to the natural range on the island of Nihoa in the Hawaiian archipelago.

COMMON NAME Nihoa, for the natural range. Finch, see *Telespiza cantans*.

Tetraogallus himalayensis   Himalayan Snowcock

SCIENTIFIC NAME *Tetraogallus*, from the genus *Tetrao*, from Latin *tetrao*, a name for several kinds of gamebirds, and the genus *Gallus*, *gallus*, Latin for a farmyard cock. Reference is to this gamebird's large size + *himalayensis*, Latin for belonging to the Himalayan Mountains. Reference is to the natural range.

COMMON NAME Himalayan, see scientific name. Snowcock, for the snowy mountainous habitat and the bird's appearance.

Thryomanes bewickii   Bewick's Wren

SCIENTIFIC NAME *Thryomanes*, reed cup, from Greek θρυον, *thruon*, a reed or rush, and μανης, *manēs*, a cup. The cup-shaped nest is made in any available cavity with any available material; this bird is not associated with reeds by habitat or nesting site + *bewickii*, for Thomas Bewick (1754–1828), an English wood engraver who made plates for several natural history works. His best-known publication is *History of British Birds* (1797).

Thryomanes bewickii, Bewick's wren

COMMON NAME Bewick's, see scientific name. Wren, from Anglo-Saxon *wraenna*, their name for this type of bird.

Thryothorus ludovicianus   Carolina Wren

SCIENTIFIC NAME *Thryothorus*, reed rushing, from Greek θρυον, *thruon*, a reed or rush, and θουρος, *thouros*, rushing, impetuous. Reference is to the habit of moving rapidly through the underbrush while searching for food + *ludovicianus*, Latin for pertaining to *Ludovicius*, Louis, in reference to Louis XIV (1638–1715), king of France. Used here to mean from Louisiana, for the Louisiana Territory, where the type specimen was collected.

COMMON NAME Carolina, for the natural range in the southeastern United States; this used to be a general term for that area. Wren, see *Thryomanes bewickii*.

Toxostoma bendirei Bendire's Thrasher

SCIENTIFIC NAME *Toxostoma*, bow mouth, from Greek τοξον, *toxon*, a bow, and στομα, *stoma*, mouth. Reference is to the downcurved bill, thought to resemble a strung bow + *bendirei*, for Charles Emil Bendire (1836–1897), a German immigrant to the United States. He was a prolific collector, especially of bird eggs, and donated his vast collection of eggs to the Smithsonian Institution, where he was named honorary curator. He wrote *Life Histories of North American Birds* (1892).

COMMON NAME Bendire's, see scientific name. Thrasher, from English *thrusher*, like a thrush.

Toxostoma crissale Crissal Thrasher

SCIENTIFIC NAME *Toxostoma* + *crissale*, Modern Latin for of the vent or crissum. Reference is to the rufous undertail coverts.

COMMON NAME Crissal, see scientific name. Thrasher, see *Toxostoma bendirei*.

Toxostoma curvirostre Curve-billed Thrasher

SCIENTIFIC NAME *Toxostoma* + *curvirostre*, curved billed, from Latin *curuus*, having a curved surface or outline, bent, and *rostrum*, the snout or muzzle of an animal, the beak or bill of a bird.

COMMON NAME Curve-billed, the bill is curved, but not more so than some other thrashers. Thrasher, see *Toxostoma bendirei*.

Toxostoma lecontei Le Conte's Thrasher

SCIENTIFIC NAME *Toxostoma* + *lecontei*, for John Lawrence Le Conte (1825–1883), a well-known American entomologist with an interest in birds. He was president of the American Association for the Advancement of Science. (His cousin Dr. John Le Conte [1818–1891] had a sparrow named for him; see *Ammodramus leconteii*).

COMMON NAME Le Conte's, see scientific name. Thrasher, see *Toxostoma bendirei*.

Toxostoma longirostre Long-billed Thrasher

SCIENTIFIC NAME *Toxostoma* + *longirostre*, long billed, from Latin *longus*, long, and *rostrum*, the snout or muzzle of an animal, the beak or bill of a bird. This bird looks like the brown thrasher but has a longer bill.

COMMON NAME Long-billed, see scientific name. Thrasher, see *Toxostoma bendirei.*

Toxostoma redivivum — California Thrasher

SCIENTIFIC NAME *Toxostoma* + *redivivum*, Latin for reused, second-hand, revived. This bird was first described by the naturalists on Jean François de Galaup la Perouse's (1741–1788) expedition to find the Northwest Passage (1785–1787) and placed in the genus *Promerops* because of the curved bill. It was not seen again until 1845, when William Gambel (1819–1849) described this bird and placed it in the current genus. Gambel assigned this species name because the bird had been rediscovered after a long time.

COMMON NAME California, for the restricted range and the region of the type specimen. Thrasher, see *Toxostoma bendirei.*

Toxostoma rufum — Brown Thrasher

SCIENTIFIC NAME *Toxostoma* + *rufum*, Latin for red of various shades, tawny. Reference is to the color of the upperparts.

COMMON NAME Brown, for the reddish brown upperparts. Thrasher, see *Toxostoma bendirei.*

Tringa erythropus — Spotted Redshank

SCIENTIFIC NAME *Tringa*, from Greek τρυγγας, *truggas*, a waterbird mentioned by Aristotle + *erythropus*, red footed, from Greek ερυθρος, *eruthros*, red, and πους, *pous*, foot. Reference is to the red feet and legs.

COMMON NAME Spotted, for the white spots on the tops of the wings. Redshank, for the red legs.

Tringa flavipes — Lesser Yellowlegs

SCIENTIFIC NAME *Tringa* + *flavipes*, yellow foot, from Latin *flauus*, yellow, especially pale yellow or golden, and *pes*, foot.

COMMON NAME Lesser, for the size; it is smaller than the greater yellowlegs. Yellowlegs, has yellow legs and feet.

Tringa glareola — Wood Sandpiper

SCIENTIFIC NAME *Tringa* + *glareola*, little gravel, from Latin *glarrea*, gravel, and the diminutive *-ola*. Reference is to the sandy habitat on the shores of marshy ponds.

COMMON NAME Wood, for part of the habitat, may nest in woods as well as on the tundra. Sandpiper, one who pipes on the sand. Piping is descriptive of its call, from Latin *pipare*, to chirp.

Tringa melanoleuca   Greater Yellowlegs

SCIENTIFIC NAME *Tringa* + *melanoleuca*, black and white, from Greek μελας, *melas*, black, and λευκος, *leukos*, of color, white. Reference is to the black and white colors of the plumage.

COMMON NAME Greater, for the size; it is larger than the lesser yellowlegs. Yellowlegs, see *Tringa flavipes*.

Tringa nebularia   Common Greenshank

SCIENTIFIC NAME *Tringa* + *nebularia*, relating to a cloud, from Latin *nebula*, characterized or subject to mists or clouds. Reference is to the mottled gray color and pattern of the plumage.

COMMON NAME Common, abundant in its range. Greenshank, for the greenish legs.

Tringa solitaria   Solitary Sandpiper

SCIENTIFIC NAME *Tringa* + *solitaria*, Latin for living or acting on one's own, solitary. Reference is to this bird often being seen alone.

COMMON NAME Solitary, see scientific name. Sandpiper, see *Tringa nebularia*.

Troglodytes aedon   House Wren

SCIENTIFIC NAME *Troglodytes*, from Greek τρωγλοδυτης, *trōglodutēs*, one who creeps into holes, a caveman, a wren. Reference is to the behavior of poking around holes and crevices searching for food or nesting sites + *aedon*, from Greek αεδον, *aedon*, a nightingale. Louis Pierre Vieillot (1748–1831) took this name from the myth of Aedon, daughter of Pandareos. Aedon married Zethus, king of Thebes, and they had only one child, a son. Her sister-in-law, Niobe, had six sons and six daughters. Being jealous of Niobe's fertility, Aedon decided to kill Amaleus, one of Niobe's sons. However, in the darkness she managed to kill her own son. Zeus took pity on the grief-stricken woman and changed her into a nightingale. Reference is thought to be the pleasant song of this wren, as is that of a nightingale.

COMMON NAME House, for the nesting sites in and around houses. Wren, from Anglo-Saxon *wraenna*, their name for this type of bird.

Troglodytes troglodytes   Winter Wren

SCIENTIFIC NAME *Troglodytes* + *troglodytes*.

COMMON NAME Winter, for the winter range in the southeast United States. Wren, see *Troglodytes aedon*.

Trogon elegans   Elegant Trogon

SCIENTIFIC NAME *Trogon*, from Greek τρωγω, *trōgō*, to gnaw, to nibble. Reference is to the toothlike edges on the bill + *elegans*, Latin for tastefully attractive, graceful, elegant. Reference is to the male's bright, multicolored plumage.

COMMON NAME Elegant, see scientific name. Trogon, see scientific name.

Tryngites subruficollis   Buff-breasted Sandpiper

SCIENTIFIC NAME *Tryngites*, having to do with the genus *Tringa*. Reference is to this bird looking somewhat like those in the genus *Tringa* + *subruficollis*, having a dull red neck, from Latin *subrufus*, dull red, tinged with red, and *collis*, Modern Latin for necked, from Latin *collum*, neck.

COMMON NAME Buff-breasted, for the reddish brown underparts. Sandpiper, one who pipes on the sand. Piping is descriptive of its call, from Latin *pipare*, to chirp.

Turdus grayi   Clay-colored Robin

SCIENTIFIC NAME *Turdus*, Latin for a thrush or similar bird + *grayi*, for George Robert Gray (1808–1872), a British ornithologist and author of *Genera of Birds* (1844).

COMMON NAME Clay-colored, for the dull mud-colored plumage. Robin, a diminutive of the English name Robert, their pet name for this bird.

Turdus migratorius   American Robin

SCIENTIFIC NAME *Turdus* + *migratorius*, a wanderer, from Latin *migratum*, to change one's residence, move from place to place. Reference is to the migratory behavior.

COMMON NAME American, for the natural range and to differentiate it from other birds called robins in other parts of the world. Robin, see *Turdus grayi*.

Turdus pilaris   Fieldfare

SCIENTIFIC NAME *Turdus* + *pilaris*, Modern Latin for a thrush. Carl Linnaeus (1707–1778) named this bird. His source was a translation from Greek to Latin by Theodorus Gaza (c. 1400–1478). Gaza made the original mistake when he assumed the Greek τριχας, *trikhas*, thrush, was derived from θριξ, *thrix*, hair. When Gaza changed the word to Latin, he used *pilaris*, which actually means hair.

COMMON NAME Fieldfare, from Anglo-Saxon *feld*, field, and *faran*, to fare or travel. Reference is to the habitat in open fields.

Turdus rufopalliatus   Rufous-backed Robin

SCIENTIFIC NAME *Turdus* + *rufopalliatus*, from Latin *rufus*, red of various shades, tawny, and *palliatus*, wearing a pallium, a rectangular piece of cloth worn draped over the shoulders as an outer garment, mainly by men. Reference is to the plumage pattern of the rufous back and wings.

COMMON NAME Rufous-backed, descriptive. Robin, see *Turdus grayi*.

Tympanuchus cupido   Greater Prairie-Chicken

SCIENTIFIC NAME *Tympanuchus*, to hold a drum, from Greek τυμπανον, *tumpanon*, a kettle drum, and New Latin *-ochos*, from Greek εκω, εχειν, *ekō*, *ekhein*, to have, to hold. Reference is to the bare inflatable neck sacs used in the male's mating call, which sounds like a drum. This was the intended derivation, however, another interestingly apt translation can be dissected from *Tympanuchus*: drum neck, from Greek τυμπανον, *tumpanon*, a kettle drum, and Modern Latin *nucha*, neck + *cupido*, for the winged child-god Cupid. Reference is to the small erectile feather tufts on the neck that look like small wings.

COMMON NAME Greater, for the size; it is larger than the lesser prairie-chicken. Prairie-Chicken, for the habitat and appearance.

Tympanuchus pallidicinctus   Lesser Prairie-Chicken

SCIENTIFIC NAME *Tympanuchus* + *pallidicinctus*, pale banded, from Latin *pallidus*, having a pale color, pallid, and *cinctus*, a girdle, a band, a crown or garland. Reference is to the bands on the body, which are paler than those of the greater prairie-chicken.

COMMON NAME Lesser, for the size; it is smaller than the greater prairie-chicken. Prairie-Chicken, see *Tympanuchus cupido*.

Tympanuchus cupido, greater prairie-chicken

Tympanuchus phasianellus — Sharp-tailed Grouse

SCIENTIFIC NAME *Tympanuchus* + *phasianellus*, little pheasant, from Latin *phasiana*, a pheasant, in turn from Greek φασιανος, *phasianos*, a pheasant (see *Phasianus colchicus*), and the diminutive *-ellus*. Reference is to the appearance.

COMMON NAME Sharp-tailed, descriptive. Grouse, origin unknown but thought to come from French *griais*, speckled gray.

Tyrannus couchii — Couch's Kingbird

SCIENTIFIC NAME *Tyrannus*, from Greek τυραννος, *turannos*, an absolute ruler, especially if imperious or despotic, a tyrant. Reference is to the aggressive behavior of this bird + *couchii*, for Darius Nash Couch (1822–1897), a Union general during the Civil War. Early in his career, he collected birds while serving in Texas and during the Mexican War (1846–1848).

COMMON NAME Couch's, see scientific name. Kingbird, see the genus name.

Tyrannus crassirostris   Thick-billed Kingbird

SCIENTIFIC NAME *Tyrannus* + *crassirostris*, thick billed, from Latin *crassus*, thick, and *rostris*, billed, from Latin *rostrum*, the snout or muzzle of an animal, the beak or bill of a bird.

COMMON NAME Thick-billed, has a much thicker bill than the others in this genus. Kingbird, see *Tyrannus couchii*.

Tyrannus dominicensis   Gray Kingbird

SCIENTIFIC NAME *Tyrannus* + *dominicensis*, Latin for belonging to Santa Domingo, Hispaniola. Reference is to the region of the type specimen.

COMMON NAME Gray, for the color of the upperparts. Kingbird, see *Tyrannus couchii*.

Tyrannus forficatus   Scissor-tailed Flycatcher

SCIENTIFIC NAME *Tyrannus* + *forficatus*, possessing scissors, from Latin *forfex*, *forficis*, tongs, pincers, forceps, scissors, and *-atus*, possessing. Reference is to the long tail feathers that spread in flight to resemble a pair of open scissors. When referring to a bird's tail, the appropriate use of *forficate* is when the depth of the fork equals or exceeds the length of the shortest tail feather (*Century Dictionary and Cyclopedia*, 1913).

COMMON NAME Scissor-tailed, see scientific name. Flycatcher, for the habit of catching insects in the air.

Tyrannus melancholicus   Tropical Kingbird

SCIENTIFIC NAME *Tyrannus* + *melancholicus*, from Greek μελαγχολικος, *melagkholikos*, of melancholic temperament. The Greeks used melancholy to mean sullenness or violent anger and understood this temperament to result from an imbalance of one of the four humors, in this case black bile. Reference is to the aggressive behavior of this bird.

COMMON NAME Tropical, for the natural range in Central and South America. Kingbird, see *Tyrannus couchii*.

Tyrannus savana Fork-tailed Flycatcher

SCIENTIFIC NAME *Tyrannus* + *savana*, from Spanish *zavana*, originally a Carib Indian (Lesser Antilles, West Indies) word for a treeless plain. Reference is to the habitat.

COMMON NAME Fork-tailed, descriptive. Flycatcher, for the habit of catching insects in the air.

Tyrannus tyrannus Eastern Kingbird

SCIENTIFIC NAME *Tyrannus* + *tyrannus*.

COMMON NAME Eastern, for the natural range in the United States, although it ranges well west of the Mississippi River. Kingbird, see *Tyrannus couchii*.

Tyrannus verticalis Western Kingbird

SCIENTIFIC NAME *Tyrannus* + *verticalis*, crowned, from Latin *vertex*, the crown or topmost part of the head, and *-alis*, relating to. Reference is to the orange-red crown-patch that is visible only during aggressive displays.

COMMON NAME Western, for the natural range in the United States. Kingbird, see *Tyrannus couchii*.

Tyrannus vociferans Cassin's Kingbird

SCIENTIFIC NAME *Tyrannus* + *vociferans*, I bear a voice, from Latin *vocifero*, *vocis*, genitive form of *vox*, voice, and *fero*, I bear. Reference is to the loud calls.

COMMON NAME Cassin's, for John Cassin (1813 1869), a Philadelphia ornithologist with a broad knowledge of the birds of the world. Kingbird, see *Tyrannus couchii*.

Tyto alba Barn Owl

SCIENTIFIC NAME *Tyto*, from Greek τυτω, *tutō*, night owl + *alba*, Latin for white, light colored. Reference is to the white face and underparts.

COMMON NAME Barn, for a favored nesting site. Owl, from Anglo-Saxon *ule*, owl, and from Latin *ululo*, to cry out.

Tyto alba, barn owl

Uraeginthus bengalus   Red-cheeked Cordonbleu

SCIENTIFIC NAME *Uraeginthus*, long-tailed *Aegintha*, from Greek ουρα, *oura*, tail, properly of animals, should not be used for birds, and the genus *Aegintha*, the waxbills. Reference is to the long blue tail + *bengalus*, for Bengal, where Matthew Jacques Brisson (1723–1806), who named the bird, thought it originated.

COMMON NAME Red-cheeked, for the male's red cheek-patches. Cordonbleu, from French *cordon*, a cord, and *bleu*, blue. Reference is to the long blue tail.

Uria aalge   Common Murre

SCIENTIFIC NAME *Uria*, from Greek ουρια, *ouria*, a waterbird mentioned by Athenaeus + *aalge*, Danish for an auk.

COMMON NAME Common, abundant in its range. Murre, a type of auk, guillemot, or puffin, depending on the geographic region in which the word is used. The word is of obscure origin; the earliest printed reference in English as a name for this type of bird is 1602.

Uria lomvia   Thick-billed Murre

SCIENTIFIC NAME *Uria + lomvia*, the Faeroese (Faeroe Islands), Danish, and Swedish name for this type of bird.

COMMON NAME Thick-billed, has a thicker bill than the common murre. Murre, see *Uria aalge*.

Vanellus vanellus   Northern Lapwing

SCIENTIFIC NAME *Vanellus*, a little fan, from Medieval Latin *vannus*, a winnowing basket or fan, and the diminutive *-ellus*. Reference is to the slow wingbeats, reflecting the up and down speed of a winnowing basket. The second *n* should not have been dropped when the diminutive was formed from *vannus + vanellus*.

COMMON NAME Northern, for the natural range in the Northern Hemisphere. Lapwing, from Anglo-Saxon *hleapewince*, a lapwing, from *hleapan*, to leap, dance, run, and *winc*, to totter or waver. Reference is to the irregular flight pattern.

Vermivora celata   Orange-crowned Warbler

SCIENTIFIC NAME *Vermivora*, worm eater, from Latin *vermis*, a worm, maggot, or other small creature of similar appearance, and *voro*, to swallow ravenously, to devour + *celata*, Latin for concealed. Reference is to the inconspicuous orange crown.

COMMON NAME Orange-crowned, descriptive. Warbler, for the trills and quavers of the song.

Vermivora chrysoptera   Golden-winged Warbler

SCIENTIFIC NAME *Vermivora + chrysoptera*, golden winged, from Greek χρυσος, *khrusos*, gold, and πτερον, *pteron*, feather, bird's wing. Reference is to the bright yellow wing-panel.

COMMON NAME Golden-winged, see scientific name. Warbler, see *Vermivora celata*.

Vermivora crissalis   Colima Warbler

SCIENTIFIC NAME *Vermivora + crissalis*, Modern Latin for of the vent or crissum. Reference is to the orange undertail coverts.

COMMON NAME Colima, for Sierra Nevada de Colima, Mexico, where the type specimen was collected. Warbler, see *Vermivora celata*.

Vermivora luciae   Lucy's Warbler

SCIENTIFIC NAME *Vermivora* + *luciae*, for Lucy Hunter Baird (1848–1913), the daughter of Spencer Fullerton Baird (1823–1887), secretary of the Smithsonian Institution and author of *Catalogue of North American Mammals* (1857) and *Catalogue of North American Birds* (1868).

COMMON NAME Lucy's, see scientific name. Warbler, see *Vermivora celata*.

Vermivora peregrina   Tennessee Warbler

SCIENTIFIC NAME *Vermivora* + *peregrina*, Latin for foreign, alien, exotic, wandering. The type specimen was a migrant collected in Tennessee. The summer range is mainly Canada and the northern United States.

COMMON NAME Tennessee, for the region of the type specimen. Warbler, see *Vermivora celata*.

Vermivora pinus   Blue-winged Warbler

SCIENTIFIC NAME *Vermivora* + *pinus*, Latin for a pine tree. The type specimen for this species was collected by William Bartram (1739–1823) and sent to George Edwards (1693–1773), who mistakenly identified it as the pine creeper of Mark Catesby (c. 1679–1773), an English naturalist who collected and explored in Virginia and the Carolinas, and thus assigned this species name. The actual habitat of this warbler includes brushy fields, woodland edges, and neglected pastures.

COMMON NAME Blue-winged, descriptive. Warbler, see *Vermivora celata*.

Vermivora ruficapilla   Nashville Warbler

SCIENTIFIC NAME *Vermivora* + *ruficapilla*, red haired, from Latin *rufus*, red of various shades, tawny, and *capillus*, the hair of the head. Reference is to the male's red crown-patch.

COMMON NAME Nashville, the type specimen was collected near Nashville, Tennessee. Warbler, see *Vermivora celata*.

Vermivora virginiae   Virginia's Warbler

SCIENTIFIC NAME *Vermivora* + *virginiae*, for Mary Virginia Anderson (f. 1858), the wife of William Wallace Anderson (1824–1911), a U.S. then

Confederate Army surgeon. He collected the type specimen and asked Spencer Fullerton Baird (1823–1887) to name the bird for his wife.

COMMON NAME Virginia's, see scientific name. Warbler, see *Vermivora celata*.

Vestiaria coccinea 'I 'Iwi

SCIENTIFIC NAME *Vestiaria*, Latin for concerned with or relating to clothes. Reference is to the bright red plumage and sharply contrasting black wings, making this bird appear well dressed + *coccinea*, Latin for scarlet dyed, in turn from Greek κοκκινος, *kokkinos*, scarlet. Reference is to the bright red body.

COMMON NAME 'I 'Iwi, the Hawaiian name for this bird.

Vireo altiloquus Black-whiskered Vireo

SCIENTIFIC NAME *Vireo*, from Latin *vireo*, to be green, New Latin for a small green bird + *altiloquus*, the original intent was to speak high, from Latin *altus*, high, and *loquor*, *loqui*, to speak. Reference is to the high-pitched twittering call. Strictly interpreted, this should translate to speak loudly or deeply. *Altus* means high or deep when used to describe vertical distances and deep or loud when referring to sounds; thus, to speak from a high place is another possible translation.

COMMON NAME Black-whiskered, for the dark lateral throat-stripe. Vireo, see scientific name.

Vireo atricapillus Black-capped Vireo

SCIENTIFIC NAME *Vireo* + *atricapillus*, black haired, from Latin *ater*, black, and *capillus*, the hair of the head. Reference is to the black on the head, especially noticeable on the male.

COMMON NAME Black-capped, see scientific name. Vireo, see *Vireo altiloquus*.

Vireo bellii Bell's Vireo

SCIENTIFIC NAME *Vireo* + *bellii*, for John Graham Bell (1812–1889), a taxidermist who accompanied John James Audubon (1785–1851) on his Missouri River trip of 1843.

COMMON NAME Bell's, see scientific name. Vireo, see *Vireo altiloquus*.

Vireo cassinii   Cassin's Vireo

SCIENTIFIC NAME *Vireo* + *cassinii*, for John Cassin (1813–1869), a Philadelphia ornithologist with a broad knowledge of the birds of the world.

COMMON NAME Cassin's, see scientific name. Vireo, see *Vireo altiloquus*.

Vireo crassirostris   Thick-billed Vireo

SCIENTIFIC NAME *Vireo* + *crassirostris*, thick billed, from Latin *crassus*, thick, and *rostrum*, the snout or muzzle of an animal, the beak or bill of a bird. This bird has a thicker bill than the other vireos.

COMMON NAME Thick-billed, see scientific name. Vireo, see *Vireo altiloquus*.

Vireo flavifrons   Yellow-throated Vireo

SCIENTIFIC NAME *Vireo* + *flavifrons*, yellow front, from Latin *flauus*, yellow, especially pale yellow or golden, and *frons*, forehead, front. Reference is to the yellow throat and breast.

COMMON NAME Yellow-throated, descriptive. Vireo, see *Vireo altiloquus*.

Vireo flavoviridis   Yellow-green Vireo

SCIENTIFIC NAME *Vireo* + *flavoviridis*, yellowish green, from Latin *flauus*, yellow, especially pale yellow or golden, and *viridis*, green. Reference is to the pale green plumage suffused with yellow.

COMMON NAME Yellow-green, see scientific name. Vireo, see *Vireo altiloquus*.

Vireo gilvus   Warbling Vireo

SCIENTIFIC NAME *Vireo* + *gilvus*, Latin for dun colored or dull grayish brown. Dun, a neutral, slightly brownish dark gray, is a much better fit for the color of this bird's upperparts.

COMMON NAME Warbling, for the trills and quavers of the song, which is different from the song of the other vireos. Vireo, see *Vireo altiloquus*.

Vireo griseus   White-eyed Vireo

SCIENTIFIC NAME *Vireo* + *griseus*, Medieval Latin for gray. Reference is to the bird's gray nape.

Vireo griseus, white-eyed vireo

COMMON NAME White-eyed, for the white irises. Vireo, see *Vireo alti-loquus*.

Vireo huttoni   Hutton's Vireo

SCIENTIFIC NAME *Vireo* + *huttoni*, for William Hutton (f. 1845), an American naturalist who collected the type specimen. John Cassin (1813–1869) named the bird in his honor.

COMMON NAME Hutton's, see scientific name. Vireo, see *Vireo altiloquus*.

Vireo olivaceus   Red-eyed Vireo

SCIENTIFIC NAME *Vireo* + *olivaceus*, Modern Latin for olive-green. Reference is to the color of the upperparts.

COMMON NAME Red-eyed, for the red irises. Vireo, see *Vireo altiloquus*.

Vireo philadelphicus   Philadelphia Vireo

SCIENTIFIC NAME *Vireo* + *philadelphicus*, of Philadelphia. Reference is to where the type specimen was collected.

COMMON NAME Philadelphia, see scientific name. Vireo, see *Vireo altiloquus*.

Vireo plumbeus   Plumbeous Vireo

SCIENTIFIC NAME *Vireo* + *plumbeus*, Latin for made of lead, leaden. Reference is to the lead gray upperparts.

COMMON NAME Plumbeous, see scientific name. Vireo, see *Vireo altiloquus*.

Vireo solitarius   Blue-headed Vireo

SCIENTIFIC NAME *Vireo* + *solitarius*, Latin for living or acting on one's own. Alexander Wilson (1766–1813) described this species from a solitary migrant specimen, hence the name.

COMMON NAME Blue-headed, for the bluish gray head. Vireo, see *Vireo altiloquus*.

Vireo vicinior   Gray Vireo

SCIENTIFIC NAME *Vireo* + *vicinior*, more neighborly, Latin comparative degree of *vicinus*, a neighbor. According to Elliot Coues (1842–1899), he selected this name for the close resemblance of this species to others in the genus *Vireo*.

COMMON NAME Gray, for the overall color of the plumage. Vireo, see *Vireo altiloquus*.

Wilsonia canadensis   Canada Warbler

SCIENTIFIC NAME *Wilsonia*, for Alexander Wilson (1766–1813), known as the father of American ornithology. He initiated the first series on birds of the eastern United States, *American Ornithology* (1808–1814) + *canadensis*, Latin for belonging to Canada. Reference is to the breeding range.

COMMON NAME Canada, see scientific name. Warbler, for the trills and quavers of the song.

Wilsonia citrina   Hooded Warbler

SCIENTIFIC NAME *Wilsonia* + *citrina*, Late Latin for lemon colored. Reference is to the bright lemon yellow of the face and breast.

COMMON NAME Hooded, for the male's black hood. Warbler, for the trills and quavers of the song.

Wilsonia pusilla   Wilson's Warbler

SCIENTIFIC NAME *Wilsonia* + *pusilla*, Latin for very small, tiny, wee. This is the smallest bird in the genus.

COMMON NAME Wilson's, see *Wilsonia canadensis*. Warbler, for the trills and quavers of the song.

Xanthocephalus xanthocephalus   Yellow-headed Blackbird

SCIENTIFIC NAME *Xanthocephalus*, yellow headed, from Greek ξανθός, *xanthos*, yellow, and κεφαλη, *kephalē*, head. Reference is to the male's bright yellow head, which contrasts sharply with the dark body + *xanthocephalus*.

COMMON NAME Yellow-headed, see scientific name. Blackbird, for the dark body color.

Xema sabini   Sabine's Gull

SCIENTIFIC NAME *Xema*, a word coined by William Elford Leach (1790–1836) of no known meaning + *sabini*, for Sir Edward Sabine (1788–1883), an English astronomer and physicist who was president of the British Association for the Advancement of Science and president of the Royal Society. This bird was named in his honor by his brother, Joseph Sabine (1770–1837).

COMMON NAME Sabine's, see scientific name. Gull, from Celtic *gullan*, *gwylan*, *gwelan*, all names for this type of bird.

Xenus cinereus   Terek Sandpiper

SCIENTIFIC NAME *Xenus*, from Greek ξενος, *xenos*, generally a stranger or foreigner, especially a wanderer. Reference is to the migratory behavior + *cinereus*, Latin for ash colored. Reference is to the pale gray upperparts.

COMMON NAME Terek, for the breeding range in the province of Terek, Russia. Sandpiper, one who pipes on the sand. Piping is descriptive of its call, from Latin *pipare*, to chirp.

Zenaida asiatica   White-winged Dove

SCIENTIFIC NAME *Zenaida*, for Princess Zenaide Laetitia Julie Bonaparte (1804–1854), wife of Prince Charles Lucien Jules Laurent Bonaparte (1803–1857); in addition to being a prince, he was a well-known French ornithologist + *asiatica*, Latin for Asian. Carl Linnaeus (1707–1778) gave this species name because the type specimen was labeled to have come from "Indiis," which he took to mean India and not the actual site of collection in the West Indies.

COMMON NAME White-winged, for the white upper-wing patches. Dove, from Anglo-Saxon *dufan*, to dive, for its irregular flight pattern.

Zenaida macroura   Mourning Dove

SCIENTIFIC NAME *Zenaida* + *macroura*, long tailed, from Greek μακρος, *makros*, long, and ουρα, *oura*, tail. According to the *Oxford Greek-English Lexicon* (1996), ουρα, *oura* should not be used for the tail of a bird but is restricted to other animals. The tail of this bird is much longer than that of the white-winged dove.

COMMON NAME Mourning, for its mournful call. Dove, see *Zenaida asiatica*.

Zonotrichia albicollis   White-throated Sparrow

SCIENTIFIC NAME *Zonotrichia*, banded thrush, from Greek ζωνη, *zōnē*, a belt or girdle, and τριχας, *trikhas*, a song-thrush. Reference is to the bands on the head of this genus + *albicollis*, white necked, from Latin *albus*, white, and *collum*, neck. Reference is to the white throat.

COMMON NAME White-throated, descriptive. Sparrow, from Anglo-Saxon *spearwa*, to flutter. Originally used to denote any small bird.

Zonotrichia atricapilla   Golden-crowned Sparrow

SCIENTIFIC NAME *Zonotrichia* + *atricapilla*, from Latin *ater*, black, and *capillus*, the hair of the head. Reference is to the black bands just below the yellow forecrown.

COMMON NAME Golden-crowned, descriptive. Sparrow, see *Zonotrichia albicollis*.

Zonotrichia leucophrys White-crowned Sparrow

SCIENTIFIC NAME *Zonotrichia* + *leucophrys*, white eyebrow, from Greek λευκος, *leukos*, of color, white, and οφρυς, *ophrus*, brow, eyebrow. Reference is to the white band above and behind the eyes.

COMMON NAME White-crowned, descriptive. Sparrow, see *Zonotrichia albicollis*.

Zonotrichia querula Harris's Sparrow

SCIENTIFIC NAME *Zonotrichia* + *querula*, Latin for full of complaints or protests, fretful. Reference is to the call.

COMMON NAME Harris's, for Edward Harris (1799–1863), a patron of John James Audubon (1785–1851) who accompanied the artist on some collecting trips. Sparrow, see *Zonotrichia albicollis*.

Zosterops japonicus Japanese White-eye

SCIENTIFIC NAME *Zosterops*, eye girdle, from Greek ζοοτηρ, *zostēr*, a warrior's belt, anything that goes round like a girdle, and οψ, *ops*, the eye, face, appearance. Reference is to the white ring around the eyes + *japonicus*, of Japan, from French *Japon*, Japan, and *-icus*, of. Reference is to the natural range.

COMMON NAME Japanese, for the natural range. White-eye, for the white ring around the eyes.

BIBLIOGRAPHY

Alsop, Fred J., III. 2001. *Birds of North America, Eastern Region*. Smithsonian Handbooks. New York: R. R. Donnelley and Sons.

Alsop, Fred J., III. 2001. *Birds of North America, Western Region*. Smithsonian Handbooks. New York: R. R. Donnelley and Sons.

American Ornithologists' Union. 1998. *Check-list of North American Birds. 7th ed. Washington, D.C.: American Ornithologists' Union. On-line version* (http://www.aou.org/aou/birdlist.html) *accessed January 2003; this version incorporates changes made in the 42nd (2000) and 43rd (2002) Supplements to the Check-list.*

Baicich, Paul J., and Colin J. O. Harrison. 1997. *A Guide to the Nests, Eggs, and Nestlings of North American Birds*. San Diego, Calif.: Academic Press.

Bell, Robert E. 1991. *Women of Classical Mythology: A Biographical Dictionary*. Oxford: Oxford University Press.

Bent, Arthur Cleveland. 1992. *Life Histories of North American Woodpeckers*. Bloomington: Indiana University Press.

Brown, Roland W. 1956. *Composition of Scientific Words*. Washington, D.C.: Smithsonian Institution Press.

Byers, Clive, Jon Curson, and Urban Olsson. 1995. *Sparrows and Buntings*. Boston: Houghton Mifflin.

The Century Dictionary and Cyclopedia. 1913. New York: Century Company.

Choate, Ernest A. 1985. *The Dictionary of American Bird Names*. Rev. ed. Boston: Harvard Common Press.

Coues, Elliot. 1881. *The Coues Check List and Ornithological Dictionary*. Boston: Estes and Lauriat.

Curson, Jon, David Quinn, and David Beadle. 1994. *Warblers of the Americas*. Boston: Houghton Mifflin.

Davidson, Gustav. 1967. *A Dictionary of Angels Including the Fallen Angels*. New York: Free Press.

Dunn, Jon, and Kimball Garrett. 1997. *A Field Guide to Warblers of*

North America. Peterson Field Guides. Boston: Houghton Mifflin.

Eckert, Allen. 1987. *The Owls of North America*. New York: Weathervane Books.

Edwards, Ernest Preston. 1998. *The Birds of Mexico and Adjacent Areas*. Austin: University of Texas Press.

Forshaw, Joseph M. 1989. *Parrots of the World*. Melbourne: Lansdowne Editions.

Friel, John P., ed. 1965. *Dorland's Illustrated Medical Dictionary*. 25th ed. Darien, Ill.: W. B. Saunders.

Giare, P. G. W., ed. 1997. *Oxford Latin Dictionary*. Oxford: Clarendon Press.

Gotch, A. F. 1995. *Latin Names Explained*. New York: Facts on File.

Gould, John. 1990. *John Gould's Hummingbirds*. Secaucus, N.J.: Wellfleet Press.

Griscom, Ludlow, and Alexander Sprunt Jr., eds. 1957. *The Warblers of America*. New York: Devin-Adair.

Gruson, Edward S. 1972. *Words for Birds: A Lexicon of North American Bird Names with Biographical Notes*. New York: Quadrangle Books.

Harrison, Hal H. 1975. *A Field Guide to Birds' Nests of 285 Species Found Breeding in the United States East of the Mississippi River*. Peterson Field Guides. Boston: Houghton Mifflin.

Harrison, Hal H. 1979. *A Field Guide to Western Birds' Nests*. Peterson Field Guides. Boston: Houghton Mifflin.

Harrison, Peter. 1983. *Seabirds: An Identification Guide*. Boston: Houghton Mifflin.

Hawaiian Audubon Society. 1997. *Hawaii's Birds*. 5th ed. Honolulu: Hawaiian Audubon Society.

Hopkins, Daniel J., ed. 1997. *Merriam-Webster's Geographical Dictionary*. 3rd ed. Springfield, Mass.: Merriam-Webster.

Hornblower, Simon, and Anthony Spawforth, eds. 1996. *The Oxford Classical Dictionary*. Oxford: Oxford University Press.

Howell, Steve N. G., and Sophie Webb. 1999. *A Guide to the Birds of Mexico and Northern Central America*. Oxford: Oxford University Press.

Hughes, Joan, ed. 1991. *The Australian Reference Dictionary*. South Melbourne: Oxford University Press.

Hunter, Robert. 1897. *Encyclopaedic Dictionary*. Rev. ed. Philadelphia: Syndicate Publishing Company.

International Trust for Zoological Nomenclature. 1999. *International Code of Zoological Nomenclature*. 4th ed. London: International Trust for Zoological Nomenclature.

Jaeger, Edmund C. 1978. *A Source-Book of Biological Names and Terms*. 3rd ed. Springfield, Ill.: Charles C. Thomas.

Joblin, James A. 1995. *A Dictionary of Scientific Bird Names.* Oxford: Oxford University Press.

Jordon, Michael. 1993. *Encyclopedia of Gods.* New York: Facts on File.

Kaufman, Kenn. 2000. *Birds of North America.* Boston: Houghton Mifflin.

Kazmierczak, Krys. 2000. *A Field Guide to the Birds of the Indian Subcontinent.* New Haven, Conn.: Yale University Press.

Kilman, Lawrence. 1983. *Woodpeckers of Eastern North America.* New York: Dover.

Liddell, H. G., and R. Scott. 1996. *A Greek-English Lexicon.* Oxford: Clarendon Press.

Lipton, James. 1991. *An Exaltation of Larks.* 3rd ed. New York: Viking.

Mercatante, Anthony S. 1988. *The Facts on File Encyclopedia of World Mythology and Legend.* New York: Facts on File.

Meyers Geographischer Handatlas. 1926. Leipzig, Germany: Bibliographisches Institut.

Morris, Richard B., ed. 1961. *Encyclopedia of American History.* New York: Harper and Row.

National Geographic Society Staff. 1999. *National Geographic Atlas of the World.* 7th ed. Washington, D.C.: National Geographic Society.

Nybakken, Oscar E. 1959. *Greek and Latin in Scientific Terminology.* Ames: Iowa State University Press.

The Oxford English Dictionary. 1989. 2d ed. Prepared by I. A. Simpson and E. S. Weiner. Oxford: Oxford University Press.

Peterson, Roger Tory, and Edward L. Chalif. 1973. *A Field Guide to Mexican Birds: Field Marks of All Species Found in Mexico, Guatemala, Belize (British Honduras), El Salvador.* Peterson Field Guides. Boston: Houghton Mifflin.

Pollard, John. 1977. *Birds in Greek Life and Myth.* London: Thames and Hudson.

Proctor, Noble S., and Patrick J. Lynch. 1993. *Manual of Ornithology.* New Haven, Conn.: Yale University Press.

Quattrocchi, Umberto. 2000. *CRC World Dictionary of Plant Names.* Boca Raton, Fla.: CRC Press.

Quinn, David, and Simon Harrap. 1995. *Chickadees, Tits, Nuthatches, and Treecreepers.* Princeton, N.J.: Princeton University Press.

Rose, H. J. 1959. *A Handbook of Greek Mythology.* New York: E. P. Dutton and Company.

Seyffert, Oskar. 1904. *A Dictionary of Classical Antiquities, Mythology, Religion, Literature, and Art.* Revised and edited from the original German by Henry Nettleship and J. E. Sandys. New York: Macmillan.

Sibley, David Allen. 2000. *The Sibley Guide to Birds.* New York: Alfred A. Knopf.

Skeat, Walter W., ed. 1997. *An Etymological Dictionary of the English Language*. Reprint of 1879–1882 ed. Oxford: Clarendon Press.

Souter, Alexander. 1996. *A Glossary of Later Latin to 600 A.D.* Oxford: Clarendon Press.

Stearn, William T. 1983. *Botanical Latin*. 3rd ed. London: David and Charles.

Stokes, Donald, and Lillian Stokes. 1996. *Field Guide to Birds, Eastern Region*. Boston: Little, Brown, and Company.

Stokes, Donald, and Lillian Stokes. 1996. *Field Guide to Birds, Western Region*. Boston: Little, Brown, and Company.

Sutton, George Miksch. 1936. *Birds in the Wilderness*. New York: Macmillan.

Sutton, George Miksch. 1951. *Mexican Birds: First Impressions*. Norman: University of Oklahoma Press.

Sutton, George Miksch. 1986. *Birds Worth Watching*. Norman: University of Oklahoma Press.

Sweet, Henry. 1911. *The Student's Dictionary of Anglo-Saxon*. Oxford: Oxford University Press.

Terres, John K. 1980. *The Audubon Society Encyclopedia of North American Birds*. New York: Alfred A. Knopf.

Thompson, A. Landsborough, ed. 1964. *A New Dictionary of Birds, Covering the Birds of the World*. New York: McGraw-Hill.

True, Dan. 1993. *Hummingbirds of North America*. Albuquerque: University of New Mexico Press.

Voous, Karl H. 1989. *Owls of the Northern Hemisphere*. Cambridge, Mass.: MIT Press.

Warre Cornish, Francis, ed. 1898. *A Concise Dictionary of Greek and Roman Antiquities*. London: John Murray.

Webster's New International Dictionary of the English Language. 2d ed. 1946. Springfield, Mass.: G & C Merriam.

INDEX

'a 'o, 176
Accipiter cooperii, 13
   gentilis, 13
   soloensis, 13
   striatus, 13
Acridotheres cristatellus, 14
   tristis, 14
Acrocephalus familiaris, 14
Actitis hypoleucos, 14
   macularia, 14
Aechmophorus clarkii, 15
   occidentalis, 15
Aegolius acadicus, 15
   funereus, 15
Aeronautes saxatalis, 16
Aethia cristatella, 16
   psittacula, 16
   pusilla, 16
   pygmaea, 16
Agapornis roseicollis, 17
Agelaius phoeniceus, 17
   tricolor, 17
Aimophila aestivalis, 17
   botterii, 18
   carpalis, 18
   cassinii, 18
   quinquestriata, 18
   ruficeps, 19
Aix galericulata, 19
   sponsa, 19
'akeke 'e, 122
'akepa, 122
'akiapola 'au, 105
'akikiki, 138

'akohekohe, 141
'alae ke 'oke 'o, 97
'Alala, 76
'alauahio, Maui, 144
   Oahu, 143
Alauda arvensis, 19
albatross, black-footed, 155
   Laysan, 154
   short-tailed, 154
Alca torda, 19
Alectoris chukar, 20
   rufa, 20
Alle alle, 20
Alopochen aegyptiacus, 20
'amakihi, Hawaii, 105
   Kauai, 104
   Oahu, 104
Amandava amandava, 20
Amazilia beryllina, 20
   violiceps, 21
   yucatanensis, 21
Amazona aestiva, 21
   albifrons, 21
   amazonica, 22
   auropalliata, 22
   autumnalis, 22
   farinosa, 22
   finschi, 22
   ochrocephala, 22
   oratrix, 23
   ventralis, 23
   viridigenalis, 23
   xantholora, 23
Ammodramus bairdii, 23

[*Ammodramus*]
  caudacutus, 23
  henslowii, 24
  leconteii, 24
  maritimus, 24
  nelsoni, 24
  savannarum, 24
Amphispiza belli, 25
  bilineata, 25
Anas acuta, 25
  americana, 25
  bahamensis, 25
  clypeata, 26
  crecca, 26
  cyanoptera, 26
  discors, 26
  fulvigula, 26
  laysanensis, 27
  penelope, 27
  platyrhynchos, 28
  querquedula, 28
  rubripes, 28
  strepera, 28
  wyvilliana, 28
Anhinga anhinga, 28
anhinga, 28
ani, groove-billed, 78
  smooth-billed, 78
'anianiau, 105
Anous minutus, 29
  stolidus, 29
Anser albifrons, 29
  anser, 29
  cygnoides, 29
  indicus, 30
Anthus cervinus, 30
  rubescens, 30
  spragueii, 30
'apapane, 106
Aphelocoma californica, 30
  coerulescens, 31
  insularis, 31
  ultramarina, 31
Aphriza virgata, 31
Aquila chrysaetos, 31
Ara severa, 32
Aramus guarauna, 32

Aratinga acuticaudata, 32
  erythrogenys, 32
  holochlora, 33
  mitrata, 33
  weddellii, 33
Archilochus alexandri, 33
  colubris, 34
Ardea alba, 34
  herodias, 34
Arenaria interpres, 34
  melanocephala, 34
Asio flammeus, 35
  otus, 35
Asturina nitida, 35
Athene cunicularia, 35
Auklet, Cassin's, 174
  crested, 16
  least, 16
  parakeet, 16
  rhinoceros, 61
  whiskered, 16
Auriparus flaviceps, 35
avadavat, red, 20
avocet, American, 179
Aythya affinis, 36
  americana, 36
  collaris, 36
  fuligula, 36
  marila, 37
  valisineria, 37

Baeolophus atricristatus, 37
  bicolor, 37
  inornatus, 37
  ridgwayi, 38
  wollweberi, 38
bananaquit, 71
Bartramia longicauda, 38
Basileuterus culicivorus, 38
  rufifrons, 39
beardless-tyrannulet, northern, 55
becard, rose-throated, 140
bishop, orange, 93
bittern, American, 40
  least, 110
blackbird, Brewer's, 93
  red-winged, 17

rusty, 92
tricolored, 17
yellow-headed, 217
black-hawk, common, 46
bluebird, eastern, 185
mountain, 185
western, 185
bluethroat, 122
bobolink, 86
bobwhite, northern, 72
Bombycilla cedrorum, 39
garrulus, 39
Bonasa umbellus, 39
booby, blue-footed, 197
brown, 197
masked, 197
red-footed, 197
Botaurus lentiginosus, 40
Brachyramphus brevirostris, 40
marmoratus, 40
perdix, 40
brambling, 97
brant, 41
Branta bernicla, 41
canadensis, 41
leucopsis, 41
sandvicensis, 42
Brotogeris chiriri, 42
versicolurus, 43
Bubo virginianus, 43
Bubulcus ibis, 43
Bucephala albeola, 43
clangula, 44
islandica, 44
budgerigar, 126
bufflehead, 43
bulbul, red-vented, 177
red-whiskered, 177
Bulweria bulwerii, 44
bunting, blue, 78
indigo, 146
lark, 48
lazuli, 145
McKay's, 163
painted, 145
rustic, 88
snow, 163

varied, 146
bushtit, 170
bush-warbler, Japanese, 62
Buteo albicaudatus, 44
albonotatus, 45
brachyurus, 45
jamaicensis,45
lagopus, 45
lineatus, 45
platypterus, 45
regalis, 46
solitarius, 46
swainsoni, 46
Buteogallus anthracinus, 46
Butorides virescens, 46

Cacatua galerita, 47
Cairina moschata, 48
Calamospiza melanocorys, 48
Calcarius lapponicus, 48
mccownii, 48
ornatus, 48
pictus, 49
Calidris acuminata, 49
alba, 49
alpina, 49
bairdii, 49
canutus, 50
ferruginea, 50
fuscicollis, 50
himantopus, 50
maritima, 50
mauri, 51
melanotos, 51
minuta, 51
minutilla, 51
ptilocnemis, 51
pusilla, 52
ruficollis, 52
subminuta, 52
temminckii, 52
tenuirostris, 53
Callipepla californica, 53
gambelii, 53
squamata, 53
Calonectris diomedea, 53
Calothorax lucifer, 54

Calypte anna, 54
    costae, 54
Camptostoma imberbe, 55
Campylorhynchus brunneicapillus, 55
canary, yellow-fronted, 184
canvasback, 37
Caprimulgus carolinensis, 55
    ridgwayi, 55
    vociferous, 56
Caracara cheriway, 56
caracara, crested, 56
Cardellina rubifrons, 56
cardinal, northern, 56
    red-crested, 143
    yellow-billed, 143
Cardinalis cardinalis, 56
    sinuatus, 56
Carduelis carduelis, 57
    flammea, 57
    hornemanni, 57
    lawrencei, 57
    pinus, 57
    psaltria, 58
    tristis, 58
Carpodacus cassinii, 58
    mexicanus, 58
    purpureus, 58
catbird, gray, 86
Cathartes aura, 59
Catharus bicknelli, 59
    fuscescens, 59
    guttatus, 59
    minimus, 59
    ustulatus, 60
Catherpes mexicanus, 60
Catoptrophorus semipalmatus, 60
Centrocerus minimus, 60
    urophasianus, 60
Cepphus columba, 61
    grylle, 61
Cerorhinca monocerata, 61
Certhia americana, 61
Ceryle alcyon, 62
    torquata, 62
Cettia diphone, 62
chachalaca, plain, 139
Chaetura pelagica, 63

    vauxi, 63
Chamaea fasciata, 63
Charadrius alexandrinus, 63
    hiaticula, 64
    melodus, 64
    mongolus, 64
    montanus, 64
    morinellus, 64
    semipalmatus, 65
    vociferus, 65
    wilsonia, 65
Chasiempis sandwichensis gayi, 65
    sandwichensis, 65
    sclateri, 66
chat, yellow-breasted, 107
Chen caerulescens, 66
    canagica, 66
    rossii, 66
chickadee, black-capped, 165
    boreal, 166
    Carolina, 166
    chestnut-backed, 166
    gray-headed, 166
    Mexican, 167
    mountain, 166
Chlidonias leucopterus, 66
    niger, 67
Chloroceryle americana, 67
Chondestes grammacus, 67
Chondrohierax uncinatus, 67
Chordeiles acutipennis, 68
    gundlachii, 68
    minor, 69
chuck-will's-widow, 55
chukar, 20
Cinclus mexicanus, 69
Circus cyaneus, 69
Cistothorus palustris, 69
    platensis, 70
Clangula hyemalis, 70
Coccothraustes vespertinus, 70
Coccyzus americanus, 70
    erythropthalmus, 70
    minor, 71
cockatiel, 135
cockatoo, sulphur-crested, 47
Coereba flaveola, 71

Colaptes auratus, 71
  chrysoides, 71
Colibri thalassinus, 72
Colinus virginianus, 72
collared-dove, Eurasian, 195
Columba fasciata, 72
  flavirostris, 72
  leucocephala, 72
  livia, 73
Columbina inca, 73
  passerina, 73
  talpacoti, 73
condor, California, 102
Contopus cooperi, 73
  pertinax, 74
  sordidulus, 74
  virens, 74
coot, American, 97
  Hawaiian, 97
Copsychus malabaricus, 74
Coragyps atratus, 74
cordonbleu, red-cheeked, 210
cormorant, Brandt's, 151
  double-crested, 150
  great, 151
  neotropic, 150
  pelagic, 151
  red-faced, 151
Corvus brachyrhynchos, 76
  caurinus, 76
  corax, 76
  cryptoleucus, 76
  hawaiiensis, 76
  imparatus, 77
  monedula, 77
  ossifragus, 77
Coturnicops noveboracensis, 77
Coturnix japonica, 77
cowbird, bronzed, 129
  brown-headed, 129
  shiny, 129
crane, sandhill, 102
  whooping, 102
creeper, brown, 61
  Hawaii, 138
crossbill, red, 121
  white-winged, 122

Crotophaga ani, 78
  sulcirostris, 78
crow, American, 76
  fish, 77
  Hawaiian, 76
  northwestern, 76
  Tamaulipas, 77
cuckoo, black-billed, 70
  mangrove, 71
  yellow-billed, 70
curlew, bristle-thighed, 134
  long-billed, 134
Cyanocitta cristata, 78
  stelleri, 78
Cyanocompsa parellina, 78
Cyanocorax morio, 79
  yncas, 79
Cygnus atratus, 79
  buccinator, 79
  columbianus, 79
  cygnus, 80
  olor, 80
Cyanthus latirostris, 80
Cypseloides niger, 80
Cyrtonyx montezumae, 80

Dendragapus obscurus, 80
Dendrocygna autumnalis, 81
  bicolor, 81
Dendroica caerulescens, 81
  castanea, 81
  cerulea, 82
  chrysoparia, 82
  coronata, 82
  discolor, 82
  dominica, 82
  fusca, 83
  graciae, 83
  kirtlandii, 84
  magnolia, 84
  nigrescens, 84
  occidentalis, 84
  palmarum, 84
  pensylvanica, 84
  petechia, 85
  pinus, 85
  striata, 85

[*Dendroica*]
  tigrina, 85
  townsendi, 85
  virens, 86
dickcissel, 189
dipper, American, 69
Dolichonyx oryzivorus, 86
dotterel, Eurasian, 64
dove, Inca, 73
  mourning, 218
  rock, 72
  spotted, 195
  white-tipped, 117
  white-winged, 218
  zebra, 100
dovekie, 20
dotwitcher, long-billed, 119
  short-billed, 118
Dryocopus pileatus, 86
duck, American black, 28
  harlequin, 106
  Hawaiian, 28
  Laysan, 27
  long-tailed, 70
  mallard, 28
  Mandarin, 19
  masked, 133
  mottled, 26
  muscovy, 48
  ring-necked, 36
  ruddy, 140
  tufted, 36
  wood, 19
Dumetella carolinensis, 86
dunlin, 49

eagle, bald, 103
  golden, 31
egret, cattle, 43
  great, 34
  little, 87
  reddish, 87
  snowy, 87
Egretta caerulea, 87
  garzetta, 87
  rufescens, 87
  thula, 87

  tricolor, 87
eider, common, 186
  king, 187
  spectacled, 186
  Steller's, 168
Elanoides forficatus, 88
Elanus leucurus, 88
'elepaio, Hawaii, 65
  Kauai, 66
  Oahu, 65
Emberiza rustica, 88
Empidonax alnorum, 88
  difficilis, 89
  flaviventris, 89
  fluvifrons, 89
  hammondii, 89
  minimus, 89
  oberholseri, 90
  occidentalis, 90
  traillii, 90
  virescens, 90
  wrightii, 91
Eremophila alpestris, 91
Estrilda astrild, 91
  caerulescens, 91
  melpoda, 91
  troglodytes, 92
Eudocimus albus, 92
  ruber, 92
Eugenes fulgens, 92
Euphagus carolinus, 92
  cyanocephalus, 93
Euplectes franciscanus, 93
Euptilotis neoxenus, 93

Falcipennis canadensis, 94
Falco columbarius, 94
  femoralis, 94
  mexicanus, 94
  peregrinus, 94
  rusticolus, 95
  sparverius, 95
falcon, aplomado, 94
  peregrine, 94
  prairie, 94
fieldfare, 206
finch, Cassin's, 58

house, 58
Laysan, 200
Nihoa, 200
purple, 58
saffron, 185
flamingo, Andean, 155
Chilean, 155
greater (American), 156
greater (Eurasian), 156
lesser, 155
Puna, 155
flicker, gilded, 71
northern, 71
flycatcher, Acadian, 90
alder, 88
ash-throated, 131
brown-crested, 132
buff-breasted, 89
Cordilleran, 90
dusky, 90
dusky-capped, 132
fork-tailed, 209
gray, 91
great crested, 131
Hammond's, 89
La Sagra's, 132
least, 89
olive-sided, 73
Pacific-slope, 89
scissor-tailed, 208
sulphur-bellied, 132
vermilion, 177
willow, 90
yellow-bellied, 89
francolin, black, 95
Erckel's, 95
gray, 95
Francolinus erckelii, 95
francolinus, 95
pondicerianus, 95
Fratercula arctica, 96
cirrhata, 96
corniculata, 96
Fregata magnificens, 96
minor, 96
frigatebird, great, 96
magnificent, 96

Fringilla montifringilla, 97
frog-hawk, gray, 13
Fulica alai, 97
americana, 97
fulmar, northern, 97
Fulmarus glacialis, 97

gadwall, 28
Gallinago gallinago, 97
Gallinula chloropus, 98
gallinule, purple, 169
Gallus gallus, 98
gannet, northern, 129
garganey, 28
Garrulax caerulatus, 98
canorus, 98
pectoralis, 98
Gavia adamsii, 99
arctica, 99
immer, 99
pacifica, 99
stellata, 99
Geococcyx californianus, 99
Geopelia striata, 100
Geothlypis poliocephala, 100
trichas, 101
Geotrygon, chrysia, 101
Glaucidium brasilianum, 101
gnoma, 101
gnatcatcher, black-capped, 167
black-tailed, 167
blue-gray, 167
California, 167
godwit, bar-tailed, 119
black-tailed, 120
Hudsonian, 119
marbled, 119
goldeneye, Barrow's, 44
common, 44
golden-plover, American, 164
European, 164
Pacific, 164
goldfinch, American, 58
European, 57
Lawrence's, 57
lesser, 58
goose, bar-headed, 30

[goose]
  barnacle, 41
  Canada, 41
  Egyptian, 20
  emperor, 66
  graylag, 29
  greater white-fronted, 29
  Hawaiian, 42
  Ross's, 66
  snow, 66
  swan, 29
goshawk, northern, 13
grackle, boat-tailed, 177
  common, 178
  great-tailed, 178
Gracula religiosa, 102
grebe, Clark's, 15
  eared, 165
  horned, 164
  least, 199
  pied-billed, 165
  red-necked, 165
  western, 15
greenshank, common, 204
grosbeak, black-headed, 153
  blue, 145
  crimson-collared, 180
  evening, 70
  pine, 159
  rose-breasted, 153
  yellow, 153
ground-dove, common, 73
  ruddy, 73
grouse, blue, 80
  ruffed, 39
  sharp-tailed, 207
  spruce, 94
Grus americana, 102
  canadensis, 102
guillemot, black, 61
  pigeon, 61
guineafowl, helmeted, 134
gull, black-headed, 116
  black-tailed, 114
  Bonaparte's, 116
  California, 114
  Franklin's, 116

glaucous-winged, 115
great black-backed, 115
Heermann's, 115
herring, 112
Iceland, 115
ivory, 141
kelp, 114
laughing, 113
lesser black-backed, 114
little, 116
mew, 114
ring-billed, 114
Ross's, 180
Sabine's, 217
slaty-backed, 116
Thayer's, 117
western, 116
yellow-footed, 115
yellow-legged, 113
Gygis alba, 102
Gymnogyps californianus, 102
Gymnorhinus cyanocephalus, 103
gyrfalcon, 95

Haematopus bachmani, 103
  palliatus, 103
Haliaeetus leucocephalus, 103
harrier, northern, 69
hawk, broad-winged, 45
  Cooper's, 13
  ferruginous, 46
  gray, 35
  Harris's, 143
  Hawaiian, 46
  red-shouldered, 45
  red-tailed, 45
  rough-legged, 45
  sharp-shinned, 13
  short-tailed, 45
  Swainson's, 46
  white-tailed, 44
  zone-tailed, 45
Heliomaster constantii, 104
Helmitheros vermivorus, 104
Hemignathus chloris, 104
  kauaiensis, 104
  lucidus, 104

munroi, 105
parvus, 105
virens, 105
heron, great blue, 34
    green, 46
    little blue, 87
    tricolored, 87
Heteroscelus brevipes, 105
    incanus, 105
Himantopus mexicanus, 105
Himatione sanquinea, 106
Hirundo rustica, 106
Histrionicus histrionicus, 106
hummingbird, Allen's, 184
    Anna's, 54
    beryline, 20
    black-chinned, 33
    blue-throated, 112
    broad-billed, 80
    broad-tailed, 183
    buff-bellied, 21
    calliope, 190
    Costa's, 54
    Lucifer, 54
    magnificent, 92
    ruby-throated, 34
    rufous, 184
    violet-crowned, 21
    white-eared, 106
hwamei, 98
Hylocharis leucotis, 106
Hylocichla mustelina, 107

'i 'iwi, 213
ibis, glossy, 164
    scarlet, 92
    white, 92
    white-faced, 163
Icteria virens, 107
Icterus bullockii, 107
    cucullatus, 107
    galbula, 108
    graduacauda, 108
    gularis, 109
    parisorum, 109
    pectoralis, 109
    pustulatus, 109

spurius, 109
Ictinia mississippiensis, 110
'io, 46
Ixobrychus exilis, 110
Ixoreus naevius, 110

Jacana spinosa, 110
jacana, northern, 110
jackdaw, Eurasian, 77
jaegar, long-tailed, 191
    parasitic, 191
    pomarine, 191
jay, blue, 78
    brown, 79
    gray, 147
    green, 79
    Mexican, 31
    pinyon, 103
    Steller's, 78
Junco hyemalis, 111
    phaeonotus, 111
junco, dark-eyed, 111
    yellow-eyed, 111
junglefowl, red, 98

kakawahie, 143
kamao, 130
kestrel, American, 95
killdeer, 65
kingbird, Cassin's, 209
    Couch's, 207
    eastern, 209
    gray, 208
    thick-billed, 208
    tropical, 208
    western, 209
kingfisher, belted, 62
    green, 67
    ringed, 62
kinglet, golden-crowned, 179
    ruby-crowned, 179
kiskadee, great, 162
kite, hook-billed, 67
    Mississippi, 110
    snail, 181
    swallow-tailed, 88
    white-tailed, 88

kittiwake, black-legged, 181
  red-legged, 181
knot, great, 53
  red, 50
koloa, 28

Lagopus lagopus, 111
  leucurus, 111
  mutus, 111
Lampornis clemenciae, 112
Lanius cristatus, 112
  excubitor, 112
  ludovicianus, 112
lapwing, northern, 211
lark, horned, 91
  sky, 19
Larus argentatus, 112
  atricilla, 113
  cachinnans, 113
  californicus, 114
  canus, 114
  crassirostris, 114
  delawarensis, 114
  dominicanus, 114
  fuscus, 114
  glaucescens, 115
  glaucoides, 115
  heermanni, 115
  livens, 115
  marinus, 115
  minutus, 116
  occidentalis, 116
  philadelphia, 116
  pipixcan, 116
  ridibundus, 116
  schistisagus, 116
  thayeri, 117
Laterallus jamaicensis, 117
laughingthrush, gray-sided, 98
  greater necklaced, 98
Leiothrix lutea, 117
leiothrix, red-billed, 117
Leptotila verreauxi, 117
Leucosticte atrata, 118
  australis, 118
  tephrocotis, 118
Limnodromus griseus, 118

  scolopaceus, 119
Limnothlypis swainsonii, 119
Limosa fedoa, 119
  haemastica, 119
  lapponica, 199
  limosa, 120
limpkin, 32
Lonchura malabarica, 120
  malacca, 120
  punctulata, 120
longspur, chestnut-collared, 48
  Lapland, 48
  McCown's, 48
  Smith's, 49
loon, arctic, 99
  common, 99
  Pacific, 99
  red-throated, 99
  yellow-billed, 99
Lophodytes cucullatus, 120
Lophura leucomelanos, 121
lovebird, peach-faced, 17
Loxia cruvirostra, 121
  leucoptera, 122
Loxioides bailleui, 122
Loxops caeruleirostris, 122
  coccineus, 122
Luscinia svecica, 122

macaw, chestnut-fronted, 32
magpie, black-billed, 156
  yellow-billed, 157
mallard, 28
mannikin, nutmeg, 120
martin, purple, 169
meadowlark, eastern, 196
  western, 196
Melamprosops phaeosoma, 123
Melanerpes aurifrons, 123
  carolinus, 123
  erythrocephalus, 123
  formicivorus, 123
  lewis, 124
  uropygialis, 125
Melanitta fusca, 125
  nigra, 125
  perspicillata, 125

Meleagris gallopavo, 125
Melopsittacus undulatus, 126
Melospiza georgiana, 126
 lincolnii, 126
 melodia, 126
merganser, common, 126
 hooded, 120
 red-breasted, 127
Mergus merganser, 126
 serrator, 127
merlin, 94
Micrathene whitneyi, 127
millerbird, Nihoa, 14
Mimus gundlachii, 127
 polyglottos, 127
Mniotilta varia, 127
mockingbird, Bahama, 127
 northern, 127
Moho bishopi, 128
 braccatus, 129
Molothrus aeneus, 129
 ater, 129
 bonariensis, 129
moorhen, common, 98
Morus bassanus, 129
Motacilla alba, 130
 flava, 130
 lugens, 130
munia, tricolored, 120
murre, common, 210
 thick-billed, 211
murrelet, ancient, 198
 Craveri's, 198
 Kittlitz's, 40
 long-billed, 40
 marbled, 40
 Xantus's, 198
Myadestes myadestinus, 130
 obscurus, 130
 palmeri, 131
 townsendi, 131
Mycteria americana, 131
Myiarchus cinerascens, 131
 crinitus, 131
 sagrae, 132
 tuberculifer, 132
 tyrannulus, 132

Myioborus pictus, 132
Myiodynastes luteiventris, 132
Myiopsitta monachus, 133
myna, common, 14
 crested, 14
 hill, 102

Nandayus nenday, 133
nene, 42
Netta rufina, 133
nighthawk, Antillean, 68
 common, 69
 lesser, 68
night-heron, black-crowned, 135
 yellow-crowned, 134
nightjar, buff-collared, 55
noddy, black, 29
 blue-gray, 169
 brown, 29
Nomonyx dominicus, 133
Nucifraga columbiana, 133
nuku pu 'u, 104
Numenius americanus, 134
 phaeopus, 134
 tahitiensis, 134
Numida meleagris, 134
nutcracker, Clark's, 133
nuthatch, brown-headed, 186
 pygmy, 186
 red-breasted, 185
 white-breasted, 186
Nyctanassa violacea, 134
Nyctea scandiaca, 135
Nycticorax nycticorax, 135
Nyctidromus albicollis, 135
Nymphicus hollandicus, 135

'o 'o 'a 'a, 129
'o 'o, Bishop's, 128
 Kauai, 129
'o 'u, 171
Oceanites oceanicus, 135
Oceanodroma castro, 136
 furcata, 136
 homochroa, 136
 leucorhoa, 137
 melania, 137

[*Oceanodroma*]
  microsoma, 137
Oenanthe oenanthe, 137
'oma 'o, 130
Oporornis agilis, 137
  formosus, 138
  philadelphia, 138
  tolmiei, 138
Oreomystis bairdi, 138
  mana, 138
Oreortyx pictus, 139
Oreoscoptes montanus, 139
oriole, Altamira, 109
  Audobon's, 108
  Baltimore, 108
  Bullock's, 107
  hooded, 107
  orchard, 109
  Scott's, 109
  spot-breasted, 109
  streaked-backed, 109
Ortalis vetula, 139
osprey, 141
Otus asio, 139
  flammeolus, 139
  kennicotti, 140
  trichopsis, 140
ovenbird, 183
owl, barn, 209
  barred, 196
  boreal, 15
  burrowing, 35
  elf, 127
  flammulated, 139
  great gray, 195
  great horned, 43
  long-eared, 35
  northern hawk, 198
  northern saw-whet, 15
  short-eared, 35
  snowy, 135
  spotted, 196
Oxyura jamaicensis, 140
oystercatcher, American, 103
  black, 103

Pachyramphus aglaiae, 140

Padda oryzivora, 140
Pagophila eburnea, 141
palila, 122
Palmeria dolei, 141
Pandion haliaetus, 141
Parabuteo unicinctus, 143
parakeet, black-hooded, 133
  blue-crowned, 32
  dusky-headed, 33
  green, 33
  mitred, 33
  monk, 133
  red-masked, 32
  rose-ringed, 170
  white-winged, 43
  yellow-chevroned, 42
Paroaria capitata, 143
  coronata, 143
Paroreomyza flammea, 143
  maculata, 143
  montana, 144
parrot, blue-fronted, 21
  Hispaniolan, 23
  lilac-crowned, 22
  mealy, 22
  orange-winged, 22
  red-crowned, 23
  red-lored, 22
  thick-billed, 180
  white-fronted, 21
  yellow-crowned, 22
  yellow-headed, 23
  yellow-lored, 23
  yellow-naped, 22
parrotbill, Maui, 170
partridge, gray, 147
  red-legged, 20
Parula americana, 144
  pitiayumi, 144
parula, northern, 144
  tropical, 144
Passer domesticus, 144
  montanus, 144
Passerculus sandwichensis, 145
Passerella iliaca, 145
Passerina amoena, 145
  caerulea, 145

ciris, 145
cyanea, 146
versicolor, 146
pauraque, comon, 135
Pavo cristatus, 146
peafowl, common, 146
Pelagodroma marina, 147
Pelecanus erythrorhynchos, 147
  occidentalis, 147
pelican, American white, 147
  brown, 147
Perdix perdix, 147
Perisoreus canadensis, 147
petrel, Bermuda, 172
  black-capped, 172
  black-winged, 173
  Bonin, 173
  Bulwer's, 44
  Cook's, 172
  Fea's, 172
  Galapagos, 173
  Hawaiian, 174
  herald, 171
  mottled, 173
  Murphy's, 174
  Stejneger's, 173
  white-necked, 172
Petrochelidon fulva, 148
  pyrrhonota, 148
Peucedramus taeniatus, 148
pewee, greater, 74
Phaethon aethereus, 148
  lepturus dorotheae, 149
  rubricauda rothschildi, 150
Phainopepla nitens, 150
phainopepla, 150
Phalacrocorax auritus, 150
  brasilianus, 150
  carbo, 151
  pelagicus, 151
  penicillatus, 151
  urile, 151
Phalaenoptilus nuttallii, 151
phalarope, red, 152
  red-necked, 152
  Wilson's, 152
Phalaropus fulicarius, 152

lobatus, 152
tricolor, 152
Phasianus colchicus, 152
  versicolor, 152
pheasant, Japanese green, 152
  kalij, 121
  ring-necked, 152
Pheucticus chrysopeplus, 153
  ludovicianus, 153
  melanocephalus, 153
Philomachus pugnax, 153
Phoebastria albatrus, 154
  immutablis, 154
  nigripes, 155
phoebe, black, 182
  eastern, 182
  Say's, 182
Phoeniconaias minor, 155
Phoenicoparrus andinus, 155
  jamesi, 155
Phoenicopterus chilensis, 155
  ruber roseus, 156
    ruber, 156
Phylloscopus borealis, 156
  fuscatus, 156
Pica hudsonia, 156
  nuttalli, 157
Picoides albolarvatus, 158
  arcticus, 158
  arizonae, 158
  borealis, 158
  nuttallii, 158
  pubescens, 159
  scalaris, 159
  tridactylus, 159
  villosus, 159
pigeon, band-tailed, 72
  red-billed, 72
  white-crowned, 72
Pinicola enucleator, 159
pintail, northern, 25
  white-cheeked, 25
Pipilo aberti, 160
  chlorurus, 160
  crissalis, 161
  erythrophthalmus, 161
  fuscus, 161

[*Pipilo*]
    maculatus, 161
pipit, American, 30
    red-throated, 30
    Sprague's, 30
Prianga bidentata, 161
    flava, 162
    ludoviciana, 162
    olivacea, 162
    rubra, 162
Pitangus sulphuratus, 162
Platalea ajaja, 163
Plectrophenax hyperboreus, 163
    nivalis, 163
Plegadis chihi, 163
    falcinellus, 164
plover, black-bellied, 164
    common ringed, 64
    Mongolian, 64
    mountain, 64
    piping, 64
    semipalmated, 65
    snowy, 63
    Wilson's, 65
Pluvialis apricaria, 164
    dominica, 164
    fulva, 164
    squatarola, 164
po 'ouli, 123
pochard, red-crested, 133
Podiceps auritus, 164
    grisegena, 165
    nigricollis, 165
Podilymbus podiceps, 165
Poecile atricapilla, 165
    carolinensis, 166
    cincta, 166
    gambeli, 166
    hudsonica, 166
    rufescens, 166
    sclateri, 167
Polioptila caerulea, 167
    californica, 167
    melanura, 167
    nigriceps, 167
Polysticta stelleri, 168
Pooecetes gramineus, 168

poorwill, common 151
Porphyrio martinica, 169
    porphyrio, 169
Porzana carolina, 169
prairie-chicken, greater, 206
    lesser, 206
Procelsterna cerulea, 169
Progne subis, 169
Protonotaria citrea, 170
Psaltriparus minumus, 170
Pseudonestor xanthophrys, 170
Psittacula krameri, 170
Psittirostra psittacea, 171
ptarmigan, rock, 111
    white-tailed, 111
    willow, 111
Pterocles exustus, 171
Pterodroma arminjoniana, 171
    cahow, 172
    cervicalis, 172
    cookii, 172
    feae, 172
    hasitata, 172
    hypoleuca, 173
    inexpectata, 173
    longirostris, 173
    nigripennis, 173
    phaeopygia, 173
    sandwichensis, 174
    ultima, 174
Ptychoramphus aleuticus, 174
puaiohi, 131
puffin, Atlantic, 96
    horned, 96
    tufted, 96
Puffinus bulleri, 174
    carneipes, 175
    creatopus, 175
    gravis, 175
    griseus, 175
    lherminieri, 175
    nativitatis, 176
    newelli, 176
    opisthomelas, 176
    pacificus, 176
    puffinus, 176
    tenuirostris, 176

Pycnonotus cafer, 177
  jocosus, 177
pygmy-owl, ferruginous, 101
  northern, 101
Pyrocephalus rubinus, 177
pyrrhuloxia, 56

quail, California, 53
  Gambel's, 53
  Japanese, 77
  Montezuma, 80
  mountain, 139
  scaled, 53
quail-dove, Key West, 101
quetzal, eared, 93
Quiscalus major, 177
  mexicanus, 178
  quiscula, 178

rail, black, 117
  clapper, 179
  king, 178
  Virginia, 179
  yellow, 77
Rallus elegans, 178
  limicola, 179
  longirostris, 179
raven, Chihuahuan, 76
  common, 76
razorbill, 19
Recurvirostra americana, 179
redhead, 36
redpoll, common, 57
  hoary, 57
redshank, spotted, 203
redstart, American, 184
  painted, 132
Regulus calendula, 179
  satrapa, 179
Rhodostethia rosea, 180
Rhodothraupis celaeno, 180
Rhynchopsitta pachyrhyncha, 180
Ridgwayia pinicola, 180
Riparia riparia, 181
Rissa breviorstris, 181
  tridactyla, 181
roadrunner, greater, 99

robin, American, 205
  clay-colored, 205
  rufous-backed, 206
Rustrhamus sociabilis, 181
rosy-finch, black, 118
  brown-capped, 118
  gray-crowned, 118
ruff, 153
Rynchops niger, 181

sage-grouse, greater, 60
  Gunnison, 60
Salpinctes obsoletus, 182
sanderling, 49
sandgrouse, chestnut-bellied, 171
sandpiper, Baird's, 49
  buff-breasted, 205
  common, 14
  curlew, 50
  least, 51
  pectoral, 51
  purple, 50
  rock, 51
  semipalmated, 52
  sharp-tailed, 49
  solitary, 204
  spotted, 14
  stilt, 50
  Terek, 217
  upland, 38
  western, 51
  white-rumped, 50
  wood, 203
sapsucker, red-breasted, 188
  red-naped, 187
  Williamson's, 188
  yellow-bellied, 188
Sayornis nigricans, 182
  phoebe, 182
  saya, 182
scaup, greater, 37
  lesser, 36
Scolopax minor, 182
scoter, black, 125
  surf, 125
  white-winged, 125
screech-owl, eastern, 139

[screech-owl]
western, 140
whiskered, 140
scrub-jay, Florida, 31
island, 31
western, 30
seedeater, white-collared, 190
Seiurus aurocapillus, 183
motacilla, 183
noveboracensis, 183
Selasphorus platycercus, 183
rufus, 184
sasin, 184
Serinus mozambicus, 184
Setophaga ruticilla, 184
shama, white-rumped, 74
shearwater, Audubon's, 175
black-vented, 176
Buller's, 174
Christmas, 176
Cory's, 53
flesh-footed, 175
greater, 175
Manx, 176
Newell's, 176
pink-footed, 175
short-tailed, 176
sooty, 175
wedge-tailed, 176
shelduck, common, 200
ruddy, 199
shoveler, northern, 26
shrike, brown, 112
loggerhead, 112
northern, 112
Sialia currocoides, 185
mexicana, 185
sialis, 185
Sicalis flaveola, 185
silverbill, Indian, 120
siskin, pine, 57
Sitta canadensis, 185
carolinensis, 186
pusilla, 186
pygmaea, 186
skimmer, black, 181
skua, great, 191

South Polar, 191
snipe, common, 97
snowcock, Himalayan, 200
solitaire, Townsend's, 131
Somateria fischeri, 186
mollissima, 186
spectabilis, 187
sora, 169
sparrow, American tree, 189
Bachman's, 17
Baird's, 23
black-chinned, 189
black-throated, 25
Botteri's, 18
Brewer's, 189
Cassin's, 18
chipping, 190
clay-colored, 189
Eurasian tree, 144
field, 190
five-striped, 18
fox, 145
golden-crowned, 218
grasshopper, 24
Harris's, 219
Henslow's, 24
house, 144
Java, 140
lark, 67
Le Conte's, 24
Lincoln's, 126
Nelson's sharp-tailed, 24
rufous-crowned, 19
rufous-winged, 18
sage, 25
saltmarsh sharp-tailed, 23
savannah, 145
seaside, 24
song, 126
swamp, 126
vesper, 168
white-crowned, 219
white-throated, 218
Sphyrapicus nuchalis, 187
ruber, 188
thyroideus, 188
varius, 188

Spindalis zena, 188
spindalis, western, 188
Spiza americana, 189
Spizella arborea, 189
    atrogularis, 189
    breweri, 189
    pallida, 189
    passerina, 190
    pusilla, 190
spoonbill, roseate, 163
Sporophila torqueola, 190
starling, European, 197
starthroat, plain-capped, 104
Stelgidopteryx serripennis, 190
Stella calliope, 190
Stercorarius longicaudus, 191
    maccormicki, 191
    parasiticus, 191
    pomarinus, 191
    skua, 191
Sterna albifrons, 192
    aleutica, 192
    anaethetus, 192
    antillarum, 192
    bergii, 192
    caspia, 193
    dougallii, 193
    elegans, 193
    forsteri, 193
    fuscata, 193
    hirundo, 193
    lunata, 194
    maxima, 194
    nilotica, 194
    paradisaea, 194
    sandvicensis, 194
stilt, black-necked, 105
stint, little, 51
    long-toed, 52
    red-necked, 52
    Temminck's, 52
stork, wood, 131
storm-petrel, ashy, 136
    band-rumped, 136
    black, 137
    fork-tailed, 136
    Leach's, 137

least, 137
    white-faced, 147
    Wilson's, 135
Streptopelia chinensis, 195
    decaocto, 195
    risoria, 195
Strix nebulosa, 195
    occidentalis, 196
    varia, 196
Sturnella magna, 196
    neglecta, 196
Sturnus vulgaris, 197
Sula dactylatra, 197
    leucogaster, 197
    nebouxii, 197
    sula, 197
surfbird, 31
Surnia ulula, 198
swallow, Bahama, 199
    bank, 181
    barn, 106
    cave, 148
    cliff, 148
    northern rough-winged, 190
    tree, 199
    violet-green, 199
swamphen, purple, 169
swan, black, 79
    mute, 80
    trumpeter, 79
    tundra, 79
    whooper, 80
swift, black, 80
    chimney, 63
    Vaux's, 63
    white-throated, 16
Synthliboramphus antiquus, 198
    craveri, 198
    hypoleucus, 198

Tachybaptus dominicus, 199
Tachycineta bicolor, 199
    cyaneoviridis, 199
    thalassina, 199
Tadorna ferruginea, 199
    tadorna, 200
tanager, flame-colored, 161

[tanager]
  hepatic, 162
  scarlet, 162
  summer, 162
  western, 162
tattler, gray-tailed, 105
  wandering, 105
teal, blue-winged, 26
  cinnamon, 26
  green-winged, 26
Telespiza cantans, 200
  ultima, 200
tern, Aleutian, 192
  arctic, 194
  black, 67
  bridled, 192
  Caspian, 193
  common, 193
  elegant, 193
  Forster's, 193
  gray-backed, 194
  great-crested, 192
  gull-billed, 194
  least, 192
  little, 192
  roseate, 193
  royal, 194
  sandwich, 194
  sooty, 193
  white, 102
  white-winged, 66
Tetraogallus himalayensis, 200
thrasher, Bendire's, 202
  brown, 203
  California, 203
  crissal, 202
  curve-billed, 202
  Le Conte's, 202
  long-billed, 202
  sage, 139
thrush, Aztec, 180
  Bicknell's, 59
  gray-cheeked, 59
  hermit, 59
  Swainson's, 60
  varied, 110
  wood, 107

Thryomanes bewickii, 200
Thryothorus ludovicianus, 201
titmouse, black-crested, 37
  bridled, 38
  juniper, 38
  oak, 37
  tufted, 37
towhee, Abert's, 160
  California, 161
  canyon, 161
  eastern, 161
  green-tailed, 160
  spotted, 161
Toxostoma bendirei, 202
  crissale, 202
  curviostre, 202
  lecontei, 202
  longirostre, 202
  redivivum, 203
  rufum, 203
Tringa erythropus, 203
  flavipes, 203
  glareola, 203
  melanoleuca, 204
  nebularia, 204
  solitaria, 204
Troglodytes aedon, 204
  troglodytes, 205
Trogon elegans, 205
trogon, elegant, 205
tropicbird, red-billed, 148
  red-tailed, 150
  white-tailed, 149
Tryngites subruficollis, 205
Turdus grayi, 205
  migratorius, 205
  pilaris, 206
  rufopalliatus, 206
turkey, wild, 125
turnstone, black, 34
  ruddy, 34
turtle-dove, ringed, 195
Tympanuchus cupido, 206
  pallidicinctus, 206
  phasianellus, 207
Tryannus couchii, 207
  crassirostris, 208

dominicensis, 208
forficatus, 208
melancholicus, 208
savana, 209
tyrannus, 209
verticalis, 209
vociferans, 209
Tyto alba, 209

Uraeginthus bengalus, 210
Uria aalge, 210
  lomvia, 211

Vanellus vanellus, 211
veery, 59
verdin, 35
Vermivora celata, 211
  chrysoptera, 211
  crissalis, 211
  luciae, 212
  peregrina, 212
  pinus, 212
  ruficapilla, 212
  virginiae, 212
Vestiaria coccinea, 213
violet-ear, green, 72
Vireo altiloquus, 213
  atricapillus, 213
  bellii, 213
  cassinii, 214
  crassirostris, 214
  flavifrons, 214
  flavoviridis, 214
  gilvus, 214
  griseus, 214
  huttoni, 215
  olivaceus, 215
  philadelphicus, 216
  plumbeus, 216
  solitarius, 216
  vicinior, 216
vireo, Bell's, 213
  black-capped, 213
  black-whiskered, 213
  blue-headed, 216
  Cassin's, 214
  gray, 216

Hutton's, 215
Philadelphia, 216
plumbeous, 216
red-eyed, 215
thick-billed, 214
warbling, 214
white-eyed, 214
yellow-green, 214
yellow-throated, 214
vulture, black, 74
  turkey, 59

wagtail, black-backed, 130
  white, 130
  yellow, 130
warbler, arctic, 156
  bay-breasted, 81
  black-and-white, 127
  Blackburnian, 83
  blackpoll, 85
  black-throated blue, 81
  black-throated gray, 84
  black-throated green, 86
  blue-winged, 212
  Canada, 216
  Cape May, 85
  cerulean, 82
  chestnut-sided, 84
  Colima, 211
  Connecticut, 137
  dusky, 156
  golden-cheeked, 82
  golden-crowned, 38
  golden-winged, 211
  Grace's, 83
  hermit, 84
  hooded, 217
  Kentucky, 138
  Kirtland's, 84
  Lucy's, 212
  MacGillivray's, 138
  magnolia, 84
  mourning, 138
  Nashville, 212
  olive, 148
  orange-crowned, 211
  palm, 84

[warbler]
  pine, 85
  prairie, 82
  prothonotary, 170
  red-faced, 56
  rufous-capped, 39
  Swainson's, 119
  Tennessee, 212
  Townsend's, 85
  Virginia's, 212
  Wilson's, 217
  worm-eating, 104
  yellow, 85
  yellow-rumped, 82
  yellow-throated, 82
waterthrush, Louisiana, 183
  northern, 183
waxbill, black-rumped, 92
  common, 91
  lavender, 91
  orange-cheeked, 91
waxwing, Bohemian, 39
  cedar, 39
wheatear, northern, 137
whimbrel, 134
whip-poor-will, 56
whistling-duck, black-bellied, 81
  fulvous, 81
white-eye, Japanese, 219
wigeon, American, 25
  Eurasian, 27
willet, 60
Wilsonia canadensis, 216
  citrina, 217
  pusilla, 217
woodcock, American, 182
woodpecker, acorn, 123
  Arizona, 158
  black-headed, 158
  downy, 159
  Gila, 125

golden-fronted, 123
hairy, 159
ladder-backed, 159
Lewis's, 124
Nuttall's, 158
pileated, 86
red-bellied, 123
red-cockaded, 158
red-headed, 123
three-toed, 159
white-headed, 158
wood-pewee, eastern, 74
  western, 74
wren, Bewick's, 200
  cactus, 55
  canyon, 60
  Carolina, 201
  house, 204
  marsh, 69
  rock, 182
  sedge, 70
  winter, 205
wrentit, 63

Xanthocephalus xanthocephalus, 217
Xema sabini, 217
Xenus cinereus, 217

yellowlegs, greater, 204
  lesser, 203
yellowthroat, common, 101
  gray-crowned, 100

Zenaida asiatica, 218
  macroura, 218
Zonotrichia albicollis, 218
  atricapilla, 218
  leucophrys, 219
  querula, 219
Zosterops japonicus, 219